Strategic Digital Transformation

Emerging technologies are having a profound impact upon business as individuals and organisations increasingly embrace the benefits of the 'always on' attitude that digital technologies produce. The use of the web, apps, cloud storage, GPS and Internet-connected devices has transformed the way we live, learn, play and interact – yet how a business can fully benefit from this transformation is not always clear. In response, this book enables students and business leaders to take a strategic and sustainable approach to realising the value of digital technologies. It offers results-driven solutions that successfully transform organisations into data-driven, people-focused businesses capable of sustainably competing at a global level.

Split across four key parts, the material moves through understanding digital business to planning, implementing and assessing digital transformation. The current challenges facing all small organisations, including limited resources, financial pressures and the lack of dedicated IT departments, are explored. The authors consider the ways in which innovation can increase competitive advantage, how innovative business models can create new opportunities and how a data-driven perspective can release embedded value within the organisation. Contemporary international case studies and examples throughout each chapter bridge theory with practical application and systematically document the patterns of activities that enable success.

This textbook is a vital resource for postgraduate and undergraduate students of digital business, innovation and transformation. By showing how to initiate digital transformation across an organisation, it will prepare business owners, directors and management of small- and medium-sized businesses to take strategic advantage of new and emerging technologies to stay ahead of their competition.

Alex Fenton is Lecturer in Digital Business at Salford Business School, UK. He has authored a wide range of academic and practitioner articles relating to digital transformation, digital business and digital marketing. He has won an array of industry and teaching awards for his practical approach to enterprise-led, experiential education.

Gordon Fletcher is Academic Unit Head at Salford Business School, UK. Gordon's research focuses on examples and experiences of digital business, culture and practice. Gordon has published work around conflict with online finance communities, economies within virtual game worlds, digital marketing and digital transformation.

Marie Griffiths is Reader and Head of the Centre for Digital Business, Salford Business School, UK. Her research focuses on the role of digital technologies and the convergence of the 'real' and digital worlds and the social influences of technology. She also writes and teaches in the fields of emerging technologies, security and information systems.

Business and Digital Transformation

Digital technologies are transforming societies across the globe, the effects of which are yet to be fully understood. In the business world, technological disruption brings an array of challenges and opportunities for organizations, management and the workplace.

This series of textbooks provides a student-centred library to analyse, explore and critique the evolutionary effects of technology on the business world. Each book in the series takes the perspective of a key business discipline and examines the transformational potential of digital technology, aided by real world cases and examples.

With contributions from expert scholars across the globe, the books in this series enable critical thinking students to excel in their studies of the new digital business environment.

Strategic Digital Transformation
A Results-Driven Approach
Edited by Alex Fenton, Gordon Fletcher and Marie Griffiths

For more information about the series, please visit www.routledge.com/Routledge-New-Directions-in-Public-Relations--Communication-Research/book-series/BAD

Strategic Digital Transformation

A Results-Driven Approach

Edited by Alex Fenton, Gordon Fletcher and Marie Griffiths

Routledge
Taylor & Francis Group

LONDON AND NEW YORK

First published 2020
by Routledge
2 Park Square, Milton Park, Abingdon, Oxon OX14 4RN

and by Routledge
52 Vanderbilt Avenue, New York, NY 10017

Routledge is an imprint of the Taylor & Francis Group, an informa business

British Library Cataloguing-in-Publication Data
A catalogue record for this book is available from the British Library

Library of Congress Cataloging-in-Publication Data
Names: Fenton, Alex, editor. | Fletcher, Gordon, editor. | Griffiths, Marie, editor.
Title: Strategic digital transformation : a results-driven approach / edited by Alex Fenton, Gordon Fletcher and Marie Griffiths.
Description: New York : Routledge, 2020. | Series: Business and digital transformation | Includes bibliographical references and index.
Identifiers: LCCN 2019035256 | ISBN 9780367031060 (hardback) | ISBN 9780367031077 (paperback) | ISBN 9780429020469 (ebook)
Subjects: LCSH: Business enterprises—Technological innovations. | Strategic planning. | Organizational change.
Classification: LCC HD45 .S8467 2020 | DDC 658.05—dc23
LC record available at https://lccn.loc.gov/2019035256

ISBN: 978-0-367-03106-0 (hbk)
ISBN: 978-0-367-03107-7 (pbk)
ISBN: 978-0-429-02046-9 (ebk)

Typeset in Bembo
by Apex CoVantage, LLC

Visit the eResources at: http://digital-transformation-book.org.uk/

Contents

Figures

Tables

Part I

Understanding the digital in business

1 Why do strategic digital transformation?

Gordon Fletcher, Alex Fenton and Marie Griffiths

Preface

Many organisations and their leaders are currently struggling to understand the threats and opportunities for digital transformation. As individual consumers we have all developed high expectations of digital technology that heavily influences our perceptions of technology within the organisation. This creates a very real risk for organisations, including public and third-sector institutions. Ignoring the pace of overall technological change brings the prospect of negative – or even fatal – impact on an organisation's very existence. This chapter highlights how all organisations can benefit from digital transformation. However, in order to realise these benefits, they need to adopt a strategic approach to digital transformation that embeds dynamic, innovative and even entrepreneurial ways of leading, managing and thinking. Throughout this book, we draw upon digital transformation examples of micro, small, medium and large organisations to demonstrate the value of improved organisational efficiency as well as internal cultural and behavioural change that fully engages customers and consumers. The ultimate goal of digital transformation is to create innovative working environments and business models that support a data-driven and people-focused organisation.

1.1 Businesses are struggling to adapt

A former Cisco CEO made the claim in 2015 that "at least 40% of all businesses will die in the next 10 years . . . if they don't figure out how to change their entire company to accommodate new technologies" (Ross 2015). As frightening as this prospect of imminent doom sounds, there are many tangible benefits to be discovered by those organisations ready to commit to strategic digital transformation.

As a starting point we draw upon changes in the retail consumer experience as familiar examples to both students and business owners. Consumer digital technologies are also heavily used as examples in the first section of this book, as these represent some of the most visible and heavily referenced examples of digital transformation.

Recent high-profile failures of household brand names in the UK High Street (Main Street in the US) hallmark the degree to which organisations are struggling to adapt to the challenge of digital transformation. The cause for these failures vary in their details, but two key interrelated themes are particularly visible. In each case the retailer blamed wholly, or in part, competition from online retailers who are not burdened with large and expensive high-profile real estate or complex supply chains. Reading between the lines, these statements are a diplomatic placing of blame on the power of e-commerce including Amazon and Alibaba.

A cause of failure less commonly acknowledged by retailers has been an inability to overcome their own legacy. Physical retailers have large and complex organisational structures that often employ thousands of staff who interact with multiple suppliers and intermediaries across many locations. Managing this complexity has resulted in a range of disparate locations, processes, practices and communications that – in their totality – prove very difficult to change or even understand. Attempts at creating organisational leanness and agility quickly stall when confronted by such scale of legacy.

Reports in the UK of 200 shopping centres under risk of failure in a twelve-month period (Harby 2018) combined with 5,855 shops closing in one year alone all document the scale of change. The reduction in the physical retail offering coupled with a 3% overall loss of footfall in the High Street year-on-year (BIDS 2018) hints at an unstoppable spiral of decline. The reassuring enclosed environments of shopping centres were once an attractive safe space in contrast to the more chaotic traditional High Street (Staeheli & Mitchell 2006). However, the challenge of online retail has now stripped away even this advantage to leave a heavy financial burden that has proven to be an insurmountable legacy for many retailers. The fate of High Street retail shows how difficult it is to overcome organisational legacy in the pursuit of a digital transformation.

Although the UK High Street is a visible indicator of the rapidly changing organisational environment, the challenge of overcoming legacy is found in all sectors. Those sectors traditionally tied to physical infrastructure, such as construction, still tend to dismiss the organisational benefits of digital technologies as something primarily confined to the office environment or "IT" functions.

With the largest technology companies moving into the real estate sector (Garfield 2018) as investors and developers, it will only be a matter of time until "technology" companies also begin to disrupt the construction sector. When construction is reconsidered as primarily a data problem, the most consciously data-driven organisations will become real competitors that are capable of building to specifications, timeframes and budgets in ways not previously experienced. The barriers to entry for a data-driven organisation that is challenging traditional business models in the physical domain have been reduced even further as robotics, artificial intelligence and machine learning all become suitable for mainstream use. In the construction industry, the bricklaying robot is already available (*Construction Index* 2018) and capable of output equivalent to five humans. As data is given the arms and legs to interact, physical work will no longer be the exclusive domain of people's direct labour.

In other sectors, data-driven change will similarly disrupt existing legacy processes and whole sectors. The development of autonomous goods vehicles threatens the transport and haulage sector. It is not only the threat to 3.5 million truck-driving jobs in the US alone (US Special Delivery 2017), but with an estimated 9% of these drivers reported as owner-operators this is also a direct threat to over 300,000 small businesses in the sector. Extending the risk still further, autonomous vehicles will also bring about the demise of traditional ancillary services such as service stations and independent garages. Eventually, this transport technology also reduces the need for sole direct ownership of vehicles by consumers. The ripple effect of these changes will have major consequence across all developed economies.

The lessons from all these examples, admittedly a cliché, is that change is inevitable. Extending this observation further, continuous change should now be the expectation in all organisational planning and operations. To complicate this situation even further,

Vision and Mission
(transparent and genuine)

**Business
Environment
Challenges**

Legacy
(systems, processes, people)

Competition
(sector-level digital leaders)

Figure 1.1 Current business environment challenges

political and economic volatility, uncertainty, complexity and ambiguity have become increasingly commonplace, making traditional forms of business analysis of the external environment difficult. Change in the external environment now a) is facilitated by consumer and organisational digital technologies, b) is unexpected and c) regularly comes from outside any of a sector's current competitors. Organisations will struggle to respond to change when burdened by a legacy of processes, systems and their people's current skills.

The broader external changes that now bear down on all organisations offer a third reason why so many organisations struggle to adapt (Figure 1.1). Vision and mission statements can no longer be vague or variable marketing straplines but must be an inherent part of how the organisations collectively thinks and functions. The value of persisting and remaining focused on a genuine vision also explains the rediscovery of iconic retail heritage brands such as Doctor Martens and Burberry in the UK. Genuinely shared organisational beliefs and vision provide certainty against the backdrop of changeable markets, can be adapted for application within new sectors and assists in strengthening the loyalty of brand advocates.

In effect, overcoming the challenges of the current organisational environment requires strategic digital transformation to

- Emphasise the vision of the organisation
- Address the legacy of systems, processes and people's skills
- Create and evolve an innovating organisational environment
- Constantly internalise external stimulus (from competitors and other sectors)
- Dynamically shift and introduce business models in response to new opportunities
- Proactively define the expectations for goods or services in the organisation's chosen market.

Any one of these above points represent a significant challenge to an organisation and in total offers an explanation as to why organisations are struggling to adapt.

1.2   The risks of failing to adapt and potential responses

The origins of digital transformation can be traced back at least thirty years when roles in typing pools and typesetting were forever consigned to being backdrops in historical television dramas. These early victims to transformation were rapidly followed by the demise of printed encyclopaedias, photographic film companies and video rental stores. Now traditional banking outlets and post offices are also changing in response to the transforming business environment. Society and organisations have changed to such an extent in developed economies that people undertake their everyday lives oblivious to the necessary presence of digital technologies.

The most dramatic failures brought about by the transformational effects of digital technology are easy to identify with the benefit of hindsight. However, none of the directors at, for example, Kodak or Blockbuster would have been able to identify the beginning of the end for their own businesses. The collapse of these organisations occurred slowly through incremental changes in the external environment that were out of sync with the internal dynamics of the organisation. In defence of the directors of these specific examples, when the extent of their situation became clear, corrective actions were taken in an attempt to turn around what had become, as it ultimately transpired, an irrevocable decline.

Organisational failure resulting from transformational change in the external environment must be read instructively as a warning against inaction while also emphasising the need to avoid attempting to predict an inevitably indefinite future. Kodak could not, as a single organisation, have envisaged the full extent of the uptake of digital photography, that its primary device for delivery would be the mobile phone, or the pivotal importance of photography within social media. Rather than creating a complete plan for a particular future, organisations can only face what is coming by continuously evolving their structure and business models in ways that amplify their vision and mission.

The current state of the external environment can be described with the terms VUCA and the 4Vs. VUCA – Volatility, Uncertainty, Complexity and Ambiguity – describes the current state of developed economies (Bennett & Lemoine 2014) in which we find ourselves individually, collectively and organisationally. The state of VUCA is continuously accelerating and has largely been brought about by increasing adoption of consumer digital technology. However, it is equally important to recognise that accelerating VUCA has been occurring since the first Industrial Revolution (Bennis & Nanus 1985).

The 4Vs – Velocity, Volume, Variety and Veracity – describe the aspects of data that continue to increase in an accelerating VUCA world. Data is the primary focus for the 4Vs, and increasingly this is the way in which the world is understood and defined – as data points and data problems. This data-oriented view can be usefully applied in the widest possible sense. For example, lack of consideration to some or all of the 4Vs explains the recent failure of a number of High Street retailers. Toys R Us persisted with a business model based on the traditional supermarket long after the online retailers could respond more rapidly to changing demands for toys from consumers. This situation was a case of failing to adapt to an increased velocity in toy trends brought about by increasing consumer use of social media. Maplin Electronics lost sight of its origins in providing specialist electronics components to make way for toys and gift lines on the sales floor. Losing sight of mission and vision can be regarded as a veracity issue. However, in combination with the retailing of electronic components being better served through e-commerce the reality of the situation struck at the very heart of the business creating an unpalatable reality that the board was not prepared to address.

The 4Vs can be used to understand an organisation's relationship with the external environment where the connections could be read as, for example, the "volume of goods available", the "velocity of interaction", the "variety of transactions", the "veracity of communications" and other possible combinations. It is not always the case that the aim of understanding the 4Vs should be to increase each "V". The value of the 4Vs are to systematically identify the relationships between the organisation and the changeable external environment. Any measurement of success is made through the fifth "V" – the value being created by the organisation.

Together, VUCA and the 4Vs frame our description and understanding of the organisational environment (Figure 1.2). While VUCA highlights many of the negative aspects that come from the increasing use of consumer digital technology, the 4Vs can identify what the organisation is responding to in shaping a strategy for transformation. Recognising the impact of the VUCA world as specific challenges to the organisation and the use of the 4Vs to frame and focus an organisational response is a crucial consideration in becoming a data-driven, people-focused organisation.

Issues brought into the organisation from the external environment are described here as VUCA challenges. Almost inevitably, these VUCA challenges can be framed in terms of one or more of the 4Vs. As a general example, the increasing variety, velocity and volume of consumer complaints requires an organisational response and is a direct result of the increasing consumer expectation that all goods and services are fit for purpose around a very narrow range of tolerance.

Managing an organisation's response to the VUCA world can also be aided by identifying systems quality – or what are sometimes described as non-functional requirements (Figure 1.3). The primary purpose of systems quality are to define and prioritise the individual capabilities in a system – or in an organisation. In identifying the capabilities of an organisation there is also an acknowledgment that it cannot be "best" at everything.

Some existing and current qualities in the organisation will also be challenged through digital transformation including predictability and durability. Although the most desirable organisational qualities for strategic digital transformation will vary by sector and size, some common themes can be described. With the rise of consumer power, there is a need to enable greater transparency and, in a broader sense, permeability in the organisation.

Figure 1.2 VUCA and the 4Vs in relation to the organisation

Figure 1.3 VUCA, 4Vs and systems qualities

Table 1.1 A sample of system qualities relevant to organisational strategic digital transformation and responding to the VUCA world

Accessibility	Agility	Efficiency	Integrity
Learnability	Portability	Precision	Resilience
Responsiveness	Simplicity	Transparency	Usability

The need for permeability also captures the increased pressure that consumer power has placed on organisations to collaborate with their customers. There is also a need to collaborate with other organisations to develop new products and services that better fit existing or envisaged needs. There are many other qualities that can support an organisation's response to the 4Vs and the VUCA world (Table 1.1).

1.3   Who benefits from digital transformation

Digital transformation has many facets that impact on all parts of an organisation in some way. Every organisation, particularly in the most developed economies, uses digital technology either directly or indirectly. Rainie and Wellman (2012) emphasise the arrival of a "triple revolution" of consumer technologies. That is, the combination of social media platforms, fast Internet and smartphones has created a social change in the way we communicate, network and conduct business. On the simplest level, this revolution is hallmarked by the use of smartphones to accelerate all forms of personal and organisational communications. Ryan (2017) presents an example of a non-digital business with a sole trader who sells milk in the Lake District of England on a fixed delivery round. They deliver milk each day to a pre-defined group of people who pay cash left at each delivery point. As a result there is no need for a website or social media to further promote or grow the organisation. They have used a paper-based system for the last thirty years and continue to do so.

In this fictional example it is difficult to imagine how even this micro business will resist the use of digital technology as time progresses. Milk delivery micro-businesses increasingly accept payment through Internet-based bank transfer. This form of transaction removes the need to physically handle cash or visit a bank while also automating the organisation's bookkeeping. Digital channels of communication enable customers to order based on their day-to-day needs. This type of ordering can then determine the exact load for the truck at the beginning of the day. With dynamic route-planning, vehicle fuel consumption can be optimised by avoiding current road blockages, delivering the biggest (and heaviest) orders first and travelling in the opposite direction to the busiest high-traffic routes. All of these actions bring greater labour efficiency, cost savings and environmental improvements to the organisation without it necessarily aspiring for growth. Increasingly technology-conscious consumer also expect digital channels to be their first option to be able to communicate, interact and pay.

It is possible to take this transformation of a milk delivery micro-business still further. With further integration, the milk being produced by individual cows on individual farms can be linked to the choices consumers make when ordering. Tracking on the delivery vehicle can also enable consumers to keep an eye on their delivery as it progresses towards them.

Now the milk delivery can not only be customised by a required daily volume but by additional factors such as offering a narrower timeframe for delivery as well as the farm origin and the breed of cow producing the milk. Being able to describe the very specific details of the product and allowing consumers to order against their personal requirements transforms this milk delivery business into a transparent and data-driven organisation. These changes in the organisation also address the earlier VUCA challenge of meeting consumer expectations for goods and services against very tightly defined specifications.

Any organisation can benefit from this type of holistic digital transformation in its underlying structure and in its business model. The roadmap to transformation can vary widely between organisations from the small, incremental and low budget to far more dramatic interventions and investments with shorter timelines. However, ad hoc digital transformation is not an automatic panacea. Replacing processes that already work for the sake of digital transformation is itself a poor rationale. Even replacing an existing sub-standard organisational function through digital transformation requires careful and strong leadership (Westerman et al. 2014). Without a strategic approach that considers the impact of change on the organisation and all of its people, any transformation can be worse than what has been replaced.

It is people, both external and internal to the organisation, who are pivotal to digital transformation and who are the ultimate beneficiaries – or victims. The negative effects of transformation on an individual are well documented and can range from a poor user experience to complete job loss (Collinson 2019). Transformation may streamline an organisation and make it more profitable, but the impact on people is a necessary criteria for measuring the success of strategic digital transformation (Harari 2017).

The authors asked professionals attending executive education programmes over a period of twelve months who they saw as the key beneficiaries of digital transformation.

	Partners	Internal	External
Who	Partners Suppliers Industry Distributors	Staff Employees Environment	Consumers Clients Customers Agencies Public Authorities
How		Change Easier Efficiencies	Improve Experience

Figure 1.4 Who benefits from digital transformation?

Although the professionals came from a range of large and small organisations representing a wide variety of sectors, their responses were consistent (Figure 1.4). The three groups of beneficiaries can be grouped as partners and the internal and external environments. However, the ways in which partners would benefit was left entirely undefined by the respondents.

1.4   What are the benefits

The potential list of benefits brought from transformation is as long as the ever growing list of consumer digital technologies. Digital transformation can facilitate internal cultural and behavioural changes and can provide deep, real-time insights that engage and encourage new consumers, customers and influencers. Westerman et al. (2014) interviewed 157 executives and identified several thematic benefits of digital transformation. In all of the themes discovered, the most significant were data related. Better data – improved veracity – lets an organisation better understand the continuously changing external environment including their market position, consumer behaviour and customer experience. Internally, better data improves the sharing of knowledge, contributes to business continuity, creates transparency and builds a better, more transparent organisational culture.

The increasing use of consumer technologies such as mobile and wearable devices within the organisation can further streamline processes and improve internal and external communications. The impact of these devices on the concept of the workplace are evidenced by the European Court of Justice's decision (*BBC* 2015) to regard commuting time as work time for employees with no fixed office. Further research argues for an extension of this decision to include all workers (Faragher 2018). The conclusions offered by this research is only possible now as a direct result of the widespread prevalence of mobile technology. Employees can now access greater volumes and variety of organisational data with greater veracity and at greater velocity than was previously possible sitting at a desk inside their own organisation.

The wide use and acceptance of social media channels adds variety to the sources of data available to an organisation, extending the value of these channels beyond marketing activities. Social media offers insight into the dynamic external environment, including the actions of competitors and the threats of new developments, as well as offering a means to continuously horizon scan for new organisational opportunities.

Process digitisation and automation can bring improvement at all levels and scales of the organisation's operations. Small incremental improvements can be introduced as "grass-roots" transformation, such as using a web-based data entry to capture organisational data rather than a multitude of unlinked spreadsheets or, going further, using automation to scan incoming email and avoid the need for the double entry of data received through document attachments. Any one action completed automatically is trivial in terms of the time saved, but in organisations that are large or where the time of skilled employees is at a premium this can represent significant efficiency improvements over time.

The improvement described by the web data entry and automated email scanning examples above are labour saving at the point of input, but with the resultant increased data veracity this efficiency is also recognisable at many points of output. Larger process improvements that deploy large-scale organisational technologies – most likely introduced as "top-down" transformation – for example in the manufacturing sector, can optimise entire supply chains, speed up the manufacturing process itself or optimise delivery to customers. Reconciling the operational pressures for "grassroots" change that uses consumer technology to tackle existing legacy with the desire to introduce "top-down" improvements that respond to external pressures is a key challenge for a successful digital transformation. A strategic approach to transformation once again brings a need to align all these forms of change around a shared organisational vision (Figure 1.5).

To initiate digital transformation, an organisational review of existing business models can recognise the new application of existing technologies to improve internal processes. At the very least, a review will indicate where gaps in capacity and capability may lie. Beyond bringing efficiency, this can also lead to new products and services. Collaborative models can take advantage of the combined computing resources in the hands of existing

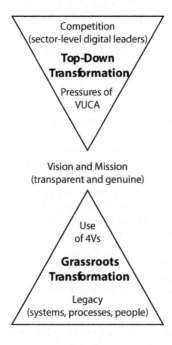

Figure 1.5 The challenge for strategic digital transformation

customers and consumers. New businesses are already taking advantage of gaps in the market that could not have existed without the widespread availability use of consumer digital technology.

1.5   Changing cultures in digital workplaces

The key message from this chapter is that it is not technology itself that creates or drives strategic digital transformation. It is the application and exploitation of these technologies to address the VUCA challenges felt by the people in an organisation that creates successful transformation. The dominant view of digital transformation is one of driving organisational efficiency, but the reality is that successful transformation must benefit people both inside and outside the organisation. Where people have been recognised as the beneficiaries of digital transformation, the focus tends solely to be turned towards the external stakeholders, often couched in terms of improvements to the customer journey. However, with increased transparency – effectively a lowering of the barriers between the inside and outside of the organisation – the need for commitment to organisational vision necessitates that digital transformation should also bring benefits to those people inside the organisation.

Seventy percent of change management projects fail to meet their goals because of internal resistance to change and/or a lack of management commitment (Beer & Nohria 2000). This figure has not significantly changed since 1995 (Hammer & Champney 1995) and has remained consistent for decades (Ashkenas 2013). There are many large and small organisations that overlooked the internal people aspects of the change process. If it is acknowledged that change in the context of digital transformation is a continuous one, then there are real risks in not addressing the concerns of internal stakeholders. Not ensuring adequate preliminary consultation, overlooking the need for appropriate training at all levels of skill or lacking sound internal communications tactics are all portents for project failure. Similarly, transforming too quickly can build up people's resistance to change. The 4Vs (and organisation qualities) are once again useful in recognising the people-oriented challenge of the transformation process (Table 1.2), with the goal of change being to generate greater value (the fifth "V") for the organisation.

Table 1.2 Considering people in the process – the 4Vs applied to the transformation project with SMART objectives and organisational qualities

Volume	The number of planned changes should be **measurable** against individual and organisational KPIs and **achievable** for the people in the organisation. Where internal capacity does not exist, training should be part of the change programme to change existing skill sets (measurability, deployability, learnability).
Variety	The changes should make **sense** to the people in the organisation and be sufficiently familiar and **specific** to them while avoiding becoming generic or overly ambitious (credibility, simplicity).
Velocity	The pace of change cannot over-extend the current organisational culture and must come with specific **time-bound** outcomes (even if these are intermediate steps). Cultural change must keep pace with other forms of change (responsiveness, robustness).
Veracity	Transparency and openness ensures that the project remains **relevant** and **motivating** for internal stakeholders and can be delivered in a **timely** fashion (integrity, relevance, timeliness).

Previous research (Ewenstein et al. 2015) shows that organisations which have focused on transforming their internal culture are more likely to succeed in the transformation project. The McKinsey research identified three cultural changes that need to be nurtured and embedded for a change programme to succeed. These changes can be summarised as organisation-wide openness to taking and accepting risk, organisation-wide commitment to breaking down silos and organisation-wide focus on the customer. None of these changes should represent a surprise, but what is important is the focus on understanding that change management is now a continuous process requiring the support and participation of all within the organisation.

1.6   New models and goals

Strategic digital transformation changes the structure of an organisation, and it also has a significant impact on the business models used. The business model sits on top of the organisation's structure as the dynamic combination of its resources and vision to offer a value proposition to a specifically defined set of consumers and customers. All organisations have at least one business model regardless of how it is actually documented or articulated. However, it is a common experience for many organisations to not understand or recognise their own business model. Without the explicit recognition or articulation of a model, there is also reduced likelihood that any organisational vision or mission is shared and understood. There is an increased risk to the digital transformation project without an understanding of the vision or business model across the organisation.

There are many definitions of a business model that can be cited, but acknowledgement of the benefits of business models is more instructive: "A better business model often will beat a better idea or technology" (Chesbrough 2007). This is illustrated by considering how many of the household brand names offer the "best" option. Consider, for example, Walmart or Tesco within the retailing sector, Dell for consumer PCs, Samsung for mobile phones, Uber in ride hailing or Ryan Air in budget airlines. A rare counterexample to this claim is worth acknowledging with Dyson, which has a significant research and development commitment, and its business model is built on leading its sector through continuous innovation.

To build better business models, the starting point is to understand the organisation and what is being sought through strategic digital transformation. When we asked professionals, a common range of thematic phrases emerged (Table 1.3).

The outcomes of digital transformation (Table 1.3) can be read as the various ways that each organisation expects to response to the core question for all businesses. That question is the one provoked by all business models. "How can we realise what is described by this model?" More recently this question is more regularly qualified to ask, "How can we realise what is described by this model through digital technologies?"

Table 1.3 Expected outcomes from digital transformation

Digital Ability	Greater Value	Improved Data
Process Alignment	Profit Growth	Quicker Engagement
Reducing Costs	Right Information	Right Skills
Wider Access		

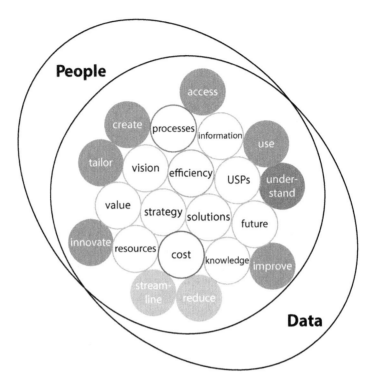

Figure 1.6 Why do digital transformation?

This observation regarding the expected outcomes of transformation brings the chapter full circle in asking the question "Why do digital transformation?" The professionals we asked presented a consistently clear view on the reasons for digital transformation (Figure 1.6). Invariably, their desire to see improvements in the people and data of the organisation was the rationale for undertaking digital transformation. Some aspects were presented negatively or in a neutral way. However the views of the professionals were primarily positive, with many different combinations. Figure 1.6 can be read with any combination of three words. Three examples are sufficiently instructive to enable readers to further construct their own combinations: "People create vision", "Data reduce[s] cost" or "People innovate resources".

Key takeaways

- The external environment is volatile, uncertain, complex and ambiguous – the VUCA world
- The VUCA world cannot be managed
- The VUCA world continuously challenges the organisation
- Digital transformation is the strategic response to VUCA and its challenges
- The goal of strategic digital transformation is to produce a data-driven, people-focused organisation

References

Ashkenas, R. (2013) "Change management needs to change", *Harvard Business Review*, https://hbr. org/2013/04/change-management-needs-to-change

BBC (2015) "Travel to work ruling: Who is affected and how?", 11th Sep, www.bbc.co.uk/news/ uk-34217549

Beer, M., & Nohria, N. (2000) "Cracking the code of change", *Harvard Business Review*, May–June, 87–96, http://ceewl.ca/12599-PDF-ENG.PDF#page=87

Bennett, N., & Lemoine, J. (2014) "What VUCA really means for you", *Harvard Business Review*, 92(1/2), https://ssrn.com/abstract=2389563

Bennis, W., & Nanus, B. (1985) *Leaders: The Strategies for Taking Charge*. New York: Harper & Row.

BIDS (2018) britishbids.info/publications/national-bid-survey-2018

Chesbrough, H. (2007) "Business model innovation: it's not just about technology anymore", *Strategy & Leadership*, 35(6), 12–17, https://doi.org/10.1108/10878570710833714

Collinson, P. (2019) "Automation threatens 1.5 million workers in Britain, says ONS", *The Guardian*, 25th Mar, www.theguardian.com/money/2019/mar/25/automation-threatens-15-million-workers-britain-says-ons

Construction Index (2018) "Brick-laying robot reaches the UK", 23rd Jan, www.theconstructionindex. co.uk/news/view/brick-laying-robot-reaches-the-uk

Ewenstein, B., Smith, W., & Sologa, A. (2015) *Changing Change Management*, McKinsey and Company, www.mckinsey.com/featured-insights/leadership/changing-change-management

Faragher (2018) "Commuting time should be counted as part of the working day", *Personnel Today*, 30th Aug, www.personneltoday.com/hr/commuting-time-should-be-counted-as-part-of-the-working-day/

Garfield, L. (2017) "Facebook, Google, and LinkedIn are investing hundreds of millions in housing projects across North America", *Business Insider*, 8th Jan, uk.businessinsider.com/tech-companies-housing-silicon-valley-2018-1

Hammer, M., & Champney, J. (1995) *Reengineering the Corporation: A Manifesto for Business Revolution*. London: Nicholas Brealey.

Harari, N. (2017) "Yuval Noah Harari challenges the future according to Facebook", *Financial Times*, www.ft.com/content/ac0e3b20-0d71-11e7-a88c-50ba212dce4d

Harby, J. (2018) "More than 200 UK shopping centres 'in crisis'", *BBC News*, www.bbc.co.uk/news/ uk-england-45707529

Rainie, L., & Wellman, B. (2012) *Networked: The New Social Operating System*. Boston: MIT Press.

Ross (2015) "Why 40 percent of businesses will die in the next 10 years", *Ross & Ross International*, 6th Oct, www.rossross.com/blog/40-percent-of-businesses-today-will-die-in-10-years

Ryan, D. (2017) *Understanding Digital Marketing: Marketing Strategies for Engaging the Digital Generation* (4th ed.). London: Kogan Page.

Staeheli, L., & Mitchell, D. (2006) "USA's destiny? Regulating space and creating community in American shopping malls", *Urban Studies*, 43(5–6), 977–992, https://doi.org/10.1080/00420980600676493

US Special Delivery (2017) "How many trucking companies in the US", 23rd Feb, www.usspecial.com/ how-many-trucking-companies-in-the-usa/

Westerman, G., Bonnet, D., & McAfee, A. (2014) *Leading Digital: Turning Digital into Business Transformation*. Cambridge MA: Harvard University Press.

2 How to critically understand the digital landscape

Gordon Fletcher, Alex Fenton and Marie Griffiths

Preface

This chapter advocates the use of systems-based thinking in order to understand and respond to the external organisational environment. Starting with a discussion of the difference between traditional and digitally enabled organisations, we focus on using the 4Vs as an aid to understand. A systems perspective emphasises the use of the 4Vs to frame how an organisation responds to the challenges of the VUCA world. The response shapes all aspects of the organisation's structure incorporating people, communications, data and procedures/processes alongside hardware and software. The chapter extends the traditional use of systems to advocate the inclusion of elements regarded as external to the organisation itself. The systems-based approach provides a way to critically examine an organisation and how it will respond to the external business environment.

2.1 The digital difference

"Digital" organisations are regularly presented in the popular media as counterpoints to their "physical" equivalents. In this chapter we start with consumer digital technologies and their connected business models. From this understanding we then drill down into organisation itself to understand the many ways in which technology has impact upon all the elements of all organisation.

Presenting digital organisations as being opposite to their "bricks-and-mortar" competitors relies heavily on examples from familiar consumer e-commerce such as Amazon and Alibaba. This presentation of digital is problematic and unhelpful for many reasons. Most importantly, these established e-commerce organisations are the earliest forms of a business model that relies upon an internal digital infrastructure coupled with the need for consumers having access to digital technology to buy the business' goods. The digital difference, in this case, was to take an existing retail business model and directly translate it into an online marketplace. Shifting the locus of business-to-consumer (B2C) interaction in a well-established business model is the sole innovation of early e-commerce and the one that has become the most visible example of digital organisation to consumers. At the same time this innovation should not be regarded as surprising or unexpected. Prior to the mid-1990s, there were already many available predecessors to e-commerce with, for example, the Sears catalogue in the US and the Littlewoods catalogue in the UK. Web pages "simply" enabled these catalogues to be more accessible without the need for printing or distribution.

As time and technology progressed, the goods being advertised through online catalogues could then be directly purchased through the same web pages. E-commerce had become a reality. While e-commerce is a significant change to earlier retail experiences through this single innovation, consumer e-commerce still faces many of the challenges that are similar to other retailers that sell physical goods. Inevitably, the need to manage and transport physical items tie them to the complexities of warehousing and the logistics of completing deliveries to individual customers. At this point, the digital difference between e-commerce and bricks-and-mortar retailing disappears.

Better evidence of innovation and the digital difference can be found in e-commerce models that evolved from these initial experiments to deliver purely digital goods and services. It can be seen in these examples that each substitution of a previous practice with the application of digital technology introduces the potential for innovation and transformation in the business model.

The highly visible and now aging example of e-commerce, however, neglects to recognise digital transformation that can occur deep within the organisation and its structure hidden from the direct view of consumers or competitors. Discussion of consumer-oriented organisation and technologies tend to focus on those most visible aspects of an organisation; however, this only documents a fraction of the range of changes and opportunities that transformation can realise.

The most successful exploitation of digital difference are so significant that they can define entirely new business models or even entire new sectors. In the mid-1990s this was also true of e-commerce. Changes of this scale are now popularly described as an "Uber moment" – when an organisation shakes up an entire sector with a business model that uses the latest technology (Flinders 2017). Increasingly, the most obvious gaps (at least in hindsight) and the simplest of opportunities have become harder to find, need wider technological change throughout the organisation and require equivalent transformational shifts in people, processes and communications as well as in the use of data.

Another example of the disruption made possible by exploiting the digital difference – other than that of Uber itself – can be found with Netflix. Netflix and its business model has significantly influenced how broadcast media is now consumed. While Netflix is now a vast organisation, there are still innovations that continue to be created by competitors who extend and experiment with this established business model. For example, the San Francisco-based Kanopy has shifted away from the direct consumer revenue streams used by Netflix to instead use an intermediary approach that is directed at institutional subscribers such as public libraries and universities. These institutional subscribers then determine the criteria that allow their own members to access films. Over time, still more new consumer media business models will develop as organisations recognise themselves as more data-driven and people-focused.

Understanding the digital difference – and explaining the success of Netflix – can be done with the concepts of VUCA and the 4Vs that were introduced in Chapter 1. VUCA describes the continuously changing state of the external environment. For consumers this acceleration is evident in many different ways, but in the most positive sense the phenomena is represented by ever-increasing choice. At an organisational level, VUCA represents the challenge to become more responsive to those same ever-changing consumer needs and desires and to have an internal structure that is resilient to the dynamic external environment. Even the definition of where the external environment begins and ends has become increasingly problematic. Through increasing consumer demand for transparency and genuinely collaborative organisation practices, the VUCA world continually works to blur the boundaries between what is inside or outside the organisation.

The organisational response to the VUCA world is dynamically (re)formulated business models that exploit digital difference not by attempting to control the external environment but by offering ways to respond to, interact with or order it. Extending the earlier example slightly, Netflix's on-demand delivery and AI-driven recommendations are part of a business model that let consumers manage the specific VUCA of broadcast media. A side effect of the popularity of this model has been to make binge-watching a common consumer experience (Bulkley 2018). Many producers and streaming providers now acknowledge this behaviour pattern by releasing television series at one time rather than through the more traditional sequential weekly play out of episodes.

The ways of managing VUCA within the structure of an organisation and as the basis for new business models can be defined through the 4Vs. With data at the heart of the digital difference, the 4Vs frame the VUCA challenges that must be strategically managed by an organisation. The 4Vs provide a consistent and systematic way of describing the digital difference in a business model and in an organisation's own underlying structure. Acknowledging the ever presence of VUCA and by managing each of its challenges framed as a response to one or more of the "Vs" shifts understanding of digital difference from being a simple binary decision between a digital or physical option.

VUCA labels the environment that organisations must respond to by making their own internal environment less volatile and more certain, simple and unambiguous. In other words the organisation needs the internal qualities of predictability, accuracy, stability and simplicity (the "PASS" organisation). The most likely responses to the VUCA world will include digital technologies in their descriptions. The digital difference defines the new opportunities that can be introduced through technologies to every aspect of the business model and structure of the organisation.

2.2   The organisation as a system

To understand the impact of the digital difference on the structure of the organisation itself we present the organisation as a system (Figure 2.1). This perspective provides a consistent way of describing an organisation's structure without becoming locked into

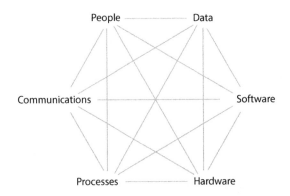

Figure 2.1 Simplified view of the organisation as a system

thinking about specific organisation functions or departments. The organisation as a system is an holistic view that avoids, for example, identifying communications as something that "marketing does" while data becomes something that "IT does". Being locked into functional thinking steers an organisation towards insular perspectives that encourage individuals to push away problems and challenges (or opportunities) to other parts of the organisation.

An organisation can be understood as being formed around the six interacting elements of people, data, software, hardware, processes and communications. Each of these elements must work with the other parts of the organisation to be sustainable and successful. Any breakdown in the relationship between elements can have major repercussions across the organisation and represents key points of pain that require resolution. Data is intentionally represented in this way within the organisation, as it is can only be realised as information through its interaction and connection with the other elements of the system.

As an example, a mid-sized business may have a process that involves regularly emailing its employees with requests for information regarding their personal skill set. Instead, employees can be empowered to personally manage and update their own details in their personnel file in a way that then can be queried as required. This single change in the use of software and a revised process then also enables new communications to individual employees that are based on specific criteria within their personnel file. The ability to create finer granularity of actions inside and outside the organisation is a key benefit of strategic digital transformation. Granular actions produce targeted efficiency that avoids the need for every interaction to begin from low levels of shared understanding. In effect, the organisation uses data in combination with other elements of the system to recommence each of its interactions at the point where it ended.

People and data in the organisation are the elements that are most distinct from those found in other organisations. It is people and data that are also an organisation's greatest assets. As a consequence, it is a realistic goal of digital transformation to make the organisation data-driven and people-focused. Reading downwards from the people and data in the organisation, the other elements become increasingly less distinctive and in larger organisations may be more readily "bought in", outsourced or delivered as a distinct project managed by consultants (Figure 2.2).

At this point it is worth acknowledging the popular fears concerning job losses with digital-transformation programmes. Figure 2.2 graphically identifies the basis for these fears. At immediate threat are those jobs within the organisation that use the labour of people to solely deliver processes. These processes are unlikely to be unique to the organisation and are prime opportunities to be transformed through a different combinations of people, data and software. However, the organisation might use an intermediate solution and outsource the processes to external people. Examples of this approach include international call centres used by banks where operatives work from a pre-set script. An intermediate solution of this type is made possible by technology that minimises the cost of global phone communications while taking advantage of the lower wages in developing economies. Becoming people-focused and data-driven does not just seek to reduce costs or increase revenues but asks instead the much broader question as to how people, data and other elements of the system create value for the organisation.

The question of creating value is the people-focused aspect of transformation. People create greatest value in their response to the VUCA challenges that cannot be entirely managed or automated through the other elements of the organisational system. This regularly resolves to the human elements of interaction. The example of Zappos is noteworthy as

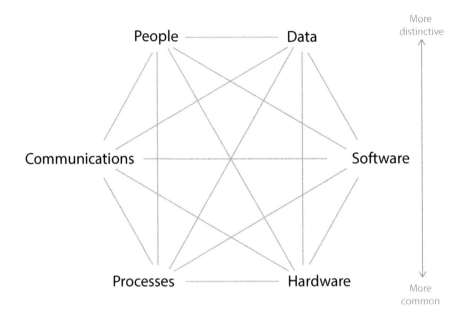

Figure 2.2 The organisation as a system highlighting the more distinctive elements

a people-focused organisation (Evans 2014). The e-commerce operation is owned by Amazon but retains its operating independence. And the difference is noticeable. There are no call-centre scripts, with a claim that one customer was once on the phone for ten hours (Feloni 2016). This radically shifts the familiar call-centre process into the elements of communications and people within the structure of Zappos. Zappos also has a primary emphasis on the happiness of employees. Ensuring that the people in the organisation have the right skills and knowledge becomes a concern of the people-focused organisation that is solved through ongoing training and development. This organisational culture is in contrast to reliance upon the continuous presence of an external surplus of labour resources who can be used to replace existing unsuitable people in the organisation at any time. Committing to people within the organisation also partially redresses the Marxian question of where the surplus value created by people's labour goes. For Zappos, at least some of this surplus value is returned in the form of support for skills development as well as supporting employee wellbeing and happiness.

Questions of labour and the creation of value raise questions about the economic inter-relationship of the elements within the organisational system. It is people that create value. The other aspects of the system enable, support, amplify and simplify this creation of value. The organisational system is structured to differentiate organisational elements that are more cultural (and people-oriented) from those elements that are more infrastructural (Figure 2.3). People, communications and processes of the organisation are more cultural elements and as a result are the points more likely to introduce VUCA-related challenges directly into the organisation, but they are essential to creating value. The organisation is supported and balanced by data, software and hardware that represent more infrastructural elements of the organisation. Although not exclusively the case, it is the tendency for organisational infrastructure to be the element best suited to mitigating the influences of

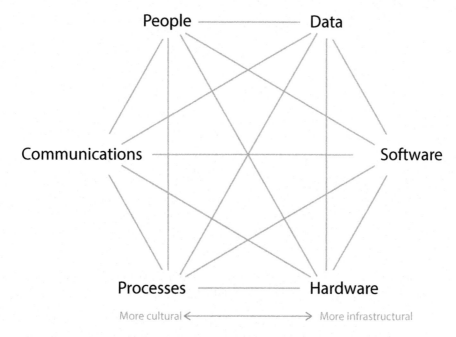

Figure 2.3 The infrastructural and cultural elements of the organisation as a system

the VUCA world. For example, it is primarily (although not exclusively) through software that the data available to an organisation (and not just the data "owned" by the organisation) can be managed into meaningful information for use by its people.

The distinction being made between infrastructure and culture is present as a continuum rather than a binary classification. It is important to acknowledge that the infrastructure of an organisation has cultural meaning and significance as the "solid" or "fixed" forms of cultural practice and preference. This distinction as "fixed" culture makes the organisation's infrastructure more resistant to the VUCA world, but with this advantage, it also has a tendency towards being less dynamic in the forms of response that these elements of the organisation's system can offer.

The relationship between infrastructure and culture explains the benefits of an organisation becoming data-driven. The data of an organisation is its most important infrastructure. As a permanent record of the organisation, including its relationships, its decisions and its performance, it is the data of the organisation that represents its solidified culture and by extension the degree to which it has lived up to its vision and mission. An organisation that is not able to call upon its data to do these things ultimately reflects a gap in its knowledge. This position also echoes the relevance of the DIKW (Data, Information Knowledge, Wisdom) triangle discussed by knowledge management scholars (iScoop n.d.) within the organisation.

Although the organisation as a system views draws upon traditional information-systems thinking, an important addition and distinction in this model is that the system's boundary between what is internal and external do not mirror the boundaries of the

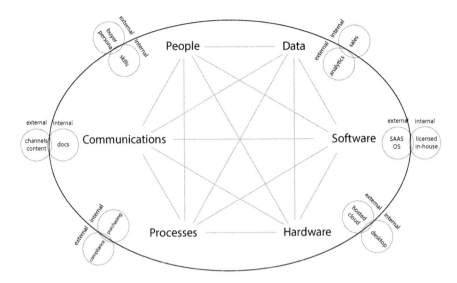

Figure 2.4 The different boundaries between the organisation as a system and the organisation itself. Elements outside the organisation remain part of the system.

organisation itself (Figure 2.4). This emphasises a key digital difference that enables – even encourages – organisations to reach beyond their own barriers to work with consumers, influencers and other organisations by using collaborative actions such as co-production and co-creation.

The organisation as a system takes collaboration beyond simple supply or sales arrangements to deeper, more robust relationships. Examples of this deeper collaboration include the success of the LadBible business model which is built on the use, availability and relative flexibility of Facebook effectively providing this startup with its key consumer-facing hardware, software and communications structures. Without Facebook, LadBible could not have the business model that it uses.

Cloud computing also exemplifies the different boundaries between the organisation and its system. Cloud facilities are generally external to the organisation but are an integral aspect of the system. As hardware, cloud computing is both infrastructural and among the most generic elements of the system but equally is an increasingly important element for many organisations. The positioning of cloud computing within the system but external to the organisation itself also helps to explain why so many third-party cloud-computing vendors currently exist.

A further extension to the system of the organisation over earlier thinking is the inclusion within the hardware element of all aspects of the physical infrastructure of the organisation. Even the most completely digital business models have hardware commitments. An entirely automated and collaborative business model could describe its hardware as being the devices that consumers and customers use to access digital content and the third-party data servers used to store its content. But inevitably this organisation also requires physical space for its developers and management to "touch down".

Hardware can be considered more broadly to include the buildings, furniture and fixtures that provide a space for the people and data of the organisation. Shifting the

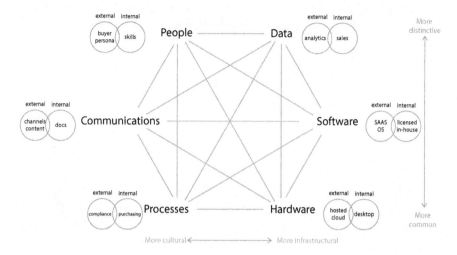

Figure 2.5 The complete organisation as a system – an organisational system

relative importance of the physical estate of an organisation is appropriate. For example, homeworking, virtual working and the rise of bring-your-own-devices and other digitally enabled practices all reduce the role of the fixed physical estate in ensuring business success.

The observation that the system's boundary extends beyond that of the organisation is also relevant to its hardware element. The need for flexible and variable "touch down" spaces has become a popular business model for physical office space. For example, WeWork and its competitors let businesses satisfy their organisational needs for estate in new ways. By offering flexible physical locations and group meeting spaces without the same traditional commitment to leasing or fixed floor space, these business models represent their own transformational "Uber moment" in the commercial real estate sector.

While it is data and people that are the key focus for strategic digital transformation, this goal necessarily requires holistic attention to the interactions of the whole organisational system (Figure 2.5).

2.3   Understanding and applying the organisation as a system

With the structural view of the organisation recognised as a more expansive system, the relationship of the organisation to the VUCA world can also be understood in more detail (Figure 2.6). As the underlying structure of the organisation, the organisational system may be largely invisible to consumers, but it is the essential platform for the delivery of the business models to customers and consumers.

With the system extending beyond the boundaries of the organisation itself, each element of the system has parts exposed to – and are part of – the VUCA world. The degree of this exposure will vary between each element and from organisation to organisation. These complex relationships have been acknowledged in literature including, for example, the body of work developed around the concepts of clustering (Porter & Bond 1999)

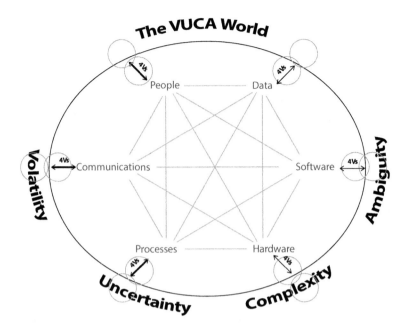

Figure 2.6 The organisation as a system within the VUCA world

just-in-time processes and open-source software (Raymond 1999). The presence of digital technology – like so many aspects of organisation – has only amplified the potential advantages of an organisation integrally working beyond its own boundaries. Digital technologies have also deepened the extent to which the internal and external activities can be successfully mixed together.

Defining organisational exposure to VUCA through each of the six elements brings a strategic advantage. With each element combining features that are external and internal to the organisation, the system can be finely balanced to be both dynamic to taking opportunities from changes in the VUCA world while also making use of the organisation's best internal qualities to buffer the internal environment from the influence of extreme VUCA challenges. The relationship between the internal and external attributes of the organisational system will be variable and may vary over time from a strong tension to complete alignment. Such variability itself reflects the dynamic nature of the VUCA world. Table 2.1 offers some examples of how this balancing might be seen within each organisational element through a variety of VUCA challenges framed in terms of the 4Vs that can be considered in relation to each element of the organisation.

Granularity at the level of organisational system elements also opens up more detailed examination of the qualities that are most important for the organisation and those that the organisation is best at delivering. Table 2.1 suggests some of the qualities that should be emphasised by an organisation when facing the types of VUCA challenges being described.

More direct examples of the organisational response to VUCA challenges are also instructive at this point (Table 2.2). While the examples only highlight a single challenge

Table 2.1 Examples of managing VUCA through the organisational system and qualities

VUCA challenges	The **volume** of customised consumer requests	The **variety** of sizes consumers are requesting	The **velocity** of consumer queries requesting support	The **volume** of consumers wanting premium delivery	The **veracity** of consumer data received through social media channels	The **variety** of devices available to consumers
Element	Desirable internal attributes		Internal qualities (+/-)	Desirable external attributes	External qualities (+/-)	
People	Engaging consumers as people		+Resilience	Prioritise and triage consumer requests based on urgency and priority	+Flexibility	
Data	Focused data collection that supports increasing organisational knowledge		+Integrity	Capture all consumer feedback and correctly tag for AI-based response	+Correctness, +Credibility	
Communications	Data-driven external personal communications		+Timeliness	Customised responses based on previous consumer behaviours	+Scalability	
Software	Data-driven query interface that shows holistic consumer information (rather framed by individual departmental needs)		+Efficiency	Gather consumer feedback from multiple external sources/formats	+Compatibility	
Processes	Processes informed by current challenges and issues		+Modifiability, +Adaptability	Consistent processes for dealing with the most common consumer feedback	+Transparency	
Hardware	Mobile working regime that enables data to be queried anywhere		+Accessibility	Enable consumer devices	+Flexibility	

and the response in a single element of the organisation's structure, the principle can be extended to all six elements and prioritised in terms of the potential value of the response.

The structural view of the organisation

- highlights the importance interlinkage of elements in their response to individual VUCA challenges
- emphasises that transformation also occurs within the "hidden" aspects of the organisation away from the business model itself
- shows how emphasising and aligning the "best" organisational qualities within each of the six elements can guide the development of strategy

Table 2.2 Real VUCA challenges and the organisational responses

VUCA challenge	Framed in terms of the 4Vs	Organisational element response	Organisational qualities (+/−)
Lack of highly skilled employees	The **volume** of skilled employees has not kept pace with other developments	People: Develop internal skills and encourage a lifelong learning that motivates and engages existing employees	+learnability
Too many choices (in terms of goods and services)	The **variety** of consumer options distracts from your own organisation's offerings	Communications: Share the genuine vision of the organisation and encourage consumers who also share this vision to collaborate	+relevance
Climate extremes impacts on supply chains for primary produce	A consistent production **velocity** cannot be maintained	Software: Machine learning in combination with good external data sources can predict coming dips in supply with sufficient notice to locate alternate suppliers or build up a surplus from the current suppliers	+adaptability
Political turmoil makes consumers caution about international travel	The **veracity** of political decisions reduces interest in specific products	Processes (with new business model): Build value-added products that encourage consumers to reflect and share previous international experiences (to "bank" their desire to travel for when things are more certain).	+upgradability

Key takeaways

- The digital difference is not a binary relationship with the physical world
- The digital difference labels all the benefits that strategic digital transformation can bring to any organisation's structure and its business models
- An organisation's structure are the aspects largely hidden from consumers
- The business models used by an organisation describes its visible consumer aspects
- The 4Vs assist in defining VUCA challenges to the organisation and the ways that they can be managed
- Systems qualities – or non-functional requirements – define what the organisation does well in responding to the VUCA world

References

Bulkley, K. (2018) "Binge-watching culture no longer just a streaming service phenomenon", *Royal Television Society*, rts.org.uk/article/binge-watching-culture-no-longer-just-streaming-service-phenomenon

Evans, J. (2014) "The future of work: Amazon vs. Zappos", *TechCrunch*, https://techcrunch.com/2013/08/10/the-manichaean-labors/

Feloni, R. (2016) "A Zappos employee had the company's longest customer-service call at 10 hours, 43 minutes", *Business Insider*, 26th July, www.businessinsider.com/zappos-employee-sets-record-for-longest-customer-service-call-2016-7

Flinders, K. (2017) "When that 'Uber moment' becomes a 'Ryan Air' moment", *Computer Weekly*, 9th Oct, www.computerweekly.com/blog/Fintech-makes-the-world-go-around/When-that-Uber-moment-becomes-a-Ryan-Air-moment

iScoop (n.d.) "The DIKW model for knowledge management and data value extraction", www.i-scoop.eu/big-data-action-value-context/dikw-model/

Porter, M., & Bond, G. (1999) "The California wine cluster", *Harvard Business School Case*, Case number: 799–124, June.

Raymond, E. (1999) *The Cathedral and the Bazaar*. Sebastopol, CA: O'Reilly & Associates.

3 What is digital business maturity?

Alex Fenton, Gordon Fletcher and Marie Griffiths

Preface

The concept of digital business maturity is presented in this chapter as a straightforward tool to make comparative snapshot assessments of an organisation's preparedness to digitally transform against its current capabilities and its external competitors. But beneath this quick positioning there is a depth of detail to consider. This chapter also includes a discussion of the rationale, benefits and insights for an organisation that a maturity model can provide. Closely linked with the previous chapter's discussion, there is an emphasis here on the need for all functions and parts of an organisation to interact and work together towards a common level of maturity. It is only when a common baseline has been achieved that the overall organisation can itself be considered to have achieved this level of maturity. This observation emphasises that an organisation can only be as 'digital' as its least 'digital' function.

3.1 Understanding digital maturity

This chapter presents a simple model to understand an organisation's digital maturity. Digital maturity has been assigned a variety of meanings and is represented in many different ways. This is particularly true of the consulting firms such as McKinsey (Caitlin et al. 2015), Deloitte (2018) and Gartner (Lyengar 2018) who all offer varying digital business maturity models. The potential for confusion is enormous. In this book we use an approach that labels the stages of digital maturity that develop an organisation towards the stated goal of digital transformation to be data-driven and people-focused.

Digital maturity, in this way, is the degree to which an organisation makes appropriate use of technology to both maximise the advantage that can be gained from its data as well as maximising the benefits to its people. Digital maturity is a question about the key 'V' for all organisations: how does technology create value for the organisation and for its customers? This definition should not be read as simply a case of 'giving everyone tablets'. Getting the structure of the organisation right and ensuring that business models are fully realising the benefits of the digital difference all take greater priority over that of providing individual consumer devices.

To support this thinking, we adopt the digital maturity model first proposed in Heinze et al. (2016), where it was used to primarily focus discussion about digital marketing techniques (Figure 3.1). The original sentiment and value of the model is equally applicable in the context of strategic digital transformation and encourages further extension of the model to recognise the different types of transformative actions that are used within the different levels of digital maturity.

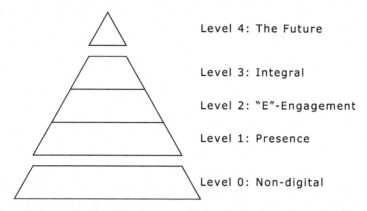

Level 4: The Future

Level 3: Integral

Level 2: "E"-Engagement

Level 1: Presence

Level 0: Non-digital

Figure 3.1 The simplified Digital Business Maturity Model
Source: Heinze et al. (2016)

The model represents digital maturity as a series of levels that positions organisations in a hierarchy from a base level with no adoption (Level 0) through to full adoption (Level 3), with a further final level labelled as an always unreachable (at least for mainstream business models) and aspirational 'future'. This final level of digital maturity acknowledges that transformation is a continuous process and that the capability for technology to bring new benefits to an organisation are practically unlimited and constantly developing. The presence of the future in the model also indicates that the criteria by which the present is understood and defined is continuously changing. However, organisational change operates at a slower pace than consumer technology, and since the model was first published in 2016 there still remains a need to acknowledge that some organisations continue to function at Level 0 with no significant adoption of technology.

The Digital Business Maturity Model is primarily intended to be used as a quick gauge of the current state of technology adoption and transformation within an organisation. At first glance, the model is simple, but despite this simplicity it still provides a useful starting point from which to develop complex levels of strategic thinking and planning. It is with this latter purpose that we develop an extended version of the model to specifically support strategic digital transformation.

Drawing on the system-based view discussed in Chapter 2, it is important to recognise that all the elements of the organisation must reach the same level of digital maturity for the organisation itself to be described in this way. An holistic view of the system is important here, as any one element of the organisation functioning at a lower (or higher) level of digital maturity will be a source of friction within the overall organisation. For example, if an organisation's processes are still undertaken through paper forms, then the organisation itself can be no higher than Level 0. If digitised versions of paper forms are emailed as attachments to individual recipients, then the overall organisation may be functioning at the marginally higher Level 1 of maturity. A quick guide to the digital maturity in a local region can be gauged with a scan of the local office supply store. A count of the carbon invoice books and filing cards points to a prevalence of Level 0 organisations, while a large number of USB sticks suggests that local organisations have moved on to Level 1. Similarly, if an organisation has fully embraced digital marketing – perhaps implying a digital maturity at Level 3 – but still sends a single group-emailed newsletter internally rather than, for example, a customised data-driven individual message to each employee, then there is still transformative work to do with its communications (and other elements of the organisation). The overall digital maturity of an organisation is defined by the role that technology plays in binding the elements of the system together.

3.1.1 *Level 0 of digital maturity*

Level 0 of the model documents the world of the non-digital. An organisation that uses little or no technology at all is described with this level of maturity. In practise, this could mean that no website or social media channels are used in communication, there is little or no technology for the delivery and facilitation of processes, and the existing data of the organisation is locked up in traditional paper-based formats. This lack of digital engagement is represented by the example in Chapter 1 of the small-scale milk delivery service. While this legacy category continues to shrink in number, there are still many traditional and smaller organisations that have no plans to change existing practices and may have retained the same approach for decades. Direct marketing through the postal service, internal paper memos and printed invoice books are all evidence of the many practices used by these organisations to continue to conduct their business.

Understanding the inefficiencies of these practices and their lack of effectiveness in contrast to their digital equivalent is one of the first steps towards recognising the benefits of transformation. Substitution of an existing physical artefact (such as a paper form) by a digitally equivalent form is a common first and soft introduction for an organisation into digital transformation.

Without organisational acknowledgement of the need for change, many organisations will remain at Level 0 of digital maturity. In some cases – at the same time – these organisations remain unaware of the threat from the VUCA world that they are facing through a lack of digital transformation. How this situation can be challenged will vary considerably between organisations and sectors. There is a need for a strategic approach that combines change through the introduction of grassroots, employee-driven use of consumer technologies as well as the introduction of organisational technologies that rise to the challenges of the VUCA world.

Organisations should resist being dragged into Level 1 of digital maturity by their employees' own individual and uncoordinated actions, as this introduces more significant challenges to the development of higher levels of maturity in the future. Unfortunately, the value of the strategic route to transformation is not always recognised soon enough, and the ad hoc introduction of consumer technologies can dominate the shift in maturity from Level 0 to Level 1. Consumer technology, by its very nature, is ubiquitous and makes its introduction by employees into the organisation overly easy. Without an organisation-level strategic perspective, the appeal of Bring Your Own Device (BYOD), redirecting phone calls to personal mobile phones, using public email addresses and a variety of different shared document editing systems (all of which nonetheless are useful technologies in their own right) can rapidly lead to a muddled organisational infrastructure.

Some Level 0 organisations will develop their digital maturity through a desire to copy the observable outward-facing activities of competitors in the hope of emulating their success – what can be described as cargo cult thinking (the belief that if we simply emulate the visible effects of achievement, the real achievement will follow automatically) (Lindstrom 2018). Without an understanding of the underlying structure of the organisation they are imitating, this type of organisational change is as reactive as the ad hoc introduction of consumer technology and equally does not produce strategic or sustainable change. The most recent prevalent example of this form of cargo cult thinking has been the internal pressure for every organisation to have its own 'app'. These types of decisions are based solely on the realisation that a competitor has an 'app' and without critically questioning the value or benefits of a standalone app for the organisation's own customers. Similar examples can be recognised in the demand for a website with similar functionality and features as a competitor with no understanding of its purpose or function.

Inevitably the majority of organisations currently at Level 0 will not be drawn to change but rather will be pushed by the pressures of increased competition, falling revenue or significant change in the external environment or be dragged into change through the introduction of a variety of consumer technology by employees and individual organisational units acting independently. For a small minority of Level 0 organisations, the catalyst for change will be their own strategic recognition of the increased value that can be created through transformation.

3.1.2 Level 1 of digital maturity

At Level 1 of maturity, there is some digital activity within the organisation. Often the technology being used is piecemeal and can vary across the organisation. Much of the technology in use will be consumer-level solutions that are readily available but change rapidly on a two-to-three-year replacement cycle. The speed of this technology cycle will – in many cases – be too rapid for an organisation's own Level 1 processes and culture to keep pace.

The Level 1 organisation may have a basic website that lists some organisational information, and perhaps there is some use of social media channels to broadcast marketing messages. These type of developments will have been driven by the wide availability of accessible and free consumer-level solutions – such as WordPress – and deployed without consideration of the impact beyond the communications element of the organisation. As a result, there is a general lack of two-way technology-mediated interaction with internal and external people.

Some basic management tools such as standalone spreadsheets might be also be used in the background. The feature that is consistent through Level 1 organisations is not the specific type and form of technologies that are being used but rather the lack of integration and connections being made between the technologies that are already in place. A single unit or function within the organisation will have taken a leading role and be shaping the overall relationship of technology to the organisational culture. This focus of transformative activity will be found in, for example, marketing, accounting or logistics. In smaller organisations the focus will be more commonly found located with a single individual.

The general lack of digital maturity at this level prevents technology from being seen as an enabler for value-creating change at the structural level of the organisation or through new business models. Without an holistic systems-based and strategic view of transformation, Level 1 organisations will continue to rely on the traditional business models that have worked in the past. Some examples are those restaurants that only take cash payments or traders at exhibitions that only sell their products via email as they have yet to venture into online sales.

Without a strategy in place from Level 1, the consumer technology currently being used will fail to fully realise its potential for the organisation. There may be, for example, some basic e-commerce functions, but these may be relatively new, use an incomplete catalogue or contain out-of-date information. The UK's train network and the many online ticketing sites offer a more complex and potentially surprising example of how an overall lack of digital maturity can constrain customers. The most popular ticketing sites are independently operated by the various companies who use the train network that is managed by a separate company. As each operator's ticketing technology has developed in isolation with only shared access to the railway timetables, a range of anomalies have developed across the network. Examples of these anomalies include differential fares and conditions for the same journey with different operators. The operators' various ticketing systems can all equally manage the booking of simple direct or single change commuter journeys, but many struggle to offer a route or a fare for more complex journeys that require multiple changes and cover long distances that do not go through major city hubs. However, the national operator's own booking website will provide fares for any combination of route and, in many cases, will offer reduced fares for journeys that cannot be booked elsewhere.

A more difficult prospect – and one evidenced by the UK train network example – is that early decisions made around the deployment of technology may already introduce the burden of legacy without ever realising the intended full benefits. By experiencing the negative outcomes before realising the benefits of the technology infrastructure the organisation's cultural position will shift to a position where blame for any change programme is directed at 'IT', the 'system' or the 'techies'. This type of challenge and resistance can be recognised in a large number of organisations across all sizes, from micro-businesses and small to medium sized enterprises up to multi-national enterprises. Negative and piecemeal experience with technology also creates resistance to the initiation of further transformation and impedes the organisational shift to Level 2 of digital maturity or higher.

Recognising that further transformation must be undertaken in a more holistic and strategic manner is a more significant challenge for Level 1 organisations than those at Level 0. Having engaged with technology without seeing many (or any) of the claimed benefits elevates the presence of risk aversion in organisational culture. Raising an organisation to Level 2 of digital maturity also requires the investment and introduction of organisational level technologies that assert the strategic direction for increasing maturity. The term 'organisational technologies' broadly describes the class of digital technologies that do not normally figure within a household because they are either too expensive to deploy or make no sense to implement in a domestic context. Some examples include the 'enterprise' license for any software including Microsoft's Office 365, Google's AdWords system or specialist data analysis software such as RapidMiner.

3.1.3   Level 2 of digital maturity

At Level 2, typically, an organisation will have a more contemporary website that is e-commerce enabled (or has the capability), content managed and well indexed by search engines. Significantly, the organisation will have a wider online presence that enables forms of two-way communications through, for example, social media channels. Behind these externally facing communications the organisations at this level will also be moving towards the use of enterprise technologies that join up many of the elements of its overall system. With the organisation's digital maturity in a key transitional state, so much of the technology and thinking will be prefaced with an 'e' or 'i' that references back to earlier non-technological equivalents, for example, e-commerce, e-HRM, digital marketing or even email. Level 2 maturity also brings an understanding that technology is not just a substitution for the equivalent physical action but can go further to automate and replace people from existing processes entirely. At this level of maturity there is a wider influence on business models and processes. There is increasing recognition, for example, that the 'open' philosophies associated with technology encourages developments around organisational transparency and collaboration which in turn leads to the generation of ideas about changing ways of working and new business models.

At Level 2, the engagement aspect also acknowledges that communication technologies such as social media can be used to engage with and interact with customers and stakeholders and to improve internal communications. Social capital is "the value of the relationships built through your social networks, the connections between people and the levels of trust that exist" (Heinze et al. 2016). Social media and e-engagement therefore can be used to build social capital which can add value to an organisation.

Many organisations are now positioned at this level of maturity. But with a blend of consumer and organisational technologies shaping the organisational infrastructure, there still remain barriers to the development of their digital maturity. Increasing legacy issues and organisational silos 'owning' specific technologies can overshadow core organisational goals and prevent seamless integration of the six elements of the system. The mix of technologies now across the organisation present as many challenges to reaching higher levels of digital maturity as the specific function of the technologies that have already been deployed.

Moving any further forward without a clear strategic view on transformation is now impossible. The strategy must focus on responding to the challenges of the VUCA world, the integration of existing technologies and the removal or minimisation of legacy. The strategy at this point does not set out to introduce specific new technologies. The strategy is built upon integrating the six elements of the business system rather than attempting to link existing technologies together. As part of the strategic push for digital maturity, the emphasis on organisational qualities such as simplicity become more important. The pool of existing organisational qualities is made more prominent with the integration of its organisational elements and supports a stronger and more sustainable starting point for transformation. Knowing the qualities of the organisation that can be emphasised through internal integration is also counterbalanced by those aspects of the organisation that it cannot or should not continue to emphasise.

3.1.4 Level 3 of digital maturity

With the realisation of a broadly integrated organisational system, Level 3 of digital maturity is reached. At this level there is a more robust understanding of how the digital difference can be directly translated into more transformative objectives. The historical baggage that persists in labelling new systems as being 'e' in less mature organisation has now disappeared. Digital technologies and more significantly the use of data has become integral across the organisation. Organisations at this level are likely to have also achieved a significant level of change. At this transformative level the ubiquitous presence and familiarity with data will have also enabled entirely new business models to be introduced into the organisation. The organisational culture has been consciously altered alongside the infrastructural aspects of the organisation. With changes in the underlying organisational system, existing and new business models can be designed to exploit the advantages of digital difference and respond fully to the VUCA world.

For existing organisations progressing through the lower levels of digital transformation, the greatest challenge is the entry of competitors from other sectors or startups with this level of maturity already in place. The newer global digital organisations, for example, Facebook, Amazon, Netflix and Google as well as others including Chinese firms such as Alibaba, all represent a major threat to any sector because they are digital by default, have significant resources and, most importantly, recognise how data is pivotal to producing value within any business model.

The challenge for all Level 3 organisations is to maintain pace with the changing range of opportunities introduced by digital technology. The large global organisations maintain their position on the crest of the technological wave by shaping and guiding research and development. If their position slips from this crest by, for instance, committing resources in pursuing research that comes to a dead end, their resources enable them to buy smaller innovating organisations to reposition and redirect their efforts.

For small organisations, their own significant commitment to research and development is not a viable option to maintain pace. This is when alternative options, including strategic clustering, continuous horizon scanning, close consumer collaboration and professional networks all become increasingly important.

3.1.5   *Level 4 of digital maturity*

Level 4 of digital maturity is the future and is a constant reminder that continuous technological change intersects with an organisation's level of digital maturity. Over time the wide base at Level 0 and Level 1 of maturity may contract to reflect the position of the majority of organisations. Organisational change, however, moves at a much slower pace than that of consumer technology and still remains relatively unchanged as a viable model since it was first presented in 2014.

The future offers the prospect of, for example, human-computer integration where the distinction between people and their devices are increasingly less pronounced. There are already coarse examples of this type of integration, with 3,000 Swedes being reported to have had a chip placed directly under their skin to enable seamless payments and building access (Pettit & Pinkstone 2018). The use of biometrics such as iris scanning, while not necessarily commonplace, is equally charting a less invasive path to human-computer integration. The popular rise of consumer DNA testing kits to become 2018's 'hot' Christmas gift (Estrada 2018) points to other avenues through this type of integration that could occur.

The interrelationship between consumer and organisational technologies that can be recognised within lower levels of the maturity model can also be recognised within the future level. At lower levels the relationship may be interpreted as a tension between getting things done and more strategic perspectives. With Level 4, consumer-oriented technologies, including their incorporation of the processes of co-design and co-funding, offer insight to future technologies available for smaller organisations. Crowdfunding sites such as Indiegogo and Kickstarter provide insights into the direction being taken by near-future consumer technologies.

At the scale of organisational technologies, the velocity of change and volume of adoption is noticeably accelerated. The rapid development and acceptance of machine learning and artificial intelligence at the end of the end of the 2010s is an example of how rapidly future technologies can move into the mainstream activities of Level 3 mature organisations. For smaller organisations, this is a second front to their horizon scanning. However, the important questions regarding transformation remain the same irrespective of the technologies being identified. The external stimulus must be internalised and considered in relation to the organisations own needs and current maturity with the same primary question: "How does this technology add value to my organisational structure or (current and future) business models?"

3.2 Strategic transformation and digital business maturity

The Digital Business Maturity Model and its levels align closely with the various forms of actions that are grouped under the label of transformation (Figure 3.2). The different levels of the model also provide guidance as to the relative position, merits and relationship of these actions. At Level 0 there are no digital transformation actions associated with digital technology. Level 1 introduces the most commonly experienced form of transformation through direct substitution. At this level, digital transformation will be framed in the context of taking an existing element within the organisation and replacing it with its digital equivalent. Using web pages instead of printed catalogues was the example used in Chapter 2 to consider the innovation and impact of the earliest forms of e-commerce. E-commerce was initially nothing more than a substitution of a printed catalogue for a web-based equivalent. Many of the paper forms that were digitised in the UK's e-government programme simply substituted the existing form with a web-based form without changing its format or structure or altering the back-end processing that was undertaken following its submission.

The key actions associated with Level 2 of maturity are task automation and labour displacement. These forms of action replace a person with technology or use technology

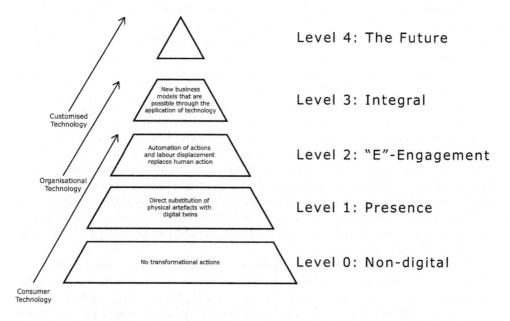

Figure 3.2 Digital transformation actions showing their relationship to digital maturity

to shift the labour to the consumer. Associating Level 2 of digital maturity with automation and displacement indicates that these types of actions generally create no additional value or benefits for the organisation of the consumer. Examples of Level 2 transformation actions are plentiful within the retail and consumer sector. Self-scan checkouts, auto-teller machines (cash machines) and vending machines are all everyday examples where person-to-person engagement has been removed from the earlier equivalent action.

Displacing the labour role within an action onto a consumer can also be identified in many consumer-level interactions. The use of open customer forums by many mobile (cell) phone providers is one example, with more experienced consumers offering the first line of support for enquiries based around incentivising the participants with points or other forms of recognition. Consumer-oriented apps and web services also use labour displacement in a variety of ways. An early – now disbanded – example can be seen with the original CAPTCHA system that challenges 'humans' with two words scanned from a book. The first word in the CAPTCHA was known and confirmed that the operation was being undertaken by a person. The second word was unknown, and the CAPTCHA system was using the many people accessing a service to help identify the word accurately. A key reason that the CAPTCHA system was changed was a result of consumer backlash when it was recognised that everyone using the CAPTCHA system was performing unpaid labour. The result was that many consumers preferred to insert a random second word – often a profanity – into their response and, as a result, rendered the accuracy of the crowdsourced identification of the word invalid (Havel 2015).

At Level 3 the actions associated with digital transformation are strategic and genuinely transformative. The use of technology extends beyond the direct substitution or replacement of existing actions to create additional value and new business models that would be impossible without technology. In most cases these new business models enable ways in which at least one of the 4Vs can be managed in response to the VUCA world. Consumer-focused business models also provide value to their consumers by enabling them to manage some aspects of their own VUCA world. Some indications of what Level 3 transformation can look like are found with the business models of the 'pure play' technology companies. These are iconic – and now large – companies that founded their business models on the opportunities that only technology can deliver and includes Google, LinkedIn, Facebook and Netflix.

The future and Level 4 of the maturity model can also be associated with transformative actions. The distributed autonomous organisations (DAO) describes an organisation that is entirely driven through technology. The role of people in these organisations is entirely reversed from that of other levels of maturity. People become disruptors in the system as the mechanisms that introduce random impetus and inspiration into entirely data-driven operations. From the point of view of the transformation process its goal is now complete. The organisation is managed through data-driven decision-making processes that makes its people the only differentiator. As a result it is people who are also the only source for defining key differences from other similarly transformed organisations.

The Digital Business Maturity Model (Figure 3.3) is a tool for making a comparative assessment of an organisation's digital maturity. It also assists in creating a roadmap for an organisation's strategic aspirations. Chapter 2 highlights that simple binary distinctions between digital and physical organisations are unhelpful. The staged approach found in this model argues instead for a continuum of experience that highlights the varying opportunities and benefits for organisations at different levels of maturity.

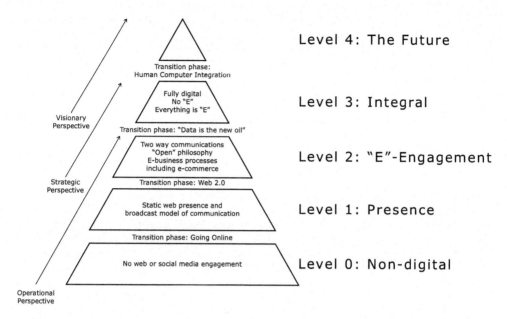

Level 4: The Future

Transition phase:
Human Computer Integration

Level 3: Integral

Fully digital
No "E"
Everything is "E"

Visionary
Perspective

Transition phase: "Data is the new oil"

Level 2: "E"-Engagement

Two way communications
"Open" philosophy
E-business processes
including e-commerce

Strategic
Perspective

Transition phase: Web 2.0

Level 1: Presence

Static web presence and
broadcast model of communication

Transition phase: Going Online

Level 0: Non-digital

No web or social media engagement

Operational
Perspective

Figure 3.3 The Digital Business Maturity Model
Source: Adapted from Heinze et al. 2016

A systems-oriented approach to strategic digital transformation points to the need for all functions of an organisation to be operating symbiotically to reach higher shared levels of maturity. It is only with a shared level of maturity across all the elements of the entire organisation that it can itself be considered to have achieved the same level of maturity. This realisation further emphasises the need for an holistic, systems-focused and strategic view of the organisation and its trajectory.

Key takeaways

- Digital maturity labels an organisation's current situation in relation to digital technology and is not an organisational goal in its own right
- Digital maturity is a continuum of organisational experience
- The levels identified by the Digital Business Maturity Model refer to the overall state of the organisation – an organisation is only as digitally mature as its least mature element
- Consumer technology and operational activities at the lower levels of maturity must eventually give way to strategic perspectives and the deployment of organisational technologies
- Transformation actions being undertaken within an organisation are indicative of its current levels of maturity

References

Caitlin, T., Scanlan, J., & Willmott, P. (2015) "Raising your digital quotient", *McKinsey*, June, www.mckinsey.com/business-functions/strategy-and-corporate-finance/our-insights/raising-your-digital-quotient

Deloitte (2018) "Digital maturity model achieving digital maturity to drive growth", Feb, www2. deloitte.com/content/dam/Deloitte/global/Documents/Technology-Media-Telecommunications/ deloitte-digital-maturity-model.pdf

Estrada, M. (2018) "DNA tests are the hottest Christmas gifts of the season, and there's still time to get one on sale", *BGR*, 22nd Dec, https://bgr.com/2018/12/22/dna-test-deals-last-minute-christmas-sale/

Havel, J. (2015) "Recaptcha: The genius who's tricking the world into doing his work", *The Hustle*, 3rd Dec, https://thehustle.co/the-genius-whos-tricking-the-world-into-doing-his-work-recaptcha

Heinze, A., Fletcher, G., Rashid, T., & Cruz, A. (eds.) (2016) *Digital and Social Media Marketing: A Results-Driven Approach.* London: Routledge.

Lindstrom, L. (2018) "Cargo cults", in Stein, F., Lazar, S., Candea, M., Diemberger, H., Robbins, J., Sanchez, A., Stasch, R. (eds.) *The Cambridge Encyclopedia of Anthropology*, www.anthroencyclopedia.com/ entry/cargo-cults

Lyengar, P. (2018) "Digital business maturity model: 9 competencies determine maturity", *Gartner*, 24th Oct, www.gartner.com/en/documents/3892086

Pettit, H., & Pinkstone, J. (2018) "Would you have a microchip implanted under your SKIN? 3,000 Swedes with electronic tags embedded into their hands risk their personal data being 'used against them'", *MailOnline*, 14th May, www.dailymail.co.uk/sciencetech/article-5726197/Would-microchip-SKIN-3-000-Swedes-electronic-tag-embedded-hands.html

4 Who are my competitors and what is my relationship to them?

Marie Griffiths, Alex Fenton and Gordon Fletcher

Preface

External innovation and the ability to internalise stimulus is a key driver for change and transformation within organisations. The proliferation of consumer digital technologies, connectivity, GPS, cheap mobile devices and increasingly demanding consumers has created the opportunities and rationale for transformation. To be successful in the digital transformation of an organisation there is a need to create an innovating environment that includes changing behaviours in the C-suite. The internalising of stimulus changes the traditional perception and role of the competitor – with the potential to reconsider them as collaborators. This chapter presents the concept of the "braided river" of an organisation as an analogy to the complex ecosystem that all organisations work within and the challenges they face to become innovative. The "braided river" also contextualises the role of failure in innovation and the need for multiple deep and shallow innovations in order to succeed as an organisation.

4.1 Competitor analysis

Competitor analysis is nothing new and has always been an important aspect of conducting business. Learning how to improve by observing the practice of others and avoiding the pitfalls experienced by competitors is as old as business itself. In 1980, Porter outlined the importance of competitor analysis in *Competitive Strategy*, but at the same time he highlighted that this activity is not always undertaken in a strategic way (Porter 1980). In the challenging VUCA world, strategic and ongoing analysis of the competition has never been more important. The ready availability of organisational data and the tools to interpret this data have increased significantly since Porter made his observations, but the core thinking behind this analysis has not necessarily evolved at the same pace.

What has changed at considerable pace is the ability to rapidly – even automatically – visualise and compare competitor's data with a few clicks. But even this change in being able to access high volumes of data with greater velocity and veracity can make competitor analysis even more intimidating for an organisation – particularly smaller ones. The nervousness around competitor analysis is understandable, as it involves, by definition, looking outwards at the VUCA world and attempting to make sense of what is found. The currently available tools for analysis open up a range of different views into the VUCA world and systematise what is seen through the filtering of one or more of the 4Vs. The value of filtering what is seen out in the VUCA world is to transform this data into relevant and actionable insight for the individual organisations.

Sloan Management Review (2018) highlights a "Darwinian shaking out" of organisations, effectively reducing the challenge of competitors into two major categories of mergers or technology. The competitors that continue to thrive will emerge and evolve through strategic transformation and increasing digital maturity. This categorisation also reinforces the observation made in Chapter 1. Change in the external environment now a) is invariably facilitated through consumer and organisational digital technologies, b) is unexpected and c) regularly comes from beyond the current competitors in the sector.

Undertaking competitor analysis with the development of a new organisation, business model, service or product is a given. What is less commonly found, and reflecting Porter's (1980) observation about the lack of strategic competitor analysis, is the ongoing scanning that is needed to keep an organisation competitive and innovating. The general availability of relevant data, the rapid pace of organisational change, the ready sharing of ideas globally and the heightened expectations of consumers all argue in favour of ongoing, strategic and systematic competitor analysis.

An hour with a web browser and a search engine can reveal current competitors on a local, national and global scale for any particular market segment and even more precisely for any given search term. Social media adds another layer of accessible data for competitor analysis. The increased transparency brought by these channels makes it possible to see exactly what competitors are doing with their customers on a day-to-day basis. Activities and engagement that has previously been hidden can now be readily and easily examined. The ability to dive even more deeply into a competitor's strategy is made possible with the sharing of materials such as webinars, whitepapers and product roadmaps. As Chaffey observes, "the implications of this dynamism are that competitor benchmarking is not a one-off activity while developing a strategy, but needs to be continuous" (Chaffey & Ellis-Chadwick 2015, 89).

However, the challenge to organisations goes beyond simply appreciating the need for a continuous form of competitor analysis – this should be a given. Richer competitor analysis should endeavour to get beneath direct engagement to build a picture of the underlying organisational structure that shapes the competitor's activities alongside its current business models. With so much data available to any organisation, the challenge is to understand what can be gained from competitor analysis and to systematise the analysis in order to make the activity sustainable and an integral aspect of being an innovating organisation. With advocacy for a sustainable and systematic approach, the answer to the key question "why do competitor analysis?" is multifaceted. The tactical response remains the same as always: to know what competitors are currently doing. The strategic response is that deep and wide-ranging competitor analysis supports the transformation of the organisation into an innovating organisation.

4.2   Systematic and sustainable competitor analysis

A sustainable approach to competitor analysis requires a systematic understanding of the external environment. A strategic approach to competitors requires examination beyond the most immediate threats to the organisation to include a wider range of organisations, including current partners and those outside the sector including larger organisations as well as innovations from individuals and small startups. What should be examined also extends beyond the interactions that competitors have with customers. Building on the systems-based understanding we have developed in Chapters 2 and 3 the value of obtaining insight about another organisation's system, business models and even operational details holds potential value for your own organisation. This is increasingly possible with the prevailing attitudes for openness and transparency that innovating organisations encourage rather than advocating the undertaking of industrial espionage.

To understand the VUCA world, it has to be broken down in ways that relate to the organisation itself. The primary dimension for this compartmentalising of the external world is in the relationship to the organisation itself. All organisations have a close relationship with at least some other businesses that they interact with regularly including competitors, suppliers and customers. These partners will be an integral aspect of existing business models and may be part of a supply chain, supplier or distributor or may collaborate even more closely. The potentially greater levels of access and data available from these organisations gives the opportunity for deeper levels of analysis beyond that of customer-facing activities. Having visibility into the structure and operations of an organisation offers broader scope to a competitor analysis and builds more strategic insight. Acknowledging the organisational norm of "free" as the optimum price point (Pattuglia & Mingione 2016) that has been brought by the prevalence the "open" philosophy means that many organisations are more closely tied to one another than ever before. One example of how relationships can be developed with "free" things can be found with construction firms that give away project management software to their suppliers in order to improve their own supply chains. As a result, understanding the business of these partner organisations becomes an important part of competitor analysis for all the organisations tied into this relationship.

There is an implied threat of competition from partners, too. Changes in their business models, including the development of greater digital maturity and rapid transformation, can represent as much of a threat as the introduction of a new product or service from a known competitor. The threat of disintermediation is ever present and very real in data-driven environments. The purpose of the close-quarters scanning of partners is to understand and recognise the balance of opportunities and risks and to build a strategic response. In general, the advantages of working together will outweigh any negative impact or risks, and the analysis of partners and collaborators should not be paralysing to the organisation's own strategic transformation.

Traditional competitor analysis tends to focus on direct competitors that are in the same sector and offer a directly comparable specific product or service. This focus of attention developed in a data-poor era as a compromise between the general lack of external data that could be easily obtained or was available in a pre-digital era combined with the most pressing need for specific insight about immediate commercial threats. Focusing attention on the most obvious current threats is a pragmatic method but counteracts the likelihood that competitor analysis will become a strategic activity within the organisation. Immediate threats provoke short-term reactions.

Taking a broader view of competitors has become an increasingly important necessity. The challenge to existing organisations is that the threat of new products and services comes unexpectedly from outside the sector. This necessitates wider scanning with an eye to organisations that may not have previously been regarded as competitors. The large technology companies are a key avenue for these explorations, with many such as Google (experiments.withgoogle.com) and Twitter (www.macrumors.com/2019/02/20/twitter-prototype-testing-app/) keen to share their innovations in order to encourage user involvement. Other, generally larger organisations are developing and sharing new products and services that may not represent immediate direct competition, such as Uber's AI platform Ludwig (eng.uber.com/introducing-ludwig/), but these actions themselves show that when any problem can be defined as a data problem there is a very real and constant threat of new entrants into the sector.

At a similar distance from the developments and experiments of large technology organisations, there is also a constant process of new technical development occurring with small startups and even individuals. Because obtaining access to finance is the greatest barrier to developing new ideas and products, there are many sources of data and insight. Crowdfunding sites including Indiegogo (www.indiegogo.com) and Kickstarter (www. kickstarter.com) reveal ideas and technology that are on the cusp of realising their commercial reality. The Pebble Watch, Fidget Cube and a number of new game experiences are all examples of successful crowdsourcing concepts that have become significant new competitors in existing markets.

Combining the scanning of partners, direct competitors and those ideas and organisations that are further on the horizon implies a need for the organisation to maintain a critical perspective on its own activities (Table 4.1). Without a willingness to internally recognise the need or value of change in response to competitor analysis, any response will tend to perpetuate and accentuate current internal business models as a form of resistance to the many external challenges. An innovating organisation, in contrast, is permeable to the VUCA world and open to the introduction of new ideas and concepts.

With a digital transformation focus there are further dimensions to the organisation's relationship with the external VUCA world that are defined by the comparative digital maturity of the competitor. Without recognising the difference in digital maturity that exists in another organisation, competitor analysis may stimulate innovation that is not currently possible with the current capacity of the organisation.

Acknowledging varying levels of digital maturity in the competitor analysis provides for better positioning of a competitor's operational and structural business model and consumer engagement differences against the specific actions that may be required internally by the organisation doing the analysis. More digitally mature organisations may be able to take direct inspiration, for example, from emerging ideas and incorporate them as additional features into existing business models. A less digitally mature organisation may use its competitor analysis to recognise aspirational endpoints in their process of becoming more digitally mature. Competitor analysis that is digitally aware also highlights the value

Table 4.1 The elements of a competitor analysis

Internal comparison with	Partners	Existing sector competitors	Large technology R&D	Emerging ideas & concepts
Operational insight	?/4			
Structural insight	?/4	?/4		
Business model insight	?/4	?/4	?/4	?/4
Consumers/Customer/ Influencer engagement insight		?/4	?/4	?/4
Partner scanning (operational)				
Competitor scanning (tactical)				
Horizon scanning (strategic)				

of strategic transformation as a mechanism to broader change rather than being seen as a necessity for its own sake.

4.3   Internalising stimulus and the innovating organisation

The purpose of conducting a strategic competitor analysis is to internalise the external stimulus that is found in the VUCA world. The need for an organisation to be permeable to external stimulus is an essential prerequisite for successful competitor analysis. Competitor analysis should not be reduced to an opportunity to copy existing ideas – what can be described as a cargo cult approach to competitor analysis.

An explanation of cargo cult thinking is useful at this point as a mechanism for highlighting what should not be done. Cargo cult thinking describes an approach to competitor analysis in which the observation of specific aspects of another organisation is then directly copied into their own operations. The problem with cargo cult thinking is that what is observed and copied is only one part of the entire operations and infrastructure of the competitor. This is a case of following observed form without acknowledging the underlying supporting content.

The most commonly cited anthropological version of the cargo cult also remains the most insightful example of the consequences of cargo cult thinking (Worsley 1957). The Tanna islanders of Vanuatu witnessed the arrival of the US infantry during the Second World War. With the troops also came the supplies, shelter and equipment of the US Army. The islanders' observations led them to believe that if they imitated the actions of the troops they too would also receive the benefits they enjoyed. As a result the islanders commenced parading in front of a star and stripes flag, painted military insignia onto themselves and crafted rifles from wood. Needless to say the expected cargo never appeared.

With hindsight, and greater knowledge of the scale and capabilities of the US Army, the Tanna islanders appear to have engaged in an extreme form of fallacious thinking. However, all organisations that engage in cargo cult thinking also lack insight into the content that lies behind the form that they observe. Other forms of cargo cult thinking have been identified, including Feynman's description of cargo cult science in 1974 (Feynman 1974) and, more recently, cargo cult programming (Fletcher 2004).

More recent technology-based examples extend the caution associated with applying cargo cult thinking. Increasingly, reports of the destructive workplace organisational cultures within the largest technology businesses, including overworked pilots at Amazon (Premack & Matousel 2019) or the low wages and recreational drug use of Facebook content moderators (Price 2019), have become a regular feature of the technology press. These two examples alone are stark warnings against directly copying the customer experiences of the largest social media channels or e-commerce retailers without recognising the organisational structure and work practices that enable this customer experience.

Knowing that cargo cult thinking is an outcome to be avoided, the key purpose for competitor analysis is to inspire the organisation and enable the formulation of a response. This also explains the cautious and limited use of the term "Uber moment" in Chapter 2 and elsewhere. It is too easy for this phrase to be misinterpreted as an invitation to copy the disruptive actions of competitors in an attempt for an organisation to remain competitive.

Internalising stimulus brings existing disruptions and ideas found in the VUCA world into the organisation and "naturalises" them through a series of filters (Figure 4.1). How these external inputs are dealt with inside the organisation reflects its own internal

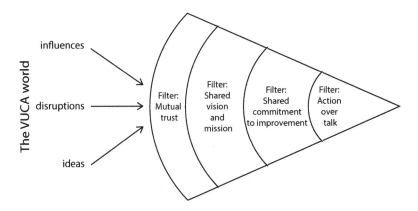

Figure 4.1 Internalising stimulus in the innovating organisation

culture – and explains why being an innovating organisation is just as important for strategic transformation as the introduction of any specific technology or processes. Internalising stimulus balances the benefits of a common shared understanding of mission and vision – which keeps everyone in the organisation pushing in the same direction – with a willingness to implement and try new ideas in ways that fit the organisation. The innovating organisation is hallmarked by mutual trust found throughout all levels of the organisation that enables colleagues to get things done with a shared commitment to doing those things in better ways. What is discovered about competitors is then understood internally as a stimulus for thinking and innovations.

Innovation that comes from attempts to internalise stimulus will inevitably be prone to occasional failure in the attempt to "do" new things within the organisation. This preparedness to occasionally fail in the process of improving emphasises a further key feature of innovating organisations. Innovating organisations are learning organisations that treat every activity as a form of knowledge exchange. Organisations that learn from its previous activities do not repeat the same failures while still maintaining a mindset to continually try new things.

4.4 The braided river of organisations

The braided river is a thinking device used to describe the VUCA world which is full of current and future competitors in ways that can be meaningful shared with an internal audience. The braided river attempts to synthesise existing conceptualisations of the external environment such as PESTLE (Political, Economic, Social, Technological, Legal and Environmental) analysis alongside internal business modelling. The individual threads discussed by different strategic tools are brought together in a linked narrative form using terms that are not tied to the jargon of a particular sector.

The original meaning of a braided river is a particular geographic form found in many locations around the world (Figure 4.2). A braided river has many different channels that flow rapidly across a wide area with relatively low banks. These type of rivers also carry a high volume of sediment and have variable rates of water discharge. The channels constantly merge and separate and are generally shallow, although it is not uncommon for a deeper main channel to predominate at various points in its course.

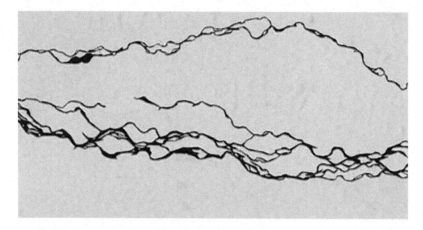

Figure 4.2 Part of a braided river in New Zealand

The path and the number of the channels changes constantly based on current environmental conditions. The conditions that influence changes in the braided river can range from large-scale storms to much smaller influences. With rapid flow across shallow courses even a fallen tree can have an influence on the form and flow of a single channel within the river. Braided rivers also have low banks that easily erode. It is this relationship with its surrounding river valley that differentiates a braided river from a meandering river.

This description of the braided river makes its potential as an analogy to the contemporary external environment more obvious if we associate aspects of the braided river with organisational practice. The braided river and the river valley that it sits within represent the entire external environment. Unlike conventional rivers, the braided river of organisations is a continuous never-ending valley and a literary device that has previously been employed in science fiction, including most famously by Philip Jose Farmer in his Riverworld series. The river itself and its many courses reflects the sector within which the organisation primarily operates. The many courses of the braided river reflect the individual variety and different products and services within the sector. Sometimes new ideas evolve into an entirely new sector (Figure 4.3). However the reverse happens at least as regularly, and an existing sector merges into another. It enters the new river as a tributary. The low bank of the river reflects the permeability of the sector – and by extension the organisation itself – to its customers.

The key component in this analogy is the organisation itself – and its competitors. These are vessels that ply the braided river. Each organisation has slightly different vessels. In highly traditional sectors there may be few differentiating features on vessels other than the flag that it flies. The shape and description of each vessel assists in coherently describing the structure of the organisation as well as the business model that it uses. Even describing the size of the vessel in combination with the current course of the river sets out an important relationship between the size of the organisation and the complexity of the sector. Similarly customer relations can be described through explanation of how and when the vessel is able to draw up to the river bank. Finally, a description of the vessel's mechanism for spotting dangers on the horizon is also meaningful.

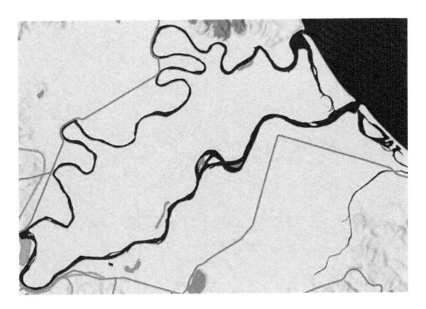

Figure 4.3 A branched braided river

The braided river of organisations can provoke a range of creative responses when discussed with delegates attending executive education courses. References to the *Titanic* are common. When pressed for details, the *Titanic* is often fitted out with a wobbly draw-bridge to access its customers and a ragged basket crow's nest. Description of the sector, the outside environment and competitors can also be revealing. Competitors' vessels are often referred to as submarines, being on jet skis or "James Bond"-style powerboats in contrast to their own. The overall river valley is described variously as a desert, an impene-trable jungle or scattered with small campsites. The valley might meet the river with steep cliffs and the river itself can vary from being the most extreme braiding to an "improved" watercourse with neat embankments.

In combination the description of the river valley, the braided river and the vessels that sail upon it are rich territory for description and even sketches that keep what can some-times become disparate aspects of analysis together in a way that encourages a common language and creative responses. Applying an analogy such as the braided river to com-petitor analysis provides focus and can even support ideas for innovation and transforma-tion by providing the buffer of a protective narrative layer over the reality of day-to-day organisational operations.

Key takeaways

- Competitor analysis should be a sustainable, systematic strategic organisational activity
- Competitor analysis should look beyond immediate threats and current competitors
- Competitor analysis should include scanning of close partners as well as more distant opportunities that are on the horizon

- At its widest extent competitor analysis is global in its scope
- Strategic competitor analysis requires an organisation to be self-aware, critical of its own situation and open to change
- An outcome of strategic competitor analysis is to develop an innovating organisation and internal organisational environment
- Analogies and storytelling techniques such as the braided river can support and contextualise the findings of competitor analysis for the entire organisation

References

Chaffey, D., & Ellis-Chadwick, F. (2015) *Digital Marketing Strategy, Implementation and Practice*. London: Pearson.

Feynman, R. (1974) "Cargo cult science: Some remarks on science, pseudoscience, and learning how to not fool yourself", *Caltech Commencement Speech*, http://calteches.library.caltech.edu/51/2/CargoCult.htm

Fletcher, G. (2004) "Cargo cults in java", www.researchgate.net/publication/238732494_Cargo_Cults_in_Java

Pattuglia, S., & Mingione, M. (2016) "Towards a new understanding of brand authenticity: Seeing through the lens of Millennials", *XXVIII Sinergie Annual Conference*, doi: 10.7433/SRECP.FP.2016.29

Porter, M. (1980) *Competitive Strategy: Techniques for Analyzing Industries and Competitors*. New York: Free Press.

Premack, R., & Matousel, M. (2019) "'It's a ticking time bomb': A pilot for one of Amazon Air's contract airlines said the company overworks its pilots", *Business Insider*, 25th Feb, www.businessinsider.com/amazon-air-pilot-contract-said-airline-company-overworked-pilots-2019-2

Price, R. (2019) "Facebook's content moderators are paid incredibly low wages, and reportedly turn to pot and office sex to cope with what they see", *Business Insider*, 25th Feb, www.businessinsider.com/facebooks-us-content-moderators-paid-low-wages-smoke-weed-sex-report-2019-2

Worsley, P. (1957) *The Trumpet Shall Sound: A Study of 'Cargo' Cults in Melanesia*. London: MacGibbon & Kee.

5 Managing the digital transformation of an organisation

Tim Griggs, Marie Griffiths and Gordon Fletcher

Preface

In order to successfully introduce strategic transformation into an organisation, a structured and systematic approach to organisational change is required. HINGE planning, which describes an iterative process of Horizon Scanning, Internal Audit, New Business Models, Gap Analysis and Evaluation, is presented in this chapter as a tool for practically managing change as part of an organisation's digital transformation. Drawing on the combined experiences of the editors and authors of this chapter, the approach acknowledges the constraints within which all organisations operate and the need for organisational fluidity in order to keep pace with external changes. HINGE offers a phased approach to digital transformation that incorporates continuous development and multiple iterations. We further evidence the benefits of the HINGE approach with a case study from the lead author's own organisation. The lead author of this chapter is Tim Griggs, Associate Director of Arup, who leads its Advanced Digital Engineering group across the north of the UK. Arup, like many organisations, is currently in the throes of its digital transformation 'journey', and Tim is best placed in offering his insight, war stories and lessons learned.

5.1 Change

The lessons learned so far from previous chapters is that change is an inevitable and a constant aspect of all organisational activities. There is also the realisation that invariably some competitors are always in some way ahead of your own current situation. There is also an inevitable legacy within the organisation that may be seen as a handbrake on future progress and on bringing the types of change that the organisation wants to realise. A further tension can often be found within an organisation, as senior management's desire for strategic change can be at odds with more grassroots pressures for short-term improvements (Dodd & Favora 2006). This internal tension for change can itself be the greatest barrier to realising a change that everybody wants (Gunduz & Semercisz 2012). With this general combination of challenges the key question is how to positively manage the organisation to take forward their digital transformation and – as a further benefit and additional challenge – to introduce a culture of innovating. It may also be worth highlighting at this point that these tensions and challenges to digitally transform are not saved for the larger or mid-sized businesses but can be felt in smaller organisations as well.

Chapter 1 highlighted the importance of organisational alignment around the key focus of its mission and vision. The importance of emphasising the existing qualities found inside the organisation also supports the creation of a more holistic alignment. Central to managing digital transformation and the organisation itself is the need to recognise and adhere to the value being expressed by this alignment through all types of strategic decision-making but most importantly with the most difficult of decisions. Beyond the adherence of a central mission and vision, everything else within the organisation should be open to consideration and change.

Many of the high-profile examples used throughout this book come from organisations that have failed to keep pace with digital transformation in their own sectors such as Kodak, HMV and may High Street retailers. These are also examples of organisations that were not open to the possibility of comprehensive internal organisational process, cultural and or structural change.

Acknowledging that change is constant and accelerating within the external VUCA world, Bennet and Lemoine (2014) emphasise the need for actions and projects that are tightly scoped, employ SMART (Specific, Measurable, Acceptable, Realistic and Time-bound) objectives and have shorter timelines. The implied urgency that comes with this approach is challenging to some organisations where the need to complete an objective in the 'right' way is a quality that is at the core to their culture (Hansen et al. 2011). Even when employing SMART objectives sometimes getting it 'right' needs to be of lesser importance to an approach that is focused on delivering a 'rapid' response. In the context of digital transformation, we suggest, a more appropriate definition for the 'A' in the SMART acronym is 'agreed' and 'R' is 'rapid' in the sense of having shared agreement and organisational alignment within the transformation project coupled with a sense of urgency to move projects along.

With the wide combination of pressures weighing on the organisation there is a risk that not recognising which task to do first will effectively neutralise everyone into inaction. HINGE is introduced here as a method of planning action that takes stated strategic goals and, through the internalising of external stimulus, produces actionable objectives. Taking this approach also supports the creation of an innovating organisation looking forward, that is permeable to ideas and that is changeable in ways that can meet shifting demands and needs. HINGE enables the setting of SMART objectives for specific transformational actions that operationalise the organisation's strategic goals. We present HINGE as an iterative process to facilitate transformation within an innovating organisation (Heinze et al. 2018)

5.2   HINGE: planning for transformation actions

The HINGE planning model for digital transformation (Figure 5.1) is developed from the collective experience obtained through a range of digital transformation projects and decades of working with technology startups and evolving SMEs. It is no coincidence that the HINGE diagram above is circular – it reconfirms the need for HINGE to be revisited and repeated regularly.

Although the acronym suggests a specific order of activities that itself implies a specific logic, each step may be done in a different order to reflect existing understandings or incomplete actions within a transformation project. Irrespective of the starting point, the actions that are undertaken in a HINGE cycle will take their impetus from a strategic decision. A major challenge facing many organisations going through transformation is the tendency to set out projects with wide scope, lots of deliverables and long deadlines. This tendency reflects a traditional approach to project management that bundles up multiple problems and may be a result of overly vague strategic decisions and objectives.

Figure 5.1 HINGE digital transformation model

Source: From Heinze et al. 2018

Large-scale transformation projects mean that while the intended outcome will bring benefit to the organisation, it may have lost some of its relevance over the intervening time-frame. Significant changes to the underlying organisational system will tend to fall into this scale of work. The advantage of HINGE is that the monolithic problem-solving can be broken down into smaller constituent parts and produce a larger number of HINGE cycles that can be potentially realised in parallel as well as producing more immediate quick wins across the organisation (Senge & Sterman 1992).

Strategic goals that are too specific offer less opportunity for internalising external stimulus or significant innovation. However, there may be a place for a small number of rapid HINGE cycles around, for example, the evolution or updating of specific business models within the organisation. This balances the need to maintain 'business as usual' against the need to change in order to keep pace with competitors. By utilising a tight HINGE cycle the organisation necessarily looks out into the VUCA world for insight. By maintaining a narrow scope the levels of risk being introduced into the organisation can be managed by setting out achievable activities that bridge existing gaps.

The strategic decision that works well combines two features. The most useful strategic decision captures a specific direction or change in combination with the broader – and more usual – aspirational desires of the organisation. This approach translates into decisions such as "Increase market share in the Point-of-Sale sector with a new customer-oriented online design tool", "Reduce overall licensing costs to suppliers by developing a complete digital research tool internally" or "Improve customer retention by offering a one-stop online high quality print service". These examples are all real strategic decisions that have been defined by SMEs and consequently have shaped projects scoped for delivery over a two-year period. Drawing these type of goals into the HINGE cycle then provides a way of turning strategy into tangible actions and projects.

The steps in the HINGE cycle are:

- **H**orizon scanning: Evaluate the external environment – discover what is happening and what is on the horizon
- **I**nternal audit: Assess the internal environment – what systems are in place, what skill sets are available, what is working and what can be improved
- **N**ew models: Define new business models by leveraging improved levels of digital maturity
- **G**ap analysis: Evaluate the current and future state of the organisation with specific emphasis on your data, people and skills
- **E**valuation of options: Testing and evaluating the different options available

The outcome of a HINGE cycle is the selection of one option for action that brings the strategic decision closer to being achieved.

5.3   Arup's digital transformation – a case study

Arup is an international firm of engineers, designers and consultants that has helped shaped the built environment for over 70 years. This contribution has been evident in challenging and complex projects that demand the highest level of problem solving and engineering skill. In many senses the company are pioneers of their craft, right back to solving the complex structural engineering challenges of the Sydney Opera House using computer modelling for the first time. But in many senses, they remain a traditional engineering firm, and a walk through any Arup office worldwide would find groups of engineers huddled around whiteboards or large print-outs of their latest project, marking up amendments by hand. Of course, this is a huge generalisation, and much of the work Arup does has already been digitised, but as industries, both engineering and construction lag somewhat behind and have an urgent need to transform, with Arup being no exception.

In 2017 the Arup Group board recognised this challenge, describing it as "an urgent and important task", and set about developing a global digital transformation strategy, which they released at their annual general meeting (AGM). It was simple and effective and remains the cornerstone of their digital transformation strategy today, but progress has been slower than they had hoped. Their strategy focused on four core goals:

1 To automate work
2 To become a data-driven organisation
3 To develop digital products
4 To be the leading digital advisor in the built environment

This was underpinned by a number of groups, councils and leaders tasked with developing and implementing initiatives to deliver these strategic goals. However, after launching the global digital strategy at the AGM in 2017, the transformation programme failed to take off, and a year later (at the 2018 AGM) it was acknowledged that the 'starter pistol' had been fired too early and that a number of key organisational changes and realignments needed to happen before the programme could begin in earnest.

5.3.1 *Lessons learned*

There were a number of key lessons learned through the initial development of the transformation programme, and these lessons have directly informed the programme's onward development. The first lesson was that firing the starter pistol in 2017 with little in the way of an agreed programme of activity or initiatives to immediately follow meant that momentum was lost. The staff had got excited by the initial buzz and potential for transformational change but quickly found other things to occupy their energies. In essence, it was business as usual and digital transformation went from 'an urgent and important task' to 'that thing we were going to do'. Another by-product of firing the pistol too soon was that many parts of the organisation went off in their own direction developing initiatives and programmes at a local level without guidance from the centre, leading to confusion and disharmony. The grassroots transformation initiatives did not always reflect the intentions set out by the overall strategic goals.

These mismatches between grassroots action and organisational goals also tapped into another lesson learned. By their very nature, Arupians are inquisitive, technically capable and highly skilled, with an ability to pick up new things very quickly. As such many fell into one of two camps in their response to the digital transformation strategy – either 'it doesn't apply to my specialist area' or 'I'm already doing it'. The strategy was proving itself to be essentially a people challenge. With the hearts and minds of many still to be convinced, winning them over became the most urgent and important task. Understanding the importance of the strategy was not just because the board had said it was a priority. For one camp it was the need to realise that digital transformation was already far more than an ill-defined existential threat in their area of operations. For the other camp, it was discovering that they needed help doing it better, faster or more efficiently – with greater strategic alignment.

What Arup had failed to do was sufficiently articulate the opportunities for digital transformation – new business models, agility, immersive outcomes, automation of process-heavy tasks, freedom to focus on creativity and more. But the organisation had also not created the burning platform in that failing to adapt could potentially make the firm irrelevant, or worse, redundant in the modern world. There was also a need for understanding context within different parts of the organisation. Communicating these push and pull factors required different mixtures for different audiences.

A further lesson learned was that in order to think differently, different perspectives are needed. Of course, in transforming a highly successful firm like Arup, the senior leaders that enabled that success have a key role to play. But often fresh thinking from outside is needed to help articulate the reasons for transforming and to develop the initiatives needed to deliver the change. This was recognised in 2018, and a number of key strategic hires were brought into Arup. The commitment to valuing this external perspective was underpinned by a newly formed and dedicated group whose full-time roles were to deliver the global transformation programme, sponsored by board-members in each region, with buy-in from business and office leaders in each Arup office across the firm. By bringing in fresh and respected industry leaders with a dedicated remit to digitally transform the firm, the new Arupians were better able to articulate the need to change and show what has been successful elsewhere. With the sharing of new ideas and thinking the new team began to get the buy-in they needed to transform the firm.

A final but key observation from this process is that scratching beneath the surface of an organisation often reveals that digital transformation is already happening at a grassroots level, despite it not being formalised. In the absence of any direction from the centre, Arup engineers had begun to figure out the answers for themselves. Across the globe, staff began to teach themselves to code, they sought internal funding to try new software and new techniques for solving problems, and they were being supported by their leaders. These early approaches were inevitably somewhat piecemeal and un-coordinated, but the global digital strategy launched in 2017 gave staff the permission to try new things and to start to transform in their own way and at their own pace, with some success. These many starting points were an unintended consequence of not launching a fully defined mature transformation programme. With hindsight there has been benefit in allowing staff to find their own way, and new pockets of digital activity, transformation and best practices are being identified across the firm.

5.4   Learning from the Arup experience

Digital transformation is essentially firstly a people challenge – it requires that people are on board with the need to change. Communicating this need to change will be based around a combination of push and pull factors that are specific to each organisation (Sanchez 2018). Different rates of development within the organisation will also mean that the messages communicating the need to change must match their audience. Pull messages emphasising the benefits of strategic transformation are going to appeal to more digitally mature audiences. Push messages may be needed to challenge the thinking of less digitally mature audience. A mixture of push and pull message are needed to explain the proposed change.

People are also key to gaining momentum for the strategy, otherwise it may fail to get off the ground. The wider the extent of the practice and thinking around digital transformation across the organisation the greater the opportunities that will be possible. Grassroots change should be encouraged where it can align with overall strategic direction of the organisation as a way of empowering people while also enabling them to focus on actions that produce high-value productivity. As more people recognise the benefits of transformation, the faster those aspects of the transformation will become business as usual.

Communicating the thinking, direction and purpose that underlies transformation is important. A significant challenge for any organisation – but particularly medium and large organisations – is to create an environment in which the strategic direction of the organisation is understood and, hopefully, shared. This also relates to the increasing expectations among younger employees that their organisation will act ethically and transparently. Sharing and continuing to discuss a vision for change is a key part of this thinking.

Scratching beneath the surface of the organisation's activities may reveal more grassroots digital activity and change. This is particularly in organisations like Arup where inquisitive and technically capable staff always look to push the boundaries of the specialisms. As a result it may not take much to pull these parts of the organisation towards a new digital future. But this fostering of pockets of digital excellence should be undertaken cautiously in order to ensure that those with the essential skills and breadth of experience are being brought along with the overall strategic direction of the organisation.

The people of the organisation are also a consideration when the need for external insight is recognised. Arup's approach was to hire new senior people into roles specifically relating to digital transformation. Other options could also be considered, including the use of graduate recruitment to bring new ideas into the organisation. Working more closely with other organisations including universities can bring the development of closer working relationships that incorporate knowledge transfer in combination with graduate recruitment. Some organisation make use of external consultants to bring in new ideas and concepts. The cost of using consultants generally prevents this option from being used in most startups or small businesses.

The HINGE planning model offers a mechanism for obtaining understanding of external changes and development by systematically bringing this insight into the organisation within the specific context of operationalising strategic goals. An organisation that can gain early efficiencies by automating existing tasks has the capacity to deploy existing employees with the tasks relating to HINGE, including the externally facing horizon-scanning task.

Key takeaways

- Managing digital transformation within an organisation is firstly and primarily a people challenge
- Multiple push and pull factors exist within every sector for doing strategic digital transformation
- Communicating the purpose of the transformation is key to its success
- The messages being communicated should vary between audiences
- Do not transform your current business processes, look forward
- A shared vision: digital transformation must be strategic and aligned across the organisation
- Grassroots transformation should be encouraged when it aligns with overall strategy
- Projects should be managed through short cycles with highly defined, quickly delivered outcomes that bring value to the organisation
- Consider the 'A' in the SMART acronym as 'agreed' to ensure a harmonised shared agreement and organisational alignment within the transformation project

References

Bennet, N., & Lemoine, J. (2014) "What a difference a word makes: Understanding threats to performance in a VUCA world", *Business Horizons*, 57(3), 311–317, https://doi.org/10.1016/j.bushor.2014.01.001

Dodd, D., & Favora, K. (2006) "Managing the right tension", *Harvard Business Review*, Dec, https://hbr.org/2006/12/managing-the-right-tension

Gunduz, E., & Semercisz, F. (2012) "The relationship between competitive tension and strategic innovation", *Procedia – Social and Behavioral Sciences*, 58, 29–30, Oct, https://doi.org/10.1016/j.sbspro.2012.09.975

Hansen, M., Pernille, A., Pernille, K., & Lars, L. (2011) "Rapid adaptation in digital transformation: A participatory process for engaging IS and business leaders", *MIS Quarterly Executive*, 10.

Heinze, A., Griffiths, M., Fenton, A., & Fletcher, G. (2018) "Knowledge exchange partnership leads to digital transformation at Hydro-X Water Treatment, Ltd", *Global Business and Organizational Excellence*, 37(4), 6–13.

Sanchez, P. (2018) "The secret of leading organizational change is empathy", *Harvard Business Review*, December, https://hbr.org/2018/12/the-secret-to-leading-organizational-change-is-empathy

Senge, P., & Sterman, D. (1992) "Systems thinking and organizational learning: Acting locally and thinking globally in the organization of the future", *European Journal of Operational Research*, 59(1), 137–150.

6 How to become a digitally enabled and visionary leader

Alex Fenton, Tina Judic and Gordon Fletcher

Preface

This chapter sets out a challenge for managers and entrepreneurs. Undertaking the digital transformation of an organisation personally requires long-term vision, self-awareness and self-reflection. In digital transformation, the preparedness to change, listen, be flexible and generally work differently is expected of everyone. These types of changes must also be reflected in the shifting day-to-day practices of the C-suite. Without full commitment to strategic digital transformation, the chances for success are limited. The chapter presents the value of vision and visionary management as the third and often unacknowledged aspect of an organisation that closely complements and works with its strategy and operations.

6.1 Visionary management

Primal Leadership (Goleman et al. 2002) lays out the central concept of visionary leadership and management. Visionary leaders have the ability to mobilise people towards defined long-term goals using persuasion, charisma and high emotional intelligence. Visionary leaders are able to articulate for any audience the future direction of the organisation and motivate and communicate to others why and how this vision can and should be reached. We present the visionary leader as a hybrid of two leadership styles that aligns with the organisation's strategic aspirations while also being capable of operating in uncertain and changing times. The visionary leader is primarily a transformational leader who is able to inspire confidence in the organisation and its vision and mission while also being, when necessary, a flexible situational leader who can adapt their style to changing circumstances, organisational resistance, new forms of challenges and new tools and opportunities without the need to completely restart or revisit the intent of the original strategy. The transformational aspects of the visionary leader recognises the need to maintain alignment with the strategic vision of the organisation, while the situational leadership perspective incorporates the pragmatic view of getting things done when they are needed.

The positive impact that the leader's presence and engagement creates for the benefit of the organisation is the reason that transformational leadership is said to surpass other potential styles (*Advance HE* n.d.). The situational leader changes their style to suit the circumstances and not the reverse situation where employees are forced to adapt to the leader's style. In an era when the pressures of the external VUCA world are pressing heavily on the organisation, it is necessary for leaders to have a strong understanding of digital transformation and the technologies that can lead to positive organisational improvements and offer clear pathways to success, irrespective of what metrics are being measured for increased growth, productivity, efficiency or innovation. The optimum perspective for the visionary leader is a clear understanding and perspective of the relationship between the wider change brought by digital transformation and their own sector.

Overall, visionary leaders require a continuous and specialised (although not necessarily detailed) knowledge of their sector. This knowledge is obtained through constantly learning, networking, interacting and developing a strong understanding of competitors and customers. In effect, leaders need the type of insight that is gained from the type of horizon scanning that is described in Chapter 7. In order for leadership to be effective, visionary managers need to gain credibility and respect from others by being an authority in their own field. It is difficult to galvanise and direct the motivations of others within an organisation without personally having the prerequisite core knowledge as well as the capability to share it with conviction. This describes the third key quality of the visionary leader; they are knowledgeable and recognised as a thought leader in their sector.

Keeping the vision and the end goals in focus are crucial for strategic success. Intermediate measures of progress such as Key Performance Indicators (KPIs) are indicators of the organisation moving in the right strategic direction. However, the necessary caveat is that KPIs must measure the right intermediate outcomes that enable movement towards the intended overall goal and should not succumb to Goodhart's Law: "When a measure becomes a target, it ceases to be a good measure." A key strategic goal such as growth or increased productivity can be reached through different intermediate SMART objectives depending on the organisation, sector and its preferred KPIs.

6.2   People

With the goal of strategic digital transformation to become data-driven and people-focused, getting the right people and the people right is essential. Visionary leadership and management is at its most effective when the right people are in place who have the right skills, current knowledge and ongoing training plans. This also feeds backwards to the importance of making the right recruitment choices initially, to ensure that new employees have the capacity and willingness to also become the 'right' people. Choosing and retaining the right people has the prerequisite need that the leaders engaging new and existing people have a clear vision of the direction and purpose of the organisation and appreciate the culture of the organisation as well as its qualities. Taking this further and more widely, the same principles also apply to working with the right partners who echo or parallel these core organisational cultural values and visions. The importance of people as the key distinctive cultural element of the organisational system described in Chapter 2 emphasises that achieving this alignment is key to realising successful digital transformation.

A good example of the application of this consideration by visionary managers is the use of a 'can do, will do, will fit' approach during the interview stage for staff. The weightings reflect the relevant significance of capability, enthusiasm and shared direction.

- Can do (25%) – can the person do the job? Do they have the correct skills and knowledge?
- Will do (25%) – will the person do the job? Do they have the motivation and aptitude required?
- Will fit (50%) – will the person fit? Do they echo the organisational culture and overall vision?

Passion and enthusiasm are important attributes among visionary leaders and the staff and partners that they employ. This does not mean being 'high on life' but a passion to succeed on a personal level combined with a willingness to embrace the values of the organisation and its vision. There is also an acknowledgement that organisational culture is always changing and is not a fixed entity – so adaptability is also an important quality for both leaders and staff. The objective, therefore, is to build an organisation that embraces people as key to success and to then empower and motivate them.

6.2.1 Working with millennials

Managing and working with millennials (those born in the last fifteen years of the 20th century) is also a key aspect of becoming a visionary leader. Typically, millennials have high expectations relating to their job roles, so it is important to support and work with them to help them maintain an alignment of their own focus and that of the organisation. Millennials also require the correct support to understand an organisation's culture and its vision. Increasingly, all employees have greater access to a wider range of information about life, politics and current issues at both micro and macro levels. Millennials – whose entire worldview has been shaped by this depth of available information – will be motivated and gravitate towards organisations that they believe in and have the right cultural fit with their own perspectives. *The Life of Y: Engaging Millennials as Employees and Consumers* (Sengupta 2017) highlights that the world's two billion millennials are rapidly becoming fundamental to the way organisations operate and conduct themselves. Sengupta (2017) suggests that the old models of dealing with younger employees need to be rethought in order to effectively engage and retain millennial staff. The key lesson from this suggestion is to create a more ethical, supportive environment where employees understand and embrace the values of the organisation that complement their own beliefs.

6.3 Trust

Working in the VUCA world is complex. Visionary leaders accept that they are not the sole drivers for transformative change but that they are key to delivering the solution. Trust is a key component in the relationship between visionary leaders, their employees and their partners. The presence of trust within the organisation ensures that everyone shares a common vision and shared understanding of how it will be achieved, coupled with the level of autonomy needed to do what is required. These sentiments couple trust with a sense of organisational openness and transparency, ensuring that there is no sense of competing agenda or purposes. Trust is also strengthened when visionary leaders treat people fairly, make time to talk to people, get to know them and mutually build social capital.

Visionary leaders understand when and what forms of trust and responsibility to place on individual employees and provide them with the necessary level of support to succeed. Support arrives in many forms and is not solely restricted to induction or keeping pace with current knowledge. Visionary leaders and employees can benefit from a tailored "personal board of advisors" (Shen et al. 2015). This approach brings together a combination of trusted individuals with the right expertise and experience to support career development by recognising that no one mentor can bring sufficient insight to the current personally unique combination of circumstances. Trust is at the heart of the mentoring relationship, and with multiple mentors this need is only accentuated.

Nobody is perfect, and visionary leaders know when to say "sorry" for errors that they are responsible for, as much as they know how to say "please" and "thank you". This sets a good example of accountability and respect from the top of the organisation and builds trust and faith. Building a strong, trusted, trusting and empowered team is as essential as ever. In a fast-paced world, where structures are flatter and expectations are higher, building a team that can grow and flourish with you is more important than ever.

6.4   Diversity

Visionary leaders also recognise the power of diversity in its many varied forms, not as a token exercise but as a means to progress and achieve strategic change. A variety of academic studies (Richard 2001; Kane 2015) show that a diverse team brings fresh ideas that can both challenge the status quo and the orthodoxy of the leader themselves. Having a mixture of genders, sexualities, ages, religions and ethnicities broadens knowledge, resources and connections for the organisation. Genuine diversity increases the social capital of everyone in the organisation, enriches individuals and lets the organisation grow in new ways.

> To compete in an increasingly digital environment, a diverse employee base can not only help provide new ideas but can also help reveal key decision-making errors that may otherwise go unnoticed. New connections with like-minded people typically don't offer new insights or alternative viewpoints that broaden one's knowledge resources.
>
> (Kane 2018)

Inclusion does not need to be something you have to actively consider; it should instead be intrinsically woven into the fabric of how a good team works together. Creating an 'ownership culture' is paramount to how people view their experience at work. There is a tangible difference between simply doing 'a job' and something that people very much feel is part of their lifestyle.

The need for diversity in the organisation does contradict the statements regarding the importance of organisational 'right fit' for new starters in section 6.2 . If an organisational culture represents a monolithic, monocultural attitude lacking in diversity, there is a need for a wider and more strategic consideration of what 'fit' the organisation wants rather than the one it already has. Lean In, a global community dedicated to helping women achieve their ambitions, recently cited in their *2018 Women in the Workplace* study (https://womenintheworkplace.com/) that "for the last four years, companies have reported that they are highly committed to gender diversity. But that commitment has not translated into meaningful progress". Diversity is still often treated as a concept or a 'nice to have' feature rather than recognizing its benefits as an accelerator to success. Other directors emphasise that their appointments are being made on the basis of the 'best' person for the job or the need for a successful candidate to have all of the prerequisite skills for the role (McKenna et al. 2019). This perspective will generally only serve to reinforce existing narrow perspectives and mindsets in organisations that lack diversity.

6.5   Work/life balance

Work/life balance is also a fundamental aspect of an organisation's culture. In the VUCA world it is easy to become overwhelmed with the volumes of unending work and streams of digital communications coming from many different channels across a global network.

Visionary leaders help to set the boundaries and expectations for the organisational culture in maintaining a balance between work and other times. This may also represent a balance between on- and off-line times across all of an employee's time. Technologies should be in place to allow flexible working and communications. Through mobile devices, staff can work offsite and can be considered to be 'always on'. But this makes it even more important to know when to switch off, and these boundaries can be guided by the expectations and own personal behaviours of the visionary leader. Flexibility is key – employees should be empowered and trusted to have flexibility in their working hours and locations as long as they are meeting the objectives of their role within the organisation. A visionary leader has a role in ensuring that a balance is being struck between an understanding and responsible audit of performance and making sure that staff skills are being developed and their wellbeing is being preserved, if not enhanced.

In 2019, accountancy firm Ernst & Young introduced new flexible working policies including 'life leave' (Ritschel 2019). The 'life leave' offering enabled employees to self-fund up to 12 weeks off per year to pursue other interests including travel, part-time work elsewhere or other interests. This option was developed partly in response to the influx of millennial employees and the need to retain people, but it also addressed the growing demand for flexible working more widely across the organisation. The benefits of mobile working and assigning maker time are also explored further in Chapter 18.

6.6   Engaging the C-suite

The C-suite are top-level executives of an organisation including roles such as the Chief Executive Officer (CEO), Chief Financial Officer (CFO), Chief Operating Officer (COO) and Chief Information Officer (CIO). The C-suite are leaders, including some who may be classed as being visionary themselves who, irrespective of their leadership styles, are crucial to the success of strategic digital transformation. In a digitally mature organisation, the C-suite all pull in the same direction towards the organisational vision, based on shared data-driven decision making around core KPIs. In other organisations that have not achieved this alignment, a digitally enabled and visionary leader may need to develop their own management capabilities and persuasion skills to engage and work with this level of the organisation.

The HIPPO effect can be considered by some leaders to be one of the greatest barriers to digital transformation and data-driven decision making (Marr 2017). Kaushik (2007) first coined the phrase HIPPO to describe the impact on decision making of the "Highest Paid Person's Opinion". In the absence of trusted and shared data, decision making is driven by the HIPPO in the room, and as a result others defer their own opinions and knowledge to this decision. This form of decision making can become a vicious cycle that builds reliance upon an individual that, in turn, becomes a barrier towards data-driven decision making. Tactics for managing the C-suite (or otherwise known as "How to Train your HIPPO") includes the use of "humble enquiry" and the art of asking rather than telling (Schein 2013).

6.7   Found – a case study

Found is a London-based, independent, digital growth agency that has grown considerably in the past few years. Found has increased its size, offering, experience and results. It has always been Found's aim to grow and develop ahead of the curve, to build an agency of the future, now. The mission is that an agency of the future is engaged, culturally aware, and is leveraging data and technology to power creativity and activity. An agency of future also makes it easy for clients to access talent and imagination in a way that is aligned and connected.

At Found, there are growth partners, digital specialists, data scientists, creative thinkers and, above all, people motivators. All of them bring a level of brilliance to the organisation that, collectively, enables the business to flourish. The agency itself is built around a simple philosophy: "be kind". This resonates through all aspects of everything at Found. For the CEO it is about being thoughtful in praise or giving negative feedback in a constructive and fair manner. This approach does not prevent asking demanding tasks of employees or having high expectations. It does ensure that there is clarity around what is expected from every employee, how they each can be supported and how Found can help them further develop their own careers.

Success for a visionary leader is borne out of a shared passion, determination and an overwhelmingly collaborative approach. To achieve success requires building a team who exude talent and ability, who are all focused on the desire to achieve optimum results and who truly believe in the company they are working for. Shared positive belief really comes down to the ability and presence of the leader.

Making money has largely been the biggest, if not sole, motivator for most companies, and Found is no different – it's an organisation that wants to make money. But making money as a primary motivation does not necessarily appeal to millennial employees or customers, and times are changing. Customers and employees are now much more engaged socially, politically and culturally than before, and buying from or working at a company that truly stands for something is increasingly important to Found and visionary leaders. Leaders, therefore, need to be clear on what they and their company stand for and what they are doing to make it happen, whether it is solving social and environmental challenges or working closely with the local community while, of course, still making money. Letting your team know what you stand for and where you are heading, and inviting them on the company journey with you, will not only empower them, it will motivate them to want to do well.

Found is an organisation that clients want to work with and a workplace where individuals and teams collectively thrive. Both leader and team have worked together diligently to transform the structure of the agency in order to ensure that there is a growth path. This path is made clearer by recognising that the digital space is fast-paced; that needs and expectations are changing rapidly; that clients are urgently looking for agency partners capable of designing and delivering integrated, end-to-end, omnichannel customer experiences; and that agencies are all having to continuously reconsider their structure and approach to be fast and agile.

As part of Found's ongoing transformation as a digital growth agency there are now four specialist quadrants: Data, Strategy, Attention and Performance. This is a structure that is relevant for internal teams but is also meaningful to clients working with or wanting to work with Found. This structure provides a perfect scalable architecture to support best-in-class delivery of services. It also provides clarity and structure to facilitate both business and personal growth over the coming years. Found has spent considerable time working with its teams to design and refine its approach. Time has also been invested in ensuring that the approach was communicated to the teams in terms of locating themselves within the organisation and in understanding the opportunities that were available as a result.

Every organisation is different, and there is no definitive 'right way' to do things. Digital visionary leaders, therefore, need to understand how to use the data available to them in order to develop while staying true to themselves and what they stand for.

Key takeaways

- Visionary leaders are thought leaders who inspire others
- Visionary leaders can shape the company vision and mission and get buy-in from the entire organisation
- Visionary leaders take responsibility for failures and share successes
- Visionary leaders build trust across the organisation
- Visionary leaders are flexible and know how to manage in different situations

References

Advance HE (n.d.) "10 x leadership styles", www.lfhe.ac.uk/en/general/lf10/ten-times-tables/10-leadership-styles.cfm

Goleman, D., Boyatzis, R., & McKee, A. (2002) *Primal Leadership: Realizing the Power of Emotional Intelligence*. Boston: Harvard Business School.

Kane, G. (2018) "Use digital platforms to cultivate diversity", *MIT Sloan Management Review*, 6th Mar, https://sloanreview.mit.edu/article/use-digital-platforms-to-cultivate-diversity/

Kane, G., Palmer, D., Phillips, A., Kiron, D., & Buckley, N. (2015) "Strategy, not technology, drives digital transformation: Becoming a digitally mature enterprise", *MIT Sloan Management Review*, 14th July, https://sloanreview.mit.edu/projects/strategy-drives-digital-transformation/

Kaushik, A. (2007) *Web Analytics: An Hour a Day*. Indianapolis: Wiley.

Marr, B. (2017) "Data-driven decision making: Beware of the HIPPO effect!", *Forbes*, 26th Oct, www.forbes.com/sites/bernardmarr/2017/10/26/data-driven-decision-making-beware-of-the-hippo-effect/#21a18e6780f9

McKenna, S., Fletcher, G., & Griffiths, M. (2019) *Hiding in the light: Recognising UK mid size businesses as a distinct category and their economic and social value to the nation*, Discussion Paper, Manchester: MSB Leaders, www.msbleaders.com/the-report

Richard, O. (2001) "Racial diversity, business strategy, and firm performance: A resource-based view", *Academy of Management Journal*, 43(2), 164–177.

Ritschel (2019) "Australian accounting company introduces 'life leave' policy that gives employees up to 12 Weeks off", *The Independent*, 18th Mar, www.independent.co.uk/life-style/life-leave-policy-holiday-australia-ernst-and-young-work-days-a8828201.html

Schein, E. (2013) *Humble Enquiry: The Gentle Art of Asking Rather Than Telling*. San Francisco: Berrett-Koehler.

Sengupta, D. (2017) *The Life of Y: Engaging Millennials as Employees and Consumers*. New Delhi: Sage.

Shen, Y., Cotton, R., & Kram, K. (2015) "Assembling your personal board of advisors", *MIT Sloan Management Review*, 16th Mar, https://sloanreview.mit.edu/article/assembling-your-personal-board-of-advisors/

Part II

Digitally transforming the organisation

The external drivers for change

7 Horizon scanning

Cautionary tales

Marie Griffiths, Alex Fenton and Gordon Fletcher

Preface

Horizon scanning is the 'H' in the HINGE model that assists in reimagining future pathways for your organisation. Horizon scanning is a key part of the process, as it helps to understand the external environment and supports the identification of innovations that can act as external stimulus for change within your organisational system and its business models. After an initial outline of the concept of horizon scanning, we argue for the need to become more responsive to client and industry insights, to be 'fit' and 'ready' for change. As a way of elaborating the concept we look back at cautionary tales of businesses that took a narrow view of responding to external change. We use three iconic multinational case studies, Kodak, Blockbuster and Nokia, to illustrate the importance of horizon scanning and the need to continuously reflect and learn from the external environment. Finally we outline some tactics for continuously identifying potential innovations (wherever they may be found) and for having appropriate internal response mechanisms.

7.1 What is horizon scanning?

As a way of defining horizon scanning we can first eliminate what this activity is not. It is not a crystal ball to predict the future, it is not rocket science and it is not scenario planning (Ogilvy 2015). There are also many different tools and frameworks offered to chart an organisation forward, such as PricewaterhouseCoopers' framework for future risk, control and assurance or Kranz's (2018) suggested ways "to future proof your business" through transformational technology capabilities. Additionally there are many classic business tools for looking forward and long-term planning, including SWOT analysis (Gürel 2017), Boston Consulting Group's (BCG) Matrix (Reeves 2014) or Porter's Five Forces analysis (Porter 1989). These options are undeniably useful for strategists and for planning within an organisation, but they fall short of acting as a catalyst to challenge static thinking or provoking innovation within an organisation.

In Chapter 4, horizon scanning has already been identified as a key tool for understanding competitors, and in this chapter we take the activity further still to position it as a change-making catalyst for organisational transformation. Horizon scanning is offered in this chapter as a lens through which to imagine a future business model as well as an even more radical tool for changing the internal organisational *status quo* and encouraging wider transformational processes. The goal of horizon scanning is to understand what is, or soon will be, affecting you, your customers and clients. It is the process of looking at a distance from your own organisational activities to identify the accelerators, disruptors, social challenges, customer trends and technologies so that they will not be a surprise when they become an immediate threat, challenge or opportunity. If the oncoming external change can be identified with sufficient time it can be mitigated or, better still, embraced and internalised into new innovative business models or processes.

The act of horizon scanning enables an organisation to internalise observed stimulus with sufficient time to proactively respond to coming challenges and opportunities rather than acting too late and becoming enmeshed in a reactive spiral of last-minute responses and decline. The interface that horizon scanning creates between the external VUCA world and the internal organisational system creates a channel for the translation of the observed external world – including dynamic consumer technologies – into enterprise-level responses. By examining examples of multinational companies that were, at their peak, recognisable household brand names, emphasis is thrown on the potential for any organisation regardless of their size to fall (or at least falter) if they fail to continuously horizon scan in relation to all aspects of their operations.

7.2   Cautionary tales

7.2.1   *Kodak*

Kodak is still today a significant multimillion dollar company. However, its current financial position with a negative operating income hallmarks a company that is a shadow of its former market power. Its continued existence after 2013 is largely a result of selling much of its intellectual property that had previously made it a leader in imaging technology to key digital companies including Google, Samsung and Apple. Kodak itself was a product of an earlier technology revolution in the 1880s when photography became increasingly popular and affordable to mass consumers. As a photographic film company it dominated its market. In traditional photography the sole disposal and interchangeable item in the process that had to be regularly changed was also its most essential component. In contrast, in the early days of photography the camera was often regarded as a once in a lifetime purchase.

In the periods of its greatest success, Kodak was also a technology innovator. It was Kodak that invented the device that brought its own demise with the digital camera being presented to company executives in 1975 (Dan 2012). As a company that could only perceive itself as a film company, the impact of this invention was not recognised and arguably was dismissed as a distraction (rather than a disruption) to its primary activities. The fact that the digital camera was an internal development may itself have served to camouflage the real risks of the technology to the photographic film business (Mui 2012).

Kodak did not, however, ignore that digital photography was a threat to its core business. In the early 1980s Kodak undertook market research that suggested it had ten years to formulate a response through its technology and its business models before the quality of digital photography would match or exceed that of traditional film products. Once again, and with the threat already recognised, Kodak contributed the technology that brought this tipping point. By the mid-1980s Kodak's own R&D department created the first megapixel digital camera. This development effectively accelerated the quality of digital images that threatened the core of Kodak's film and printing business. But technological development did not itself damage Kodak's business so much as the company's persistence in the belief that consumer behaviour would not change with the availability of digital photographic technologies (Anthony 2016). In the early 1990s, Kodak's own ten-year warning had expired. Very little had changed within Kodak's activities, and while digital cameras were generally available it was still another ten years before mobile phones incorporated cameras and still another four or more years after that before the camera mounted onto phones would have megapixel resolution (Hill 2013). Even more significantly, the iPhone and the rise of smartphones and their partner app stores would not reach consumers until 2007. From Kodak's own first internal warnings about the changing marketplace for photography to the key technology that finally opened the floodgates to this disruption can be measured over a full quarter of a century.

But even with this early warning, and as Kodak faced a changing world where more and more consumers had mobile phones with increasingly high-quality cameras, it continued to move in highly predictable ways. In 2001 it purchased oFoto, which was an early form of online photo sharing. But rather than encouraging the concepts of sharing between users, it primarily used oFoto to encourage its users to simply print more of their digital photographs. Twelve years after buying oFoto and only six years after the launch of the first iPhone, Kodak filed for bankruptcy in 2013. In the same year, the iPhone had already evolved to become the iPhone 5 and Facebook bought a different photo-sharing system in the form of Instagram for US$1 billion.

7.2.2 Blockbuster

In July 2018 two Blockbuster stores closed, leaving just one last store open in Bend, Oregon, USA. This was the end of an era that had been at its peak in the late 1990s. At the earlier high point in its history, Blockbuster had more than 9,000 stores in the USA alone. As a further indication of the size and financial success of Blockbuster, by 2004 then CEO John Antioco was trying to arrange a US$54 million leaving package, a payment that was challenged and blocked by Blockbuster's key investor Carl Icahn (Keating & Wu 2007). Antioco was also the CEO who refused the offer from a fledgling Netflix to establish a partnership that would enable Netflix to run the Blockbuster brand online and that would see cross-promotion of the new DVD-by-mail service through the physical Blockbuster stores (Satell 2014).

Antioco is now pilloried for his lack of insight, but other internal forces influenced the decision to reject Netflix. Icahn was pushing for an improvement in the share price of Blockbuster in order to realise a return on his significant investment. Netflix had begun to lose money in the early 2000s, and the stock market would never have responded to the proposed partnership as positively as the more traditional business decisions of cost cutting and efficiency improvements. Other reasons for the rejection appear sensible without the benefit of hindsight. In the early 2000s when Blockbuster was exiting its peak, Netflix was only a few years old – having started in 1997 – and was still at the time of the offer solely a DVD-by-mail operation. Partnering with Netflix would have been a seemingly pointless leap of faith for Blockbuster given its goliath status at the time. Various stories persist that Antioco both laughed at the Netflix offer and described their operating model at the time as a very small niche business.

Blockbuster was also not ignorant of streaming services and did partner with Enron Broadband to deliver video-on-demand – until scandal in the energy arm of the company brought that partnership to an end (Graser 2013). Other initiatives around online and DVD-by-mail also ended without success. The series of Blockbuster failures runs counter to the rise of Netflix. Both companies commenced streaming services in 2007. In 2010, Blockbuster filed for bankruptcy. By 2011 Netflix moved away from DVDs to become a streaming-only service and has matured to now be worth around US$153 billion, displacing Disney from being the top-performing entertainment company (Bloom 2018).

There are a number of explanations for the failure of Blockbuster. The emergence and eventual predominance of streaming services is a key reason. But there are more fundamental business model issues that are associated with the different perspectives to technology. Netflix started with no physical retail space and only used a subscription model from its beginning that did not employ any punitive fees for late returns. As Blockbuster CEO, Antioco was an experienced retailer working with a familiar business model that required thousands of retail spaces. The company also earned significant revenue from late fees that positively encouraged its customers to seek out alternative cheaper options. The need for late fees themselves also represents the limits in scale of the Blockbuster business model. Hiring a physical media item to customers meant that the individual stores could never accommodate the demand for the most popular films, while the comparative bulkiness of the items meant that the retail floor space was inevitably filled with less appealing options. A Blockbuster store that was empty was simultaneously a success (for meeting previous demand) and a failure (for being unable to meet current demand) and vice versa.

7.2.3 *Nokia*

Nokia remains to this day a multibillion dollar company. Nokia is also a company with a significant history dating back to 1865 – twenty years older than Kodak – and continues to play an important role in Finnish business culture. It is still a technology company and actively partners with key organisations worldwide including Chinese mobile technology companies such as Xiaomi. Nokia has also been actively researching and designing 5G network technologies since 2015. This current R&D activity continues Nokia long-term contribution to other key mobile technology standards including LTE and GSM.

A key question is how a company that remains one of the largest 500 in the world based on its revenues can also be regarded as a failure (Doz 2017). One indication that this company in some way failed can be found on the list of the top ten global best-selling mobile phones of all time. Seven of the ten phones are Nokia devices, including the number one position: the Nokia 1100, with 250 million units sold between 2003 and 2009 (Hamill 2018). The inclusion of built-in games on many of the early Nokia phones also defines *Snake* as the most played video game ever (Windows Blog 2013). Both of these superlatives are unlikely to ever be surpassed with the current consumer trend to shorter product cycles and app-based games that are installed after purchase.

Nokia's senior management did recognise that the increasing success of their mobile phone business had brought different pressures and challenges into the company that they and the organisation's culture were unprepared to accommodate. The concern was that the pressure to deliver products to meet increasing consumer demand for more capable technology was also coming at a time when the volume of demand was also increasing. During the 1990s and 2000s Nokia had already proven that it could deliver products at volume, but its business model was, and still is, based around longer term strategic R&D that produces revenues by being licensed to consumer-facing technology companies. Nokia was not able to deal with the increasingly tight two-year product cycles being demanded by phone carrier companies who bundled the devices with network access or the increasingly sophisticated expectations of the consumers of mobile phones.

A further burden to Nokia's situation was its link to the Symbian operating system that many of the earliest smartphones released during the 2000s. During this period, in 2003, Nokia released the first mobile phone/game hybrid with the N-gage. This system echoed some of the features of future developments with the App Store and Google Play environments, but the system never found a niche or a 'killer' game to drive sales. Despite the disappointing reception to the N-gage and the complex device-centric nature of the operating system, Nokia took the relationship with Symbian further by first becoming the largest shareholder in 2004 and then purchasing Symbian outright in 2008. Android overtook Symbian as the most popular operating system in 2010. Nokia resisted development of Android-based phones. But the company did acknowledge the shortcomings of the Symbian system and, in response, in 2011 adopted Windows Mobile for its subsequent phones. By 2013 Nokia released the 1020 device. The phone represent a significant evolution for the camera-phone concept as it incorporate a 41 MP sensor and a Carl Zeiss lens. There was also an optional camera grip accessory to further reinforce the blurring between a camera and a phone. But as a result of Nokia's newfound commitment to the Windows Mobile platform, this low-end DSLR competitor had no native applications for Instagram or Snapchat. As a semi-experimental development, the 1020 received mixed reviews as a technically superb device that was hampered by its operating system and a lack of relevance to mainstream consumers. The 1020 is almost an icon of what went wrong with Nokia.

For Nokia the failure was one of scale and ambition. Although the company's 2018 annual revenue was €22 billion, this is only a tenth of another relative latecomer to the mobile phone industry. As a contrast, Apple's revenue was US$265 billion for the same period. In 2007 – the year of the iPhone's introduction – Nokia had 50% of the global phone market, but significantly Apple had already gained 5% in the same market in its first 12 months. Within six years, the same year that Kodak filed for bankruptcy and the 1020 was released for sale, Nokia sold its mobile phone division to Microsoft in an attempt to offset spiralling loses (Brand Minds 2018).

In some ways Nokia's history could be read simply as the rise and fall of an R&D company in and out of the consumer mainstream. However, there are also aspects of failure that should be considered in the Nokia story. Nokia persisted with long development cycles, ensuring that the products were 'right' at their consumer release. This was increasingly at odds with Android and even Apple-based releases that were bringing quick incremental design changes over the same period. In this rapidly changing environment, Nokia also persisted with its own operating system which lacked the flexibility, extensibility, scalability and openness of Android. Organisational fear of Android pushed Nokia to adopt Microsoft's platform, but the new system mirrored many of the issues faced by Symbian and was not the Android-killer needed by the company. Technical and process inefficiencies were compounded by the organisational culture of Nokia itself (Doz 2017). Mistrust and misunderstandings between layers and functions of the company impacted on the resulting responsiveness of the organisation and the relevance and impact of the strategic decisions that were being made. When Nokia finally sold its phone division to Microsoft, it was not acting as a single organisation with a shared mission and vision but rather as a cluster of competing rivals.

7.3   The lessons learned from cautionary tales

The three cautionary tales all offer insight into the value and purpose of horizon scanning. In all three cases the external threats did not come as a surprise to the organisation, and they cannot be accused of lacking internal response or awareness of the potential scale of the threats they were facing. All three organisations endeavoured to respond to the external threat with new products or services that in some ways attempted to capture the sentiment of the changing external environment. Arguably, all three came close to forming a reasonable response that could have worked. The most significant failure of the three was the complete demise of Blockbuster, which was also the company that was the closest to getting its response right with its Enron broadband partnership and development of its own DVD-by-mail products. It could even be argued that the three companies were all doing the right things with their horizon scanning. However, this conclusion would rewrite history by not identifying the cause of failure as being within each company and assumes the narrowest definition of horizon scanning as a mechanism for scenario planning or predicting the future.

Considering horizon scanning as the catalyst for transformational organisational change highlights a different conclusion to the three stories. In each case, the organisation's response to the challenge of external change was to continue to pursue the same product trajectory that had always succeeded in the past. Kodak produced new products that encouraged printing rather than engaging consumers online, Nokia continued to focus on delivering high-quality telephone devices rather than flexible mobile data devices and Blockbuster persisted with the assumption that physical interactions and media were the primary mechanisms for delivering films rather than breaking free of these limiting and tangible items. These positions all reconfirm the importance and benefits of the type of visionary leadership described in Chapter 6 and reinforce the potentially damaging influence of the HIPPO effect.

Horizon scanning was not a catalyst for change in these companies but rather served to further reinforce existing organisational legacy. The response of reinforcing the old reveals the lack of preparedness to change internally as part of the process of looking out into the VUCA world.

What was absent in the horizon scanning conducted by the three companies was an observation of the wider organisational cultures and systems qualities that hallmarked the alternative development of competing products and services that were threatening their sector-wide dominance. Horizon scanning cannot be restricted to recognising the products and services of competitors and must extend to an attempt to understand the organisational culture and qualities that has produced these competing offers. This is what all three of the companies failed to see in their horizon scanning. In each case the company failed to realise the different organisational perspectives that produced Windows Mobile vs Android, photo sharing vs photo printing and DVD lending vs media streaming. Internalising the external stimulus is part of the horizon-scanning process that acknowledges the wider and holistic circumstances for externally observed innovation and knowing that cannot simply be copied into the organisation.

7.4   Practical rules for horizon scanning

The three cautionary tales highlight a series of practical rules for horizon scanning. Horizon scanning is of no value if the organisation is not prepared to change as a result of the learning that is brought back into the organisation. The organisation itself is not attempting to duplicate the products or services that are observed in its horizon scanning. Instead, horizon scanning is the catalyst for internal change that brings forms of innovation that are mediated through the filter of existing organisational culture. Horizon scanning must happen regularly – even continuously – and be part of business as usual. What is learned from horizon scanning is not necessarily new products and services that the organisation should copy, emulate or resist but new ways of being the same business in better ways. This learning is a far more challenging and complex level of input for an organisation.

Key takeaways

- Don't bring your current situation into the future – the actions of your people and the use of your data is what makes you distinctive
- Ask questions, don't restrict yourself to solving current or immediate problems.
- Horizon-scanning process should be a catalyst to challenge static thinking
- There is no definitive methodology or template for horizon scanning – but it is not just a checklist of competing products
- Horizon scanning has to be viewed as a credible process by all key stakeholders
- Horizon scanning should support (the creation of) an internal culture of innovation
- Horizon scanning should be reported in a format for communicating internally, and it should be written in plain language and in a style that focuses on the results
- Horizon scanning requires justification of the findings if they are to challenge the *status quo*

References

Anthony, S. (2016) "Kodak's downfall wasn't about technology", *Harvard Business Review*, 15th July, https://hbr.org/2016/07/kodaks-downfall-wasnt-about-technology

Bloom, D. (2018) "Netflix really worth more than Disney or Comcast?", *Forbes*, www.forbes.com/sites/dbloom/2018/05/26/netflix-disney-comcast-market-capitalization-valuation/

Brand Minds (2018) "Why did Nokia fail and what can you learn from it?", *Medium*, https://medium.com/multiplier-magazine/why-did-nokia-fail-81110d981787

Dan, A. (2012) "Kodak failed by asking the wrong marketing question", *Forbes*, 23rd Jan, www.forbes.com/sites/avidan/2012/01/23/kodak-failed-by-asking-the-wrong-marketing-question/

Doz, Y. (2017) "The strategic decisions that caused Nokia's failure read", *Knowledge*, 23rd Nov, https://knowledge.insead.edu/strategy/the-strategic-decisions-that-caused-nokias-failure-7766

Graser, M. (2013) "Epic fail: How blockbuster could have owned Netflix", *Variety*, 12th Nov, https://variety.com/2013/biz/news/epic-fail-how-blockbuster-could-have-owned-netflix-1200823443/

Gürel, E. (2017) "Swot analysis: A theoretical review", *Journal of International Social Research*, 10(51), 994–1006, doi: 10.17719/jisr.2017.1832

Hamill, L. (2018) "What are the best-selling cell phones of all time?", *Decluttr*, 13th July, www.decluttr.com/blog/2018/07/13/what-are-the-best-selling-cell-phones-of-all-time/

Hill, S. (2013) "From J-Phone to Lumia 1020: A complete history of the camera phone", *Digital Trends*, 8th Nov, www.digitaltrends.com/mobile/camera-phone-history/

Keating, G., & Wu, T. (2007) "Blockbuster CEO to leave with lower pay package", *Reuters Business News*, 20th Mar, www.reuters.com/article/us-blockbuster-antioco/blockbuster-ceo-to-leave-with-lower-pay-package-idUSWEN559320070320

Kranz, M. (2018) "How to Future-Proof your Business", Maciej Kranz blog, 29th Oct, www.maciejkranz.com/how-to-future-proof-your-business/

Mui, C. (2012) "How Kodak failed", *Forbes*, 18th Jan, www.forbes.com/sites/chunkamui/2012/01/18/how-kodak-failed/

Ogilvy, J. (2015) "Scenario planning and strategic forecasting", *Forbes*, www.forbes.com/sites/stratfor/2015/01/08/scenario-planning-and-strategic-forecasting/

Porter, M.E. (1989) "From competitive advantage to corporate strategy", in Asch, D., Bowman, C. (eds.) *Readings in Strategic Management*. London: Palgrave.

Reeves, M. (2014) "BCG classics revisited: The growth share matrix", *Boston Consulting Group*, 4th June, www.bcg.com/publications/2014/growth-share-matrix-bcg-classics-revisited.aspx

Satell, G. (2014) "A look back at why blockbuster really failed and why it didn't have", *Forbes*, www.forbes.com/sites/gregsatell/2014/09/05/a-look-back-at-why-blockbuster-really-failed-and-why-it-didnt-have-to/

Windows Blog (2013) "10 things you didn't know about mobile gaming", 16th Jan, https://blogs.windows.com/devices/2013/01/16/10-things-you-didnt-know-about-mobile-gaming-2/

8 The challenge of new, ever-changing technology and how to keep up

Marie Griffiths, David Kreps and Gordon Fletcher

This chapter links with the previous chapter and advocates looking beyond the hardware and software of new technology to recognise the core organisational advantages that are being created and the value that these advantages bring. Organisations now have access to massive computing power and endless software solutions that can be delivered through handheld devices and the Internet of Things. The challenge is how these emerging technologies alter organisational structures, change leadership perspectives and the resulting requirements for new skills and talent.

8.1 Re-imagining your future organisation

Most organisations are responding in some way to the shift to an increasingly digital environment. As an indicator, recruitment sites and internal human resource departments are awash with newly created job roles or with traditional roles that now have a prefix such as "digital", "online" or "transformation". The job market is a constantly useful barometer to examine how much the business landscape is changing. Current indications are that there is a noticeable degree of digital disruption combined with many job roles now being obsolete. The pace of this change is also indicated through the current job market. There are now job roles that did not exist five years ago but are already viewed as being business critical. Examples of these new pivotal roles include any that incorporate the term "user experience", to social media strategists, through to hybrid roles such as "digital finance" and "transformation consultant" that Accenture are seeking.

Although new digitally oriented roles are constantly emerging, and most business leaders are seeing the "writing on the wall", it is also widely acknowledged that the digital transformation is complex (Lawton 2015). The range and combination of challenges that disruptive emerging technologies introduce requires the development of robust organisational systems (see Chapter 2) that align with leadership perspectives and overall vision and mission. This combination of requirements will need new skills, new talent and a reimagining of organisation structure. This is a non-trivial task, as most organisations are faced with a shortage of talent and resources while also needing to get on with business as usual. The need for strategic and operational balance encourages digital transformation activities to be broken into bite-size projects rather than being considered as a single larger transformational piece.

As outlined in Chapter 6, it is widely acknowledged that visionary digital leaders are having to respond quickly and with insight to move forward. At the same time, the pressure to change is being driven by the forces of the VUCA world. The impact is so powerful that customer needs and demands expressed in one economy are have major implications for workers on other continents. What has changed from the earliest processes of globalisation that commenced in the latter half of the 20th century is that they are now being expressed, communicated and experienced in real time with greater degrees of precision and higher levels of expectation. All technology introduces change. The increasing acceleration of VUCA is a result of the exponential change brought about with digital technologies becoming increasingly intelligent and interconnected. Historically, leaders have always faced the challenges of change. It is how they have chosen to deal with the specific type of change that they are facing that sets apart the best from their more mediocre peers.

Different organisational demands and varying levels of external forces produce different responses. However, the observation from Davenport and Stoddard (1994) made by the Chief Information Officer of a major insurance company about the 1980s could be made of any current leader in any sector:

> In the late 1980s, I began to look at how technology was linked to our overall corporate strategy. I tried to assess how new applications impacted the enterprise; my intuition was that we were investing a lot but not getting the desired productivity. As I began to focus on what we were doing, it was clear that, generally, we did not change the processes that were being automated. Rather, we took sophisticated applications and layered them onto an old organization . . . Further, I recognized that in all of our years of focus on the technology, it was as if we had been looking through the wrong end of the telescope. Information Systems personnel needed to focus on processes, not technology.
>
> (Davenport & Stoddard 1994, 123)

Technology is therefore a constant influence on all organisations. How any technology will shape an organisation in the future can only be speculated upon, and there are many other intersecting developments to consider. The question is therefore not what technology will be predominant in five or ten years time but how can an organisation prepare for the future, maintain agility, stay current and disrupt to avoid being disrupted.

A popular approach of many digitally mature organisations is the "zoom out, zoom in" approach to strategy. This approach replaces a dogged loyalty to five-year business plans that become increasingly ineffective over time (Hagel 2018). "Zoom out, zoom in" works along two timelines in parallel. The first timeline is for the long-term horizon scanning for potential disruptions over a ten-to-twenty year period in order to prepare the organisation. The second – short-term – timeline targets a six-to-twelve month period that focuses on the present, building on those areas that might support and accelerate growth for the long-term while simultaneously shedding those areas that don't support movement along the long-term timeline. The "zoom out, zoom in" approach assumes that if the long- and short-term plans are closely aligned then the mid-range plans will also fall into place.

The analogy for this approach is the zoom lens on a high quality camera where you zoom in for the details and then zoom out for the wider picture. The approach was developed by Harvard Business School academic Rosabeth Kanter for solving problems. Kanter does warn that both of these views should be seen as momentary vantage points rather than fixed positions (Silverstone 2011). The approach does have its critics, as it is arguably impossible to predict the future. Putting the zoom-out and long-term approach into perspective, the aim of the activity is to develop a shared organisational view on what the business landscape may look like and is not an invocation to crystal ball gaze (Hagel 2018). The second challenge of the approach is gaining agreement on which one or two short-term initiatives will be used as a focus of resources to strengthen and accelerate growth. Zoom in, zoom out offers a framework for management to embed a continuously reflective culture that is both strategic and action-oriented.

8.2 Realigning your people

8.2.1 Digital leadership

There is a term and role currently being used to describe current leaders who are tackling digital transformation: the digital leader. At some time in the not too distant future, the term digital will fall away, not unlike the decline of the "e" prefix in the 2000s. Both email and e-commerce continue to highlight the legacy of an earlier and less mature period of digital technology usage. This chapter retains the term "digital leader" to describe those who are leading organisations through digital (a self-consciously awkward label given the previous statement) transformation. This must be regarded as a label of convenience for a situation that is more complex and multi-dimensional that asks for ongoing organisational evolution and change that is not a simple or a single project.

Digital leaders are at the helm of change and are no longer situated at the top of a pyramidally shaped organogram. Hierarchical structures are falling away beneath – and around – them as digital disrupts everything. These traditional structures were in place like rigid scaffolding to support stable and static established organisations. More nimble and agile digitally mature and capable organisations can behave in this way, in part, because they have flatter and faster hierarchies that are led by people with different skill sets.

Irrespective of the extent of their own personal awareness regarding the extent of the disruption that strategic digital transformation brings, successful leaders recognise that they need to be better prepared (see Chapter 6). This form of preparation is not derived from knowledge of the specific directions or challenges that their organisations will experience but in building capability within the organisation to be responsive and capable of responding to whatever changes emerge in the VUCA world.

Being aware of the parameters of coming change is not sufficient; an organisation has to be capable of being continuously ready. The challenge for most organisations is how to make sense of the volume, variety, veracity and velocity (the 4Vs) of the "noise" that digital produces within the VUCA world. A highly critical filter is needed to stay informed about the current trends coupled with a mechanism for understanding which technologies require short or longer term investment by an organisation. Horizon scanning has been discussed in a previous chapter as a technique to stay informed regarding trends and technologies happening in different sectors, and it is also essential for the "zoom out, zoom in" strategy approach discussed above.

A digital leader is the locus for this critical filter and leads the strategic prioritisation of importance that shapes decisions regarding investment. A matrix of criteria assists the digital leader in critically assessing the "noise" coming from the VUCA world (Table 8.1). This approach is drawn from narrower software-evaluation matrices (Greenhill & Fletcher 2003). The principle is similar. Criteria are scored (and weighted if necessary), with the highest cumulative score taking a higher priority for the "zoom in" timeliness. The approach can be equally applied to a software tool (e.g. selecting a cloud-based office suite),

Table 8.1 Critical assessment matrix (with indicative criteria) of technology for organisations

Criteria	Weighting (optional)	Score (1 lowest – 10 highest)
Generally regarded as safe (GRAS)/Generally regarded as mature (GRAM)		
Clear organisational use case in relation to business model (current or planned) – Value creator		
Respect or regard from similarly sized organisations (any sectors)		
Opens route to market differentiation		
Total Score		

categories of technologies (e.g. 3D printing vs cryptocurrency vs 5G) or offerings seeking crowdfunding (e.g. a new type of all-in-one 3D printer and CNC machine).

8.2.2   *Diverse workforce*

The pace of technology change, for the first time, is outstripping the pace of learning. In some disciplines, the skills gained from a traditional three-year bachelor's degree course are being superseded by emerging digital capabilities before the students graduate. However, this should not discourage organisations from turning to a younger workforce – those who are currently described as millennials and born at the end of the 20th century – to complement and fill gaps with existing organisational skill sets. Admittedly, a younger workforce comes without much needed experience and needs careful initial guidance, but the flipside can outweigh any negatives (Kappel 2016).

The millennial workforce brings fresh perspectives to the workplace, including a fresh mindset. The digital world has been the playground for millennials, so, with some constraints, they are familiar with communicating through different channels using new technologies. Another benefit is that millennials come into the world of work largely without existing legacy, prejudices or assumptions. They are already familiar with talking to their peers, but the training needed cannot be ignored to fully harness this potential.

For many organisations, the concept of diversity is still regarded as an imposed political expectation (McKenna et al. 2019). The result is that recruiting managers tend to find talent that replicates the existing mould with a similar set of characteristics. Diversity, however, is better regarded as an opportunity for finding the right talent and skills irrespective of previous incumbents or assumptions that shape the imagined "type" of person best suited for the role.

The need for diversity is a necessary part of keeping up and bridging existing talent gaps because, offsetting the pool of millennials entering the world of work, there is also a talent exodus. The exodus of highly skilled individuals has been accelerated by the viable opportunities available through startups and self-employment. If digital leaders are not given adequate resources or opportunities to thrive within their developing digital ecosystem, there are many organisations who are more than happy to support these personal expectations.

Once an organisation attracts and recruits the right talent, there is further consideration to embed the means to ensure that they stay (for at least a few years). Mitigating talent flight requires the building of a talent supply chain – similar in nature and purpose to the supply chains that are built for goods and products. This approach enables organisations to identify talent needs in advance and then address any potential disruptions in order to maintain a flow of skills as they become needed. The traditional reactive response that is enacted when a talent gap emerges increases the pressures to recruit. The result can be a perceived need for a body (anybody) even if it is not the right match, with the further danger that the race to recruit results in the organisation being prepared to pay a premium – and then doing so. The notional timeframe to fill any post is almost fifty working days, which must be factored into a project timeline to recognise the impact. In a traditional business environment, fifty days may be regarded as a relatively small timeframe within the scope of an overall project plan, but in an agile, highly iterative and increasingly digital environment, fifty days may be longer than the entire project.

Another tactic for the talent supply chain is to develop staff in house and grow the capabilities of the workforce from within. Internal development has the benefit of buffering some of the challenges coming from the VUCA world. There are a range of reasons for staff turnover, including personal ambition, aggressive recruiting practices and a surge in external job vacancies (Johnson 2018). Chilly or toxic workplaces are also major reasons for job churn, and the lack of internal opportunities or development will make other workplaces appear more attractive. To combat talent flight there is a need to have an inclusive workplace culture that is designed in a collaborative manner with a focus on employees. If you cannot beat or meet the higher salaries of larger organisations, what non-financial perks can be offered to keep your workforce happy? This could be higher value development and training, conscious knowledge exchange activities within the organisation, agile working patterns, career mapping or support for realistic promotion opportunities. All organisations require clear succession planning when key staff leave or retire, and there needs to be a strategy in place to avoid any knowledge gaps. By putting people at the heart of the organisation, the importance of talent is recognised and actions can be taken to ensure that recruitment, on-boarding, retaining and promotion are all fit for purpose.

8.3　Ready for the next trend

A major concern for many leaders is that the current organisational climate is volatile, uncertain, complex and ambiguous. Their justifiable nervousness is a result of directly dealing with the VUCA world. But this translates into real questions about how their organisation can stay relevant and remain competitive in the face of accelerating change. The source of uncertainty is not just about what specific technology is going to pose a serious threat to a specific business model. An organisation cannot predict or prepare for every eventuality; however, there is a pressing need to become agile and ever-prepared to change.

Throughout this book (see Chapters 2, 4 and 7) we suggest a number of tools that assist leaders to stay aware of emerging technologies, for example, different types of horizon scanning and the "zoom in, zoom out" technique. There are always future macro trends on the horizon that should be considered. Current long-term challenges include climate change, sustainability, an aging population, the rise of robotics and continuous political shock. All these challenges have, to a greater or lesser degree, organisational impact and should feature as innovative triggers for new products and services.

In the previous chapters there is a consistent emphasis on the power of the consumer in driving the transformation project. This is equally true for driving leadership decisions and is the prism to understand which future macro trends will be prioritised and acted upon. Engage with your customers as a digital leader to confirm your views and verify what the data is telling you. These types of discussions close the loop on becoming data-driven and people-focused. While trying to remain future fit, being reassured by the insights from the data reporting also brings the confidence to act on new insights that are being revealed.

This is a tumultuous time for all leaders. Leaders have to make big decisions and steer their organisation through uncharted waters. They have to adapt and be responsive to any signals of change that their monitoring of the horizons might bring. Consider the speed and intensity of Uber Eats' entry into the food-delivery market as a copycat and competitor to Deliveroo and Just Eats (Ram & Bond 2019). The trend for food delivery has grown exponentially and *Uber* was sufficiently responsive with its business model, irrespective of large-scale investment into long-term strategic projects, in order to establish its market presence.

SMEs are adaptable; often, learning and collaborating with other local entrepreneurs and startups. It is within these smaller organisations and collaborations where innovation flourishes and the environment from which many of the disruptive approaches and business models emerge. This SME environment describes a mechanism for larger organisations to tackle the scalability problem – doing business with early adopters who are primarily motivated by the newness of technology but being able to cross the chasm to the early majority of the population who are more interested in solutions and convenience (Moore 2014). As a leader there is a need to look outside current organisational walls (whether they are bricks or virtual) and network out in the VUCA world. Meet different people, join special interest groups, support local community initiatives in order to continuously grow your knowledge and learn from each interaction. The key message to draw from this chapter is to stay ahead by building a habit out of horizon scanning, reaching out and learning from others, listen to your customers and make innovation an integral part of your organisation.

Key takeaways

- Critically and systematically assess new technologies and trends
- Embed a process for sharing trends and future insights that are happening in your sector with your teams
- Aspire to become the 'unshockable' organisation that is up-to-date and informed
- Introduce initiatives to stem talent flight
- Encourage a happy and diverse workforce that knows they are listened to
- Adopt a new vantage position for your organisation
- Investigate the "zoom in, zoom out" approach to take a more dynamic approach to strategizing
- Constantly connect with people outside the organisation
- Place customers at the heart of your organisation

References

Davenport, T., & Stoddard, D. (1994) "Reengineering: Business change of mythic proportions?", *MIS Quarterly*, 18(2), 121–127, www.jstor.org/stable/249760

Greenhill, A., & Fletcher, G. (2003) "Utilising equipment matrices for information technology in primary school education policy", *InSITE (Informing Science) Conference: When Parallels Intersect*, June, University of Salford.

Hagel, J., & Seely Brown, J. (2018) "Take a zoom out, zoom in approach to business strategy", *Risk and Management Journal*, https://deloitte.wsj.com/riskandcompliance/2018/07/27/take-a-zoom-out-zoom-in-approach-to-business-strategy/

Johnson, T. (2018) "The real problem with tech professionals: High turnover", *Forbes Business Development Council*, www.forbes.com/sites/forbesbusinessdevelopmentcouncil/2018/06/29/the-real-problem-with-tech-professionals-high-turnover/

Kappel, M. (2016) "How your business benefits when you hire millennials", *Forbes*, www.forbes.com/sites/mikekappel/2016/09/03/how-your-business-benefits-when-hiring-millennials/

Lawton, L. (2015) "The Leader's role in managing change: Five cases of technology enabled business transformation", *Global Business and Organizational Excellence*, (Mar/Apr), 28–42.

McKenna, S., Fletcher, G., & Griffiths, M. (2019) *Hiding in the light: Recognising UK mid size businesses as a distinct category and their economic and social value to the nation*, Discussion Paper, Manchester: MSB Leaders, www.msbleaders.com/the-report

Moore, G. (2014) *Crossing the Chasm: Marketing and Selling Disruptive Products to Mainstream Customers* (3rd ed.). New York: HarperCollins.

Ram, A., & Bond, S. (2019) "Uber Eats to cut fees in battle with Deliveroo and Just Eat", *Financial Times*, www.ft.com/content/0a64006c-34f6-11e9-bb0c-42459962a812

Silverstone, S. (2011) "Zoom in zoom out on decision making", *CBS News*, www.cbsnews.com/news/zoom-in-zoom-out-decision-making/

9 Conducting a competitor analysis in the digital age

Alex Fenton, Katrina Gallagher and Aleksej Heinze

Preface

The benefits and opportunities of competitor analysis in a digital age, as well as the concept of the braided river, have already been covered in earlier chapters. This chapter now rethinks how to undertake competitor analysis in the globalised digital business environment. The chapter emphasises the need to turn the observation of success among competitors into an internal driver for innovation rather than simply copycatting and blindly adopting cargo cult thinking. The approach that is presented is undertaken using a range of data and critically evaluating differences that have brought about successful change for them. What do the competitors do, what insights can be gained from them, how relevant are these for your customers and do you want to meet or go beyond these benchmarks?

9.1 Rethinking competitor analysis

As a starting point it is useful to outline the objectives of competitor analysis.

1 Understand *who* the competitors are for each product or service
2 Understand what *strengths and weaknesses* exist in relation to their own offering
3 Use *customer* perspectives to identify and set *benchmarks* for our offerings

When undertaking competitor analysis, the objective may be to see what the competitors are doing but, more importantly, how to improve or provide an alternative to their offer. It could also identify areas where future collaborations or joint projects might be possible to benefit both organisations. Digital platforms allow for collaborative innovation which benefits multiple organisations and the industry as a whole. This is particularly true with the adoption of new technologies where sharing and learning from one another benefits not only those who learn but those who share.

Developing a standard of good practice helps organisations, their suppliers and customers. For example. in China, restaurants are increasingly offering the option to pay through the social media platform WeChat (see Chapter 20). WeChat is the largest social network in China and offers a popular mobile-payment solution (Zhou 2014). By accepting payment through WeChat, competitor restaurants remove the need to process cash and can offer faster service and convenience for their customers. From a customer perspective, if they prefer this facility for payment and it is not available in a restaurant then they might decide not to return. For restaurants in China, the benchmark has been set by the common practice of competitors. If a restaurant does not match this offer, it negatively reflects on the brand and can ultimately harm the business.

9.2 Competition, openness and sharing

Contrary to popular media depictions of never-ending cutthroat corporate battles, in many sectors there is an active practice of clustering and collaboration. This is particularly true in the digital and creative sector. Here, collaborations and joint ventures are commonplace and drive collaborative learning and sharing of 'best practice' across the industry. A regular example is the way that many smaller organisations team up with large organisations to bid for larger contracts. The large organisation might gain a particular competence which they do not have access to and a smaller business benefits from, for example, the administrative support to manage a large project, certifications or financial guarantees that are required for some larger contracts.

Trust generally increases in business when someone knows how your organisation works. If you have nothing to hide and there is nothing that commercially sensitive, then sharing your processes online can also provide good marketing material for your organisation. When and how to share also depends on the information and the industry you are in, and whatever the industry, confidentiality of customer data must always be maintained.

Game theory principles can help model how you might use the data and interact with your competitors. For a given scenario, you might work out the logical responses by you and your competitor along with the risk, reward and likelihood for each combination. For example – do you bid on your competitors' brand name in paid search engine marketing (such as Google AdWords)? It's common for there to be an understanding within certain industries that it's 'not the done thing'. If your customer notices that you're bidding on their brand, then, along with joining the bidding war and upping the price for their brand name, you may find that you have to start bidding on your own brand just to be visible.

Do you cooperate or betray the competition? If you bid on their brand and they don't retaliate, the payoff, for example, in the number of sales made, might be ten for you and zero for your competitor. If they bid on your brand but you don't, the rewards are reversed. If you bid on their brand and they retaliate, it increases the costs for both parties and both realise a more modest reward. If both refrain from bidding on one another's brands, the status quo remains and neither engages in expensive brand bidding nor 'stealing' customers from the other (Figure 9.1).

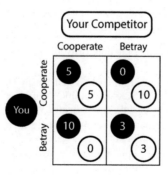

Figure 9.1 The prisoner's dilemma

Source: Adapted from Pastine and Pastine *Introducing Game Theory: A Graphic Guide*

In contrast, it is possible to evaluate the effects of sharing internal information, tips and efficiencies with competitors. If both share, both gain an advantage within the industry; if only one shares, the recipient of the information gains an advantage, potentially at the expense of the sharer.

9.3   Tools, tactics and evidence

The tools that you use to perform a competitor analysis might include an overall tracking and reporting system or dashboard with specific strategies for obtaining data about the different business areas.

You can either pull the details together into a report using a presentation tool (www. presentationload.com/competitor-analysis.html) or use a tool such as Google Data Studio. Data Studio allows you to create a dashboard for competitor monitoring as well as for tracking your own company performance. You can pull data in from digital systems automatically, as well as import offline or manually compiled information.

For example, in sales and marketing, you might identify a list of tools that can help understand the external digital presence of your competition (Table 9.1).

Using the example tools above, you could use a connector to link Google PageSpeed Insights, MOZ and/or SEMRush with Data Studio, and for the rest, you can upload to a spreadsheet or database and pull through charts and highlights.

You might break down your dashboards into the six elements of the organisation system (data, software, hardware, people, communications, processes) (see Chapter 2). Or you could create dashboards for each business function (Figure 9.2 and Figure 9.3).

When evaluating the data, it's worth noting that humans pattern match, and when something changes, we naturally look for what caused that result. There are so many interconnected factors that affect the performance of a business and it's very rarely 'just one thing'. A small change can have knock-on effects which amplify as time goes on – often referred to as the butterfly effect.

Microsoft developed a 'change audit' tool specifically for IT staff, security and compliance teams. This is used to manage changes within their technical infrastructure and teams. Based on this idea, it is possible to broaden its original scope to cover wider organisational changes that may occur (Figure 9.4). This change audit tool can be used to

Table 9.1 Descriptors of available tools

Tool	Benchmarks description
Google Trends	Identifies the popularity and seasonality of a particular search term over time
SEMrush	A competitor analysis tool, mostly search engine optimisation (SEO) focused. Keyword position, traffic rank, traffic sources, number of external links and estimated value paid advertising investment
MOZ	Website audit, business listing, rank tracker and a benchmarking tool for the number of external links
SpyFu	Comparison of organic vs paid website traffic, list of organic keyword competitors
SimilarWeb	Website analytics and ranking analysis as well as website audience overview
Google PageSpeed Insights	Tracks website performance (speed)
ahrefs	Social media and SEO metrics

Figure 9.2 Suggested dashboard elements

Marketing Dashboard

Details	Strength (1–10)	% Change ▲▼	Factors that may have impacted
Competitor 1			
Brand Exposure	x at 1		
Organic Search Presence	x at 2		
Social Media Coverage	x at 6		
Quality of Content	x at 7		
Online Reviews	x at 1		
Competitor 2			
Brand Exposure	x at 7		
Organic Search Presence	x at 8		
Social Media Coverage	x at 1		
Quality of Content	x at 1		
Online Reviews	x at 4		
Competitor 3			
Brand Exposure	x at 3		
Organic Search Presence	x at 8		
Social Media Coverage	x at 1		
Quality of Content	x at 7		
Online Reviews	x at 7		

Figure 9.3 Sample of a marketing dashboard

Figure 9.4 Sample of a change audit tool

analyse changes and their potential causes in a more scientific way in order to reduce the likelihood of drawing inaccurate conclusions.

9.4   Following or leading

Competitor analysis in a digital age offers myriad ways to understand the marketplace, products and services and new technologies. The question, therefore, is when to follow or when to lead in a new direction when identifying market opportunities and competitor moves. The objective is to avoid 'cargo cult thinking', which we define as "imitating the visible actions and behaviours of others without appreciating that what is observed is supported by far wider unseen infrastructure". An example from history is the John Frum cult in Tanna. The natives imitated the US soldiers that were stationed there in WWII, believing that if they did so the food, uniforms and equipment the soldiers received would also come to them. In terms of digital strategy, this lesson from history is to avoid blindly imitating your competition in order to achieve their perceived results. Original, data-informed action is required.

The good news in the digital age is that, as a leader, you should have access to more data and information to help you make an informed decision. Leading in a new direction can be an exhilarating but bumpy ride. Perhaps you have identified a new gap in the market – competitors moving in a particular direction or customer data demonstrating a new market need. In this case, you could execute 'first mover advantage' where you are first to market, creating a unique selling point of being the only organisation to provide this new innovation.

The balance to be struck is between being the first to do something and the quality of the product or service. From that perspective, a second mover advantage can also be beneficial, essentially, learning from the mistakes of the first mover and using feedback and data to create a superior offering. Referring back to the earlier point regarding consolidation and mergers, Weill and Woerner (2018) suggested that organisations that seek to digitally transform need to make investments that make revenue "because it seems there's a significant first mover advantage, often resulting in consolidation." Given this trend of consolidation, buy options are therefore important – investment to create new business models and acquire new technologies and even competitors. So choices need to be made – buy up the competition or be bought. In the digital era, this question is closely linked to when to follow or lead in a new direction.

The answer to the question on following or leading lies ultimately with your customers. Are they ready to embrace the offers made to them? Having identified the benchmarks it is essential to engage a representative sample of your customers and ask them for opinions about the proposed changes. This sample could be as small as five representative users testing your website or a mobile application. When developing an entirely new product or service, a customer survey could be used to get feedback on the draft ideas – ideally, these need to include around 500 participants where possible to be statistically significant. Competitor analysis can generate a number of ideas for market research which need to be explored before being implemented, as discussed in the following benchmarking evaluation tables section.

9.5   Developing benchmarks and evaluation tables

When conducting evaluations it can be easy to get confused with the range of different aspects to evaluate and rank them. The competitor analysis process itself can be very subjective – your views of the competition could be exaggerated by your personal opinions or perceptions of your customers. Even with the best use of peer evaluation tools such as TripAdvisor, it is important to be cautious that a lot of publicly available data is fake or has been manipulated by your competitors.

For example, counting Facebook, Twitter or WeChat connections can be misleading because some organisations pay for 'likes', followers and other interactions. It is also not clear which engagement rates are due to paid or organic interactions with their audience. Despite this, a number of superficial analysis tools use this method to see what competitions are up to. Any insight gained from these tools could be evaluated in combination with manual research.

For example, using an analysis tool such as ahrefs (https://ahrefs.com) – an SEO application that offers resources to grow search traffic – the top results when ordered by total shares for the term 'digital marketing training' returns three suspiciously 'thin' pieces of content. The content does not appear to be closely related and has a low volume of organic traffic and referring domains. By adding filters to a report it is possible to find higher quality posts that are more likely to have been shared organically,

Understanding how many content views are genuine organic views without any paid advertising is also not always clear. With the increasing prevalence of 'fake news' we have to exercise caution and where possible use two data sources for any variable being considered. A simple example of this would be a competitor hotel evaluation. Browsing reviews on TripAdvisor can give a feel for the kind of issues customers are highlighting, but these also should be checked with a service such as Booking.com or Expedia.

Understanding what your customers like and how important they see that technology/tool or digital interaction option helps you to make a decision – if there is a need for you to invest in this technology, time and energy. As we illustrated with the examples of Facebook and Google Reviews, both are free at the point of use, but they do still take time to promote and administer to get results.

When it comes to technologies it is not always obvious what systems and processes are being used to manage their communication with suppliers and this level of detail might be more difficult to compare. However, your customers and suppliers could be a great source of inspiration and intelligence about the experience they have with your competition. For most organisations this type of review is best undertaken on an annual basis, but for some industries it could be more frequent if the technologies they work with emerges at a fast pace.

Key takeaways

- Competitor analysis is an important ongoing process
- Do not take data at face value
- We have now more information on our competitors than ever before
- It is important to note who your competitors are in the digital space
- Your customers are the ultimate source for meaningful benchmarks

References

Weill, P., & Woerner, S. (2018) "Surviving in an increasingly digital ecosystem", *MIT Sloan Management Review*, 59(2), 26–28A.

Zhou, T. (2014) "Understanding the determinants of mobile payment continuance usage", *Industrial Management & Data Systems*, 114(6), 936–948.

10 Understanding how others see your organisation

Suzanne Kane

Preface

Armed with an understanding of influential external changes, knowledge of the value created by these changes and an awareness of what competitors are doing in response, the spotlight now turns internally to understanding your own organisation in the same way. This chapter emphasises the need to understand the internal challenges and legacies that currently impede an organisation's ability to rise to the challenges presented by the external drivers for change. Case studies are used to consider how the critical questioning of a current organisational situation can instigate radical change for rapid improvement.

10.1 From external to internal digital focus, it's all about people

Organisations must be acutely aware of external competition in order to address competitive advantage but also be open to the recognition of unexpected internal challenges that may emerge. Innovation (real or supposed) by external competitors is a strong driver for promoting some form of organisational change. However, reactive approaches that result in superficial change, which appear as innovation, simply wastes time and decreases commitment to substantial change for real long-term opportunities for organisations. Profound and lasting innovation in 21st- century organisations arises from an engaged workforce which is supported in its professional capacity as future-focused and technologically informed. 'Not doing digital' is no longer an option for organisations of any size, and 'doing digital' is dependent on human ingenuity for its technological enhancement. Hence, understanding how others see your organisation means consideration of the current expectations that society has about technology (in organisations). The expert informants for undertaking this activity might be closer than you think. Individuals are central to understanding organisational behaviour (Mullins 2013), and understanding how your present workforce views your organisation provides the inside story and illuminates areas for potential change and development.

Your competitors no longer need be High Street names with a substantial physical footprint. Their operations, supply chains and personnel all potentially exist in the 'ether' or 'cloud'. These almost magical metaphors conjure up a friendly and simplistic view of the connectivity required to support extensive digital and human networks which in turn support demanding customer expectations. Thoughtful digital transformation in organisations is not complete without organisational behavioural change. To be successful, the chief decision makers in organisations must recognise that successful digital transformation cannot be piecemeal, and substantial support may be required in their own ranks as much as elsewhere in their organisation. Long-term championing of digital transformation in organisations is necessary to support the less enthusiastic chiefs who may be considered 'digital immigrants' (Prensky 2001, 2009). But those newly entering the workforce and rising through the ranks may also continue to rely on digital champions for long-term support, as they may simply possess digital 'operational skills' and not necessarily the finesse and depth of knowledge associated with digital 'strategic skills' (Van Dijk & Van Deursen 2014). As such, the message here is that radical change for rapid improvement comes through sustained support and development of digital and technology skills championed by key personnel at all levels of the organisation. It is the people who populate the workforce that will make your organisation digital. Organisations do not live by technology alone; for long-term sustainability and competitive advantage, you require the most appropriate people.

However, it is not just your organisation that is looking for the best. Your competitors are also, of course, competing to engage the type of people that will help them to remain strong competitors in the marketplace. Digitally transforming any organisation requires professional and highly skilled personnel to support progress. Such personnel may or may not be graduates, but it is likely that a substantial number will have a university education and may have just as many expectations of the organisation as it has of them. It is expected that employers have substantial expectations of employees, but digitally skilled graduates with an existing professional profile have high expectations of employers, too. Twenty-first century graduates want to work for companies who are "fast growing and innovative" (*Bright Network* 2016/17). They want more than just a job; digital skills are part of their everyday experience and expect it to be part of their working life. "They bring a future forward outlook, in the form of digital skills and mindset" (*Accenture* 2017, 2). Therefore, part of understanding how others view your organisation is to consider why such skilled individuals would choose to work for one organisation rather than another.

10.2　Understanding internal challenges and legacies which impact upon organisations

An investigation of the organisational status quo is the starting point here. This must include all levels of the organisation in a non-judgemental approach because the strengths and weaknesses of an organisation can be unconsciously translated through stories about the workforce and management. These are informed by a cultural legacy of what has been acceptable in the past. Organisational decisions and workforce plans are based on the practical (internal) knowledge of what is possible in relation to existing and known professional skills and management support (which is often a historical understanding of what the management will support). Therefore, a review of the most recent projects and questioning the strengths and weaknesses of each from an internal perspective (of both the management and workforce) will enable greater understanding of that which has most recently been achieved and suggest areas of missed opportunities due to a mismatch of workforce skills and customer expectations.

The Cultural Web model (Johnson & Scholes 1993) provides guidance through useful section headings (which do not designate management and workforce reviews and therefore encourages information from all levels of the organisation). The model provides guidance via significant areas for focus but is also flexible enough for wide engagement (Figure 10.1). No specific professional skills are necessary, and commentary can be provided on all/any areas about which personnel have information. A range of elements are included in the model that promote descriptions of the many aspects of organisational culture. The central 'Paradigm' encourages commentary about the organisation, mindset and values. Other headings include 'Control Systems', which involves monitoring what occurs through processes; the 'Organisational Structure', which is usually well known through line managers and work flows; 'Power Structures', which show recognition of where the real power and influence is situated; and 'Symbols', from the company logo and the level of luxury in the organisation to the dress code. 'Rituals and Routines' combine acceptable behaviour and expectations of management, while 'Stories and Myths' point to the history of the organisation, including what people say inside and outside about the organisation and what an organisation chooses to promote as a story about themselves.

When utilising the Cultural Web in organisations, individuals are being asked to carry out a form of professional self-reflection in order to comment on their own perspectives of the organisation. Self-reflection is not a style of thinking that is entirely natural to some and may require support. The Gibbs Reflective Cycle (1988) affords support for this in practice (Figure 10.2), and Bassot (2016) provides a range of practical exercises and information about professional self-reflection.

The Gibbs Reflective Cycle can be used to support the construction of self-reflective accounts from the workforce based on the headings in the Cultural Web. This method allows a review of organisational issues around the strengths and weaknesses of an organisation. These may help to answer a number of important internal questions, such as What do we do well? Are we engaging with digital technology? Do we have the appropriate level of skills? Is there enough support for our managers and workforce?

Some reporting may highlight legacies, which are ideas that have been inherited about the way the organisation has always practiced. Such stories provide a starting point for development towards planned changes within the internal environment. Legacies can impede an organisation's ability to meet new challenges and as such are important areas for investigation (Chapter 13). For a defined emphasis on organisations, utilising headings from the Cultural Web provides a flexible focus that is helpful for those writing reflective statements and for the following process of analysis.

Figure 10.1 Cultural Web

Source: Adapted Johnson & Scholes 1993

Figure 10.2 Gibbs Reflective Cycle

10.3 Case study – the workforce of the future, and your future workforce

Practicing the method described above requires practical support for the self-reflection process. This study indicates the potential for this process to inform organisational practice. Digital skills as individual human capital supports organisational development, but only if you employ those that embody such skills. Understanding how your present workforce and a potential future workforce perceive your organisation provides snapshots. Will the picture of your organisation be one of ongoing developments with a digitally skilled workforce that supports demanding customers, or will those skilled professionals not be interested in working for you?

10.3.1 *Methodology*

This case is based on convenience sampling (Bryman 2016). From a class of almost 500 students in the first year of their degree course, almost half allowed access to their personal reflective statements for the purposes of research. The first level of the investigation initially focuses on fifty students. This allows a tentative insight into perceptions about digital skills development and expectations of organisational environments. It shows the potential of using self-reflection to develop an understanding of perspectives around digital skills and organisations in general. In addition to this context of convenience sampling is the use of the qualitative software package NVivo, which was employed to analyse the content of the self-reflection statements. Reading through the statements suggests potential areas of specific interest, and the software provides a digital environment to store all the reflections and supports the use of named nodes as categories. Codes for the self-reflective statements were then generated using the constant comparison technique, an approach that has been recommended for the analysis of statements (Bogdan & Bilden 1982). Initial codes were allocated following the analysis of the comments of the first statement, and the content of the second and subsequent statements were then allotted to these codes. New codes could be created for other emergent categories. NVivo software also supports coding stripes which allow the reader to highlight any part of the text and use the drag-and-drop technique to place any part of the statement into any selected node. Nodes can then be investigated for content and recognition of the percentage of text attributed to each node and overlapping nodes. At this point in the investigation, four particular areas were highlighted: reflecting on reflections, understanding of organisations, expectations of skills development and teamwork. A node was created for each of these areas.

10.3.2   Interim results of the investigation

The interim results from fifty statements forms part of a much larger cohort of a first-year university business and management module. Four categories of interest emerged from the investigation at this stage.

10.3.3   Reflecting on reflections

This case study suggests the relevance of understanding organisations through the reflections of individuals. Therefore, something of how the reflective process was viewed is relevant here. Respondents appear to be positive and suggest that reflecting on experience and practice is useful in a number of ways. Firstly, one respondent suggests, "I am now able to review my practical experiences to enhance my learning and development" (anonymous 1). Another respondent comments:

> Gibbs theory is a reflective learning cycle . . . I would do a task, see how I was feeling whether the activity was easy or difficult, then I would evaluate the activity, try and figure out what knowledge and information was gained from the task, conclude the activity and finally would be able to use the knowledge and information gained from each activity.
>
> (anonymous 38)

In addition, it is noted that

> Reflective writing enables me to identify my strengths . . . [and] . . . weaknesses . . . I now understand how to improve . . . I struggled with Gibbs Model initially . . . However, I understand the importance of being able to reflect . . . as it is a skill that will enable me to progress.
>
> (anonymous 40)

Also thoughtfully noted by another respondent: "Without reflecting and looking back . . . [it is] potential lost. It's . . . my feelings and opinions . . . that allow new situations to be tackled effectively" (anonymous 45).

While it is not suggested that self-reflection is easy, it does appear to be considered worthwhile. Many rich seams of understanding come from the reflective process, which does not occur in our usual day-to-day experience, and therefore that experience is potentially lost.

10.3.4 *Understanding of organisations*

Across all the four categories, the highest number of references, by far, were attributed to statements which related to the personal understanding of organisations.

Progress of technology was aligned with both personal and work life: "necessary skills to work digitally [are] not only essential to everyday life but also crucial for the working environment" (anonymous 1). The specific use of digital skills was also recognised as particularly important in organisations: "digital communications . . . are vital in companies, for example, emailing, video messaging . . . [and] what security they have to protect the company" (anonymous 14). It was expected that organisations would utilise "good communication to function properly" and that they would "take advantage of using communication devices to speed up their process" (anonymous 16).

Understanding how organisations reach clients is also noted as "digital communication ultimately . . . keeps businesses connected to current clients" (anonymous 20), and comments of understanding the way in which present organisations are run is not just based on skills and strategies required to support profit-making businesses. Also noted were "local councils . . . equipping locals with [digital] skills [to support] employment and other aspects of life" (anonymous 23).

In addition, reliance on technology in organisations is suggested as a way in which human error can be reduced, decision-making can be supported and distribution of information may be facilitated. Understanding of the digital world is stated as key for career progression and presents digital skills as extremely important in professional life. In regard to specific software, Excel skills were highlighted as sought after by employers and, more generally, the skills to build brand awareness via social media and also skills in online communications and collaborations. There is also an expectation of using social media apps "such as Facebook, Instagram, LinkedIn etc. to promote . . . brands and interact with customers" (anonymous 45).

It was also considered that those without digital skills would miss opportunities to "fully integrate" in social and work life. Selling practices, marketing and customer satisfaction were all aligned with the requirement for a certain level of understanding and practical knowledge of digital skills for business, as was also competitor and market analysis. Effective and efficient organisations are thought to be focused on "analytics, especially social media analytics and the Microsoft Excel software, which is both a necessary skill to have in the workplace as well as a powerful analytics tool" (anonymous 37).

Understanding organisations for this particular group of students is a blend of many factors, but unsurprisingly, technology is dominant in their view of how organisations will seek to be successful. At the heart of this is a workforce that has the requisite skills to support and utilise digital software and systems. Digital skills are described as "highly valued . . . and . . . vital . . . for future progress" (anonymous 43). They also believe that online collaboration enhances interaction: "once we connected through social media to arrange to meet, getting to know each other, ideas tend to flow, and we become more innovative when it comes to ideas and suggestions" (anonymous 45). This acceptance of working together through technology continues: "digital communications within a workplace such as virtual workplace . . . offers more flexibility and . . . it offers great productivity when people can balance work and personal life easier [these are] modern ways employees communicate with each other within businesses" (anonymous 45). Social selling, social media, blogging and vlogging are all approaches that are accepted by the cohort as normal for both personal and work-life usage. Another respondent adds: "[collaborating online] will allow me to work better in a team situation and I can pass on these skills to other people" (anonymous 50).

There is no accepted line to be crossed; the time of defined workplace technologies (such as a fax machine in the office) is a thing of the past. Social shaping previously dictated that certain technology belonged in the work environment rather than the home. However, development has decreased cost and size, allowing much of the required systems hardware to become small enough to be personal. As such, it is re-shaped and enters both our professional and private lives as personal technology and therefore belongs wherever the person resides.

One respondent clearly writes about the embeddedness of such technologies in all parts of their life:

> In my opinion, one of the most interesting workplace technologies is the ability of using social media as a major-league beneficial factor of the business . . . social media became a significant communication tool in everyone's life. [It's] replacing traditional ways such as letters, phone calls or even regular text messages with quick chats or video . . . on platforms such as Facebook, Instagram, Snapchat, Twitter and many more.
>
> (anonymous 48)

10.3.5 *Expectations of skills development*

Following from the statements that highlight the ways in which this cohort understand organisations and consider how they may fit in to such organisations in their future professional lives, it is obvious that they expect to encounter and work within digital environments. It is of no surprise that these individuals expect to increase their knowledge and practice capabilities, but along with this is likely to be an expectation that organisations will support such development long-term. One respondent states: "In terms of my future professional life, I believe digital skills are significant in helping me to achieve my goals by working efficiently and adapting to the growing increase of technology used in the workplace" (anonymous 1). Another suggests that "going forward I will aim to continuously learn and build upon my skills, to become a better-skilled individual" (anonymous 13).

The relevance of updating particular expertise was noted as "cyber security and internet safety". (anonymous 18) One respondent specifically noted that "[I have] opened my eyes to how important online safety is and . . . this made me operate with much greater caution" (anonymous 50). Another considers the importance of "awareness of security on electronic devices and how to defend yourself from malware which may attack your . . . personal information" (anonymous 43).

However, the importance of skills development isn't just relevant for the workplace where an individual works for an organisation. These are transferable skills, and some look toward building their skills to build their own business: "[I use] social media channels in order to view trends of my followers; preferably in terms of content and hopefully products if I ever launch a product line" (anonymous 23). Another respondent suggests:

> I am going to do the Master of Microsoft programme, which will enhance my communication within the workplace. To improve, I am going to vlog my life as well as blog the steps to a successful business because in the future I would like to open my own . . . firm.
>
> (anonymous 47)

It can be seen that the respondents value the development of their skill sets, which will benefit organisations they may be employed by but also, for some, their own aspirations in self-employment.

10.3.6   *Teamwork*

Teamwork was described in a number of ways by the respondents, and it was suggested that it could be extremely challenging. But many also noted that aspects of technology made a difficult situation much easier to manage and even enjoyable. One respondent said, "it was hard sharing our ideas . . . without any time together. However, to resolve this we created a project group chat in order to enhance our communication" (anonymous 11). Another stated:

> communicating with the team through the various media technologies such as instant messaging, through WhatsApp or virtually working with each other and editing the same document in real time, through One Drive by giving the group shared access while simultaneously engaging on Skype video conferences allowed me to effectively manage my time.
>
> (anonymous 37)

10.4   Conclusion

The emergent categories taken from the reflections of the respondents in this case suggest that their understanding of organisations is through the lens of omnipresent digital technology. They view digital skills as intrinsically linked with their own everyday lives and professional progress. Their expectation is of a future where they continue to increase their training and skills. At the beginning of this investigation, the cohort referred to in this case were asked in their first class about their main reason for entering a degree programme; one person cited a love of knowledge, while everyone else wanted to enhance their career opportunities. However, their reflections suggest that these two imperatives combine in their view of their future wherever that may be. Their understanding of organisations is one of technology-enhanced environments that require ongoing professional development. If that is not an accurate description of your organisation, something needs to change. Even if you haven't overtly encouraged the development of digital skills in your workforce, it is likely they have invaded your territory by default. Recognise it now, digital transformation in organisations is here to stay – it isn't a threat, it's just the new normal. Therefore, it should be asked whether established organisations are up to the challenge of providing the support which will in turn sustain technology development because the students presented here are the workforce of the future, or put another way, your future workforce.

Key takeaways

- Understanding how others view your organisation includes knowing why skilled individuals would choose to work for your organisation rather than another
- Chief decision makers must recognise that successful digital transformation cannot be piecemeal and substantial support may be required in their own ranks
- 'Not doing digital' is no longer an option for organisations of any size, and 'doing digital' is dependent on human ingenuity

- It is the people who populate the workforce that will make your organisation digital; for long-term sustainability and competitive advantage you require the most appropriate workforce
- Digital transformation in organisations is here to stay – it isn't a threat, it's just the new normal.

References

Accenture (2017) "Gen Z rising", www.accenture.com/t20170901T082427Z__w__/us-en/_acnmedia/PDF-50/Accenture-Strategy-Workforce-Gen-Z-Rising-POV.pdf#zoom=50

Bassot, B. (2016) *The Reflective Journal* (2nd ed.). London: Palgrave.

Bogdan, R., & Bilden, S. (1982) *Qualitative Research for Education: An Introduction to Theory and Methods.* Boston, MA: Allyn and Bacon.

Bright Network (2016) "What do graduates want", www.brightnetwork.co.uk/sites/default/files/what_do_graduates_want.pdf

Bryman, A. (2016) *Social Research Methods* (5th ed.). Oxford: Oxford University Press.

Gibbs, G. (1988) *Learning by Doing: A Guide to Teaching and Learning Methods.* London: Further Education Unit, GB.

Johnson, G., & Scholes, K. (1993). *Exploring Corporate Strategy.* New York: Prentice Hall.

Mullins, L.J. (2013) *Management and Organisational Behaviour* (10th ed.). Harlow: FT Publishing.

Prensky, M. (2001) "Digital natives, digital immigrants", *On the Horizon,* 9(5), 1–6, doi: 10.1108/10748120110424816

Prensky, M. (2009) "H. sapiens digital: From digital immigrant and digital natives to digital wisdom", *Innovate: Journal of Online Education,* 5(3), 1.

Van Dijk, J., & Van Deursen, A. (2014) *Digital Skills: Unlocking the Information Society.* New York: Palgrave Macmillan.

Internal motivations

Wanting to change the organisation

11 Doing a forensic internal audit of your organisation

Skills, resources, culture, resistance

Aleksej Heinze and Gordon Fletcher

Preface

It is necessary to regularly reflect on current practice and process. Following on from the previous chapter in which the external perspectives of an organisation were considered, a forensic audit sets out to identify the gaps for an organisation to undertake strategic digital transformation. Using the organisational system as the structuring perspective, every area of the organisation is considered. Not only does it position an organisation in terms of its existing digital maturity, but it also considers the extent to which an organisation presents a suitable ecosystem for innovation and if there is any existing internal agility to capitalise on emerging external stimulus.

11.1 Inside the organisation

In Chapter 7 the first element of the HINGE model highlighted the importance of being aware of the wide variety of opportunities and challenges that are constantly emerging in the VUCA world. The second element to HINGE is the internal audit in which the current organisational situation is reconciled with the external stimulus that has been discovered. This focus is on the organisational system that supports the current as well as any future business models.

As this is a forensic audit a key starting point is to determine who has responsibility for which parts of the system. Some current roles will have an obvious relationship with the system. For example, the human resource functions of the organisation line up closely with the "People" components of the system. However, reiterating the points made earlier in Chapter 2, the system refers to people both inside and outside the organisation, so the marketing function of the organisation is also key to developing an understanding of the current people situation.

The organisational system provokes a critical re-examination of the defined functions of the organisation and how they interact with one another in this context. This examination, in the first instance, may be time-consuming, but the benefit is that subsequent iterations of HINGE will only require minor modifications as a result of the impact of the actions that have come out of previous HINGE cycles.

The type of critical review that is required for the internal audit is challenging and will test the degree to which there is full commitment for change across the organisation. Barriers and resistance to the internal audit is itself an indication that more development work and different forms of leadership are required to further communicate the push and pull factors of digital transformation.

Documenting the development and findings of an internal audit are also important for consistency and for facilitating the change in the organisation towards sharing and transparency. Preventing access to the development of the audit can build resistance rather than gaining acceptance. The audit can commence with the initial mapping of the organisational system (Table 11.1). A new line is added for each new aspect discovered in the audit (column 3). The result will be a multi-line table with repetition of components, functions and possibly leaders. Duplication in column 3 may also occur if there is divided responsibility for an aspect of a component across functions (column 2) or individual leaders (column 4).

The mapping of functional leadership to organisational components immediately reveals the relative complexity or simplicity of the system. In organisations mid-sized and above there will not be a one-to-one relationship of functions to components – the lack of a Chief Process Officer or a Chief Communications Officer in any organisation is one indicator that no organisation can be this simple. An exception to this observation may be found in some family businesses where there are stronger lines of reporting and responsibility to a small number of family members. Similarly, in startups, micro and some small organisations there is a strong likelihood that one person will lead on multiple functions and possibly even multiple system components. This form of multi-function responsibility sitting with an individual, however, should not necessarily be read as a form of organisational simplicity.

Once the leadership of the components of the organisational system has been determined, the opportunity now exists to identify interrelationships. Finding the relationships between components highlights the mixture of interchanges that must occur for the organisation in its current situation to remain at *status quo*. Locating the absence of a relationship that has been identified as being needed through the audit may also offer a quick win for the organisation to implement.

Mapping the relationships will create significant quantities of documentation, as there is the potential for each component to relate to all of the other five components, and this relationship is multiplied further when multiple business functions have responsibility for an different aspects of a single component. The scale of the complexity is readily evident. If only one existing business function is mapped to each component of the system and a relationship is identified to every other component in the system this produces thirty

Table 11.1 Functions and leaders mapped to the organisational system

1. Organisation system component	2. Current organisational functions (functional areas)	3. Aspect of the component that the function leads	4. Function leaders
People			
Communications			
Processes			
Hardware (in the broadest sense)			
Software			
Data			

Table 11.2 Functional identification of system relationships

1. We give (2.) to (or) We need (2.) from	2. What	3. This component	4. Through this function	5. Because

one-way relationships. Because of this complexity, the task is best undertaken from the perspective of each of the existing functions with an eye towards what is given and what is needed (Table 11.2). Each function should attempt to document the input requirements (what they need) and the output expectations (what they produce). Each line of the responses creates an individual statement that captures all the relationships consistently across the organisation. The prototype sentence can then read as "We give 'what' to 'component' through 'function' because . . . ." or "We need 'what' from 'component' through 'function' because . . ."

Function

When completed, this identification is compiled to produce a map of the organisational system. Particular attention can then be given to duplicate relationships coming in or out of functions within a single component. This may indicate a lack of efficiency within the system that can be considered in more detail. Further consideration can also be given to mismatched expectations between the input and output of functions and their overall components. These mismatches may be capturing examples of internal under- or over-servicing that may highlight opportunities for releasing capacity to other activities or existing ability to undertake new developments.

It is also important to acknowledge in the audit that the components of the organisational system can also be external to the business itself. This means, for example, that interaction with "People" includes people both internal as well as external to the organisation.

With the organisational system mapped out, the overall organisation has a new and detailed perspective of itself that enables it to address issues with the right people. The audit also makes it possible to trace systemic and interlocking issues throughout the entire system to appreciate the necessary scope of future transformation projects.

11.2 People and skills

With the structure of the organisation mapped out in detail, there is an opportunity to examine specific parts of the organisation. Within the digital transformation agenda the key components for consideration are the most distinctive parts of the organisation: its people and its data.

The organisation has less control over external people and so can realise the greatest difference by focusing on those inside. The repeating theme that comes consistently from all research about people and digital transformation is the need for having the right skill sets (van Dijk & van Deursen 2014). These skills must service the organisation's current and future needs but should not be driven by available or potential technology. Previously, many technology development companies recruited their staff based on their knowledge, real or claimed, against a specific list of technologies. Candidates were not necessarily chosen for their ability to adapt to change, to problem solve or to position their own work within a wider context or critique their own work.

The danger with a move towards digital transformation is that other organisations set out criteria for recruits based on an awareness of specific technologies rather than higher level skills that enable them to work with people and technologies in the future in unimagined and new ways. This expectation broadly describes the qualities of any under-graduate completing their course of study, with their ability to

> determine, refine, adapt and use appropriate methods and advanced cognitive and practical skills to address problems that have limited definition and involve many interacting factors. Use and, where appropriate, design relevant research and development to inform actions. Evaluate actions, methods and results and their implications.
>
> (Phoenix 2018, 18)

Any specific skills that a new recruit may have beyond this broad set of higher level graduate skills is better seen as an added bonus and something that comes out of the value-added benefits delivered by a specific course of study or gained from previous work experience. This also contrasts markedly with the observation sometimes heard from directors and leaders that their employees need to be (or become) programmers (Bolboaca 2015). While specific situations may need this bundle of skills, the increasing rise of turnkey solutions for high-level technology functions, including artificial intelligence and machine learning, make this a priority for a very small number of businesses – such as those companies producing the turnkey technology solutions.

The statement should be better reconsidered as a call for employees to develop broader sets of skills that are often found as a combination with individual programmers. Skilled programmers are problem solvers who are able to express a solution to complex problems in systematic ways that are often adaptable to unforeseen future circumstances. Many skilled programmers are able to work and make decisions independently while also being able to critically reflect upon individual design decisions and choices that they have made.

This broader view of skills and what the organisation currently needs then feeds into an internal audit. Each of the interactions between functions that has already been mapped out can now be reviewed in light of the skills or the qualities needed by the people involved in successfully delivering this interaction. This can be done by including an additional "Skills" column to the original mapping of interactions (in Table 11.2).

Identifying the skills people need to successfully negotiate the interactions in the organisation completes the enquiry aspect of the audit. Work can now begin on cross-checking the findings of the audit. For the "People" aspect of the system, this involves examining the skills defined by the roles that undertake the interactions to ensure they are aligned with what is needed. A further and deeper examination involves assessing the actual skills of the current role-holders to reveal any potential training or development needs.

11.3 Accessing infrastructure and resources

The cross-checking of the organisational system can also be initiated for the infrastructure of the organisation. At this stage the audit moves from building an understanding of the organisation to a confirmation of its overall structure. In general, it is the end points of the interaction that are captured in the initial information gathering stage. Some of the data, software and hardware requirements may already be captured through the definition of specific interactions. However, other interactions may be more than a one-to-one relationship and require facilitation through multiple components of the system. Some of these requirements may at least be implied in the list of interactions (Table 11.2).

Most significantly, the data required for each interaction is a key consideration. This particularly includes those interactions that are currently defined as being solely "People to People". There is a need to consider the data within the interaction and how this is being captured and shared. Without recognising what suitable supporting data is that brings insight to the interaction, there is a risk of decisions being taken without a supporting evidence base. This results in interactions within the organisational system being based upon the experience and knowledge of individuals. "Gut" feeling is then the basis for decision making – potentially with some degree of accuracy – in the interaction. In the absence of this employee and their "gut", interactions will become less accurate and more prone to incorrect or unexpected outcomes.

Infrastructure also includes all the software and hardware of the organisational system and should also be documented. What is being captured are all the intangible and tangible artefacts that connect end-to-end to make each interaction work.

As with the previous assessment of skills this aspect of the audit adds a new "Infrastructure" column to each interaction (Table 11.2). Some interactions will require a significant chain of tangible infrastructure – described as hardware in the organisational system – that might require, for example, vehicles and buildings to be achieved successfully. Other interactions may be entirely based on intangible – software-based – exchanges. All interactions require some form of data to be exchanged – in some cases this may be difficult to determine and may, in the current interaction, be undertaken with a straightforward verbal exchange at a formal meeting. There may be no immediate need to alter the nature of an interaction of this type, but the audit nonetheless endeavours to capture a picture of precisely what occurs.

11.4 Taking a measure of culture

What remains to be considered are the cultural aspects of each interaction beyond the involvement of people. As with the infrastructure considerations, looking at the end points of each interaction benefits from considering the processes and communications that are required to successfully connect the two ends of the interaction. Processes and communications are proxies for direct interaction for people and need to be viewed in this way. Culture is the shared experiences of the organisation and the organisational system. People, processes and communications are what shape and define the unique culture of every organisation. Culture is important and should be a positive aspect of the organisation, but it should also serve the vision and mission.

Processes trigger the initiation and closing of interactions, while communications will be a consideration, especially when one person needs to connect with many people inside or outside the organisation. How these processes and communications are done, when they are used and why they are used directly reflect the culture of the organisation itself and shape the way that people describe and experience the organisation.

An interaction that brings with it a significant burden of process and communications may be a barrier that requires reconsideration or automation. Design friction – intentionally using processes to slow down or block interactions – may, on occasion, be a necessary inclusion to manage aspects of the organisational system. Design friction should be used rarely and only with very strong justification.

The cultural aspects of each interaction should be captured through the processes and communications that are required to enable them to be initiated and delivered. This is a further column for each interaction (Table 11.2).

11.5   Organisational behaviour and the artefacts of resistance

Within the organisation, resistance to change and to transformation specifically is an inevitable aspect of the process. The internal audit enables discovery of potential points where this resistance can or will be expressed directly. The identification of the cultural and infrastructural enablers that are necessary for each interaction will also reveal which artefacts can become a proxy for the expression of this resistance. Processes are particularly sensitive to being used as instruments for resistance. Being proxies for direct people to people interactions enables interactions to be stalled or diverted. Statements such as "that isn't our process" or "we don't have a process for that" can be expressions of resistance. Processes act as draglines on transformational change by acting in combination with people to resist removal or substitution. For people in the organisation, processes are symbols of organisational constancy and certainty irrespective of the value they produce – or the additional labour they require.

Infrastructure can also become artefacts of resistance for different reasons. The complexity, cost and interdependency of infrastructural legacy and enterprise technology will also resist change. This will again confirm the appeal of consumer technology to disruptors as being the more flexible and adaptable option.

Resistance can be positively engaged in the transformation process. Adopting the sentiments of openness, transparency and ongoing conversation can be used to encourage grassroots identification of the blockers and complexity within individual interactions. These are potentially as frustrating to those most resistant to change as they are to those seeking the most rapid change. Enabling mechanisms for communicating the pain points, capturing these consistently and clearly evidencing the actions taken as a result can all support more rapid transformation projects using the HINGE approach.

Key takeaways

- An internal audit of the organisation reveals it complexity, legacies and potential points of resistance to change
- The audit focuses on capturing and documenting the organisational system in detail
- Using the organisational system as a focus for the audit encourages a new perspective on existing functional structures
- Emphasis is on identifying the critical interactions in the organisation with focus on the most distinctive aspects of the organisation: its people and its data
- Cultural and infrastructural considerations can then be connected with these interactions

References

Bolboaca, A. (2015) "We don't need more programmers", *Mozaic Works*, 11th Dec, https://mozaicworks. com/blog/we-dont-need-more-programmers/

Phoenix, D. (2018) *Filling in the Biggest Skills Gap: Increasing Learning at Levels 4 and 5*, Higher Education Policy Institute (HEPI), www.hepi.ac.uk/wp-content/uploads/2018/08/EMBARGOED-UNTIL-23-AUGUST-2018-Filling-in-the-biggest-skills-gap-Report-110_Final-web.pdf

Van Dijk, J., & Van Deursen, A. (2014) *Digital Skills: Unlocking the Information Society*. New York: Palgrave Macmillan.

12 The value of transparency, sharing, customisation, boldness and openness

Mick Hides, Alex Connock and Gordon Fletcher

Preface

Organisations are increasingly expected to behave differently. The visibility that digital technology brings to an organisation – whether willingly or unwillingly – is also a key mechanism for bringing change to an organisational culture. The form of change that is being driven by the expectations of consumers asks that organisations genuinely embrace the following five qualities of transparency, sharing, customisation, boldness and openness. The expectations regarding data handling and privacy that have been formalised by GDPR in Europe and regulatory bodies also echo this consumer movement towards particular forms of organisational behaviour. Each of these five qualities enhance the organisational system and makes the business models that are being offered engaging, relevant and valuable to the consumer. Succeeding with this offer, in turn, generates greater long-term value for the organisation. This chapter looks at how to leverage these qualities internally and externally to support strategic digital transformation while also aligning with consumer expectations.

12.1 Transparency

We live in an age of authenticity. Every product and service has to verify its authenticity in some way to its ultimate consumer (Beverland 2005). Craft beer and cheese at the supermarket assert their authenticity through origin stories and organic ingredients lists; the latest mini-series on Netflix emphasises the CV of the director, producers and actors; and local visitor attractions display their TripAdvisor stars outside the gift shops. However, authenticity is at its best (and least awkward) when it can be immediately evidenced through the five organisational qualities of transparency, openness, sharing, boldness and customisation (Figure 12.1). Balancing high levels of each of these qualities within the organisation translates into higher perceptions of authenticity for consumers.

Transparency is the extent to which an organisation is wrapped in clear glass. Transparency also relates to the internal organisational system and the degree to which there is clear glass between the various departments that make up that system. There are a variety of acknowledged operational reasons for open-plan office working becoming commonplace, particularly financial ones (Perez 2018). However, from a strategic leadership point of view, open plan should be regarded as the symbolic and real embodiment of internal transparency practices if they are implemented with sensitivity to existing organisational cultures and subsequent to other 'people' work that diminishes siloes and creates an overall sense of shared identity. In this sense, shared office space is the final act of the process to create an integrated, highly transparent organisation (Bernstein & Turban 2018).

The combination of an increased ability to share insight and knowledge of an organisation on a one-to-many basis through digital media, the rising importance of brand reputation and greater levels of environmental awareness has changed business permanently. There are no longer any benefits for organisations to have an aura of mystery surrounding their operations. For those organisations that attempt to remain opaque, they are inevitably drawn into a form of forced transparency through sites such as Glassdoor, RateMyEmployer and TheJobCrowd or direct personal sharing of comments.

Instilling the quality of transparency and its importance within an organisation can only succeed if it is embraced by the leadership and then actively demonstrated internally. A key marker of the extent that transparency has been embraced within an organisation is the willingness to potentially fail, to be free from the fear of failing and to not revert to a traditional blame culture for failure (Lambert 2018). If the organisation can embrace and recognise failure as a learning opportunity then transparency is also itself nothing to fear. An organisation that is transparent to those who work within it on these terms will succeed in innovating and in bringing its innovations to consumers while maximising the value generated for the organisations. The organisation will also tend towards inclusivity, further reinforcing the balance of the five key qualities (Parris et al. 2016) (Figure 12.1).

Transparency is also found as a core principle of Agile Project Management (APM), which is widely favoured for digital development projects. This principle encourages an environment of honesty that is needed to successfully deliver robust software to a deadline. The relationship of Agile Project Management to organisational qualities of transparency is also revisited in Chapter 16 as an appropriate method for delivering dynamic business models. Internal transparency can be taken still further through Agile Project Management with large wall-mounted charts of current operational or project data. Larger projects benefit from a dedicated 'war room' where all of the project's information is collated and visible during meetings and for dissemination activities through the organisation more widely. These tangible interpretations of transparency highlights the importance of velocity and veracity (drawn from the 4V model discussed in Chapter 1) as being vital for a transparent organisation, with slow and inaccurate data leading to 'poor' decision making. Flawed decisions, in turn, make risks difficult to manage (Donaldson 2018).

The BBC's decision to be more transparent about the salaries it pays for its talent demonstrates some of the risks to this approach (Kentish 2018). A similar situation can be spotted in the resistance to releasing executive bonuses paid by financial institutions

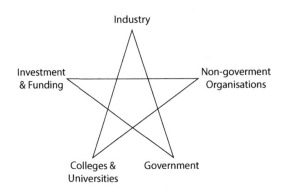

Figure 12.1 Key interconnected organisational qualities of transparency

or vice-chancellors pay within UK universities (Grove 2019). When individuals inside an organisation are uncomfortable with these levels of transparency, it reflects the degree to which there is still a journey to be travelled organisationally. If this resistance is built up within a persistent organisational culture of blame, this is a red flag highlighting the need to change. Nonetheless, the concept of transparency may be a difficult adjustment (Arringdale 2016), and arguably there are downsides to transparency (Birkinshaw & Cable 2017) that should be considered, acknowledged and mitigated carefully by all organisations.

12.2   Openness

Digital technologies provide multiple opportunities to work openly. Greater openness in an organisation creates new external perspectives and viewports on the same internal data that can bring new opportunities and bring greater value to customers and the organisation. Openness is about the permeability – and not just the visibility found with transparency – of an organisation and its data. It is not just that those on the outside can see inside the organisation, but they can also interact with what they find. Being open is about the extent to which an organisation enables access for other organisations and its own customers. Openness is also a mechanism to manage the relationship between the organisation and the VUCA world. By being consciously open, the channels between 'inside' and 'outside' can be better understood and, to some degree, managed. By opening conduits between the VUCA world and the organisation, openness also supports the creation of an internal environment in which ideas and creativity can flourish organically through the internalising of external stimulus. Both DHL and Lego have engaged with this type of co-creation thinking by encouraging customers to contribute ideas that help the companies to solve key organisational problems.

Adopting openness as a central operating tenet and a core quality of the organisation would traditionally be regarded as an act of giving up or compromising trade secrets to the competition (see Chapters 4 and 9). This form of resistance echoes older lines of thinking that positions the product or service as the entire encapsulation of the organisation's offer to the consumer. Thinking in terms of the product as the entire offer ignores the importance of the consumer's experience as well as their engagement with the brand and the organisation in informing their decisions. The organisation's relationship with the consumer is no longer solely transactional, and openness recognises that knowledge exchange that can occur with each consumer interaction. Considered pragmatically, how a product or service is created internally may be of little interest or value to competitors who will take a different approach, deploy different technology, have a different internal organisational system and focus on different value propositions for their consumers. Considered competitively, if there is little or no distinction between an organisation's offer and that of its competitors, the level of similarity raises the real risk of direct imitation or copying; then there is a need to reconfigure its value proposition to its customers. In Europe the rise of the deep discounting supermarket chains is a tangible realisation of the risks of having the customer experience entirely based around transactions of products that are easily imitated (Ashmore 2019).

Critically unpicking the reasons why openness is being resisted should be a key internal organisational project to understand what is being protected or being kept secret. Previous arguments about keeping work secrets should be scrutinised in a new light and weighed against the benefits of a more open perspective. Trust begets trust. The continuum that organisations occupy between the extremes of absolute confidentiality and complete openness can be quickly identified in the roles that they individually define. A Patents Officer or Intellectual Property Officer represents a very different organisational culture than that expressed by having an Information Sharing or Open Source Officer.

The degree of openness can be managed and throttled by the organisation. Technology development organisations that offer application programming interfaces (commonly called APIs) provide a consistent way for people outside the organisation to interact with the data that has been gathered and held internally. The most common experience of APIs is when a website, mobile app or application incorporates a social media feed from, for example, Twitter or Instagram or weather information. There are many more sophisticated examples of APIs. As an example, the data provided from a user's input on a web page can be fed into an API, processed through a separate service and then returned back to the user in a modified form. This type of API usage is generally completely invisible to the user who provides the original source data and enables sophisticated interactive third-party services to be combined and incorporated on a single webpage or through a mobile app. Examples of this interaction include geocoding locations, filtering content, confirming passwords, analysing text and tracking users.

For most organisations, the type of openness that APIs can access is something that they make use of rather than offer. Creating an API with suitably anonymised and aggregated datasets may be an entirely new opportunity and business model not currently being considered. Openness does not necessarily equate with being a free service either. High-value data offerings that can be offered through an API can also require a regular fee payment for access.

Perhaps one of the most surprising developments in organisational openness has been initiated by the KFC chain of fast food restaurants. The KFC Open Kitchen project invites guests at 300 of its restaurants in the UK and Ireland to fry their own chicken (Benjamin 2019). This means that consumers can first-hand see how the company makes its *secret* Original Recipe chicken.

12.3   Sharing

Where openness is about being permeable to the VUCA world, sharing is about recognising the value of mutually beneficial relationships and actively working to enhance these. An organisation that shares with other businesses and its customers will be more likely to generate successful relationships. In other words, organisational relationships that are built upon the mutual exchange of ideas and common learning has a better chance of succeeding over a long time than a purely transactional one. Sharing is about working together in ways that create mutually beneficial ways of dealing with the VUCA world.

Within the organisation, a shared vision, language and understanding of priorities enables people to think differently about what they have and what they can achieve. Some digital technologies enhance the ability to communicate in these terms within the organisation. Email should be primarily regarded as a broadcast technology that is counter-intuitive to organisational qualities of sharing (Wells 2018). Other forms of teamworking and collaboration systems encourage greater depth of sharing and the development of stronger levels of mutual trust. Heightened levels of sharing in turn leads to increased accountability and productivity. Improved internal sharing also propagates beyond the organisation to fuel a positive reputation externally (Arringdale 2016).

Sharing with clients helps them understand the challenges and opportunities of key internal processes in real time, which increases trust and mutual understanding while also ensuring that partners can appropriately time their own arrangements. Good production companies involve the client in the production process, and sharing can produce a competitive advantage (Lattimore 2018). This approach can be equally applied to B2C or B2B operations. A seamless supply chain is crucial to the success of any business. An organisation relies on the trust that a supplier will deliver but expects honesty about any issues they may interrupt this supply chain. Sharing in the VUCA world assists all organisations in becoming simpler and more certain. An integrated and connected digital supply chain deploying, for example, SAP or similar enterprise-level software platforms requires high levels of sharing between partners to schedule their individual contributions (such as materials, logistics or other resources) at the appropriate time and place, which also mitigates volatility and ambiguity (Thalbauer 2019).

Examples of organisational sharing of data provide some indication of the ways that sharing can bring new opportunities – without compromising on ethical behaviour or infringing upon GDPR requirements. The UK's Rail Delivery Group freely provides the timetable data for all of the train operators to developers. This has resulted in the development of innovative products that offer different ways of looking at the same data. The traintime.org.uk website offers different ways to query the timetables and also attempts to show a live map of train locations. The most common use of the data, however, is for the individual train operators to present the timetable on their own website and branded appropriately.

The qualities of organisational sharing takes many forms, but the influence of the open source software movement has shaped one of its most recognisable organisational forms. Electric cars have existed in various forms since the end of the 19th century, but it is only since 2010 that they have gained popularity. Tesla has disrupted the automobile market through its innovative electric vehicle designs coupled with a willingness to take the longer term strategic investment approach. The scale of Tesla's disruption has gone further by relinquishing patent rights. Transferring an open source philosophy to the automotive sector arguably boosts the market as a whole (Musk 2014). But sharing within the automotive sector is not a new concept. As early as the 1990s, Nissan was happy to share manufacturing expertise in the belief that once its competitors caught up they would also have developed still further and moved on.

The principles of open source software are potentially not a level of sharing that every organisation will be comfortable with (Hurley 2014). Open source software entirely exposes the entirety of the source code to external scrutiny, examination and duplication. The underlying philosophy of open source is that greater value exists and can be realised in the sharing of source code than in the locking down and direct monetisation of the code. Open source philosophy has been applied to the development of web browser technology since the 1990s and provides the core code base for the most popular browser – Chrome – which is based on the open source software project Chromium. Open source thinking has also led to Open Cola, Open Beer and Open Publishing which has become the aspirational model for all academic output.

Not all organisations will be as comfortable with a value proposition that is so abstract as offering a web browser freely for download. Organisations should determine their own comfort levels by focusing on sharing in ways that add value to their own business models (Lew 2017).

12.4   Customisation and boldness

Coupled with transparency, openness and sharing, the ability for customisation and a sense of boldness complete the five key organisational qualities of strategic digital transformation. While each quality can operate in isolation, they are best considered as an interacting set (Figure 12.1). If the organisation emphasises too heavily any one quality, there is a potentially detrimental effect on the organisational value of the others.

Boldness sets out to define the expectations for an entire sector or ultimately even all digital experiences. The Uber customer experience, for example, is such that you get to know the name of the driver, the precise time of their arrival and the average score they have been awarded by every customer they have ever driven. Coupled with the ability for drivers to rate passengers, Uber's model deploys measured quantities of sharing, openness and transparency. The use of rating metrics is now the de facto standard expectation of all millennial customer experiences. It can be seen in application with Airbnb owners, in restaurants where the Trip Advisor rankings are their primary sales driver and in countless other examples. Boldness is a complementary quality that emphasises the need for exploring a new direction within a sector and the organisational energy to make this a prominent aspect of the offering. Without boldness there would be a tendency for open and sharing organisations to drift towards a similarity and common median that could reinforce oligopoly capitalism. Boldness can 'fail fast' but it can also 'win big'.

Customisation is a quality that also complements transparency, boldness, openness and sharing. "Nike by You" is one form of a product-customisation service offered by a multinational brand. By their nature there is more opportunity for customisation in product and services offered exclusively through the digital domain. Software-based products have been developed not just with the ability to have different 'skins' but an entirely customised user experience. This data-driven customisation ranges from news feeds that 'learn' which articles and sources are read more regularly to the changing prioritisation of individuals shown on a social media feed. There are many examples of the dynamic learning for deep customisation that is possible to identify with current social media channels.

Total customisation forefronts the customer experience to such an extent that the 'same' product experienced by two customers may share no surface commonalities. Beyond the immediate user interface, a fully customised product may draw on entirely different data sources and utilise them in different ways for each individual consumer. Moving beyond social media, the business model of Vistaprint (and others) offers some hints of how customisation may look with physical products, but there are still many avenues to be explored that takes customisation beyond brand promotion and promotional products. Deloitte (2015) reported in 2015 that 20% of UK consumers would be prepared to pay a premium for customised goods or services. However, 42% of those surveyed also indicated that they would be led by brands in their customisation choices suggesting that British consumers are not yet entirely comfortable with wielding the autonomy and power that this experience offers them individually.

All five of these organisational qualities are not just sophisticated digital marketing techniques but go to the core of an organisation's business model and are representative of its core values. It is these qualities that enable collaboration and innovation within the organisation and with consumers and customers.

Key takeaways

- Transparency, openness, sharing, boldness and customisation as five hallmark organisational qualities are indicators of progress towards strategic digital transformation
- Each of the five qualities interact together
- Emphasis on any single quality potentially impedes the development of the others
- Delivering these qualities within the organisation will be a challenge to the internal culture
- The five qualities are enabled and delivered by digital technologies
- The presence of consumer digital technology in the VUCA world creates much of the imperative to have these five organisational qualities

References

Arringdale, C. (2016) "The ugly side of transparency in the workplace", *TLNT*, 19th Apr, www.tlnt.com/the-ugly-side-of-transparency-in-the-workplace/

Ashmore, J. (2019) "Aldi, Lidl and the beauty of competitive capitalism", *CapX*, 6th Mar, https://capx.co/aldi-lidl-and-the-beauty-of-competitive-capitalism/

Benjamin, K. (2019) "KFC's Open Kitchen invites guests to fry their own chicken", *Campaign*, 15th Mar, www.campaignlive.co.uk/article/kfcs-open-kitchen-invites-guests-fry-own-chicken/1579192

Bernstein, E., & Turban, S. (2018) "The impact of the 'open' workspace on human collaboration", *Philosophical Transactions of the Royal Society B*, 2nd July, https://royalsocietypublishing.org/doi/full/10.1098/rstb.2017.0239

Beverland, M. (2005) "Brand management and the challenge of authenticity", *Journal of Product & Brand Management*, 14(7), 460–461.

Birkinshaw, J., & Cable, D. (2017) "The dark side of transparency", *McKinsey Quarterly*, Feb, www.mckinsey.com/business-functions/organization/our-insights/the-dark-side-of-transparency

Deloitte (2015) *Made to Order: The Rise of Mass Personalisation*, Deloitte Consumer Report, www2.deloitte.com/tr/en/pages/consumer-business/articles/made-to-order-the-rise-of-mass-personalisation.html

Donaldson, N. (2018) "How agile transparency reduces project risk", *Boost*, www.boost.co.nz/blog/2018/11/agile-transparency-reduces-project-risk

Grove, J. (2019) "English v-cs' overall remuneration tips towards £300K", *Times Higher Education Supplement*, 12th Feb, www.timeshighereducation.com/news/english-v-cs-overall-remuneration-tips-towards-ps300k

Hurley, D.B. (2014), "Open source and transparency: Not the same thing", *Mautig.org*, 22nd Dec, www.mautic.org/blog/community/open-source-and-transparency-not-the-same-thing/

Kentish, B. (2018) "BBC gender pay gap: 170 female employees demand apology over salary differences and 'culture of discrimination'", *The Independent*, 30th Jan, www.independent.co.uk/news/uk/politics/bbc-gender-pay-gap-employees-apology-bbc-women-nuj-tony-hall-select-committee-a8184306.html

Lambert, J.-P. (2018) "Blame culture vs fail culture: What's your company's thoughts about an all-too-common situation . . .", *Medium*, 8th May, https://jp-lambert.me/blame-culture-vs-fail-culture-whats-your-company-s-52568738e686

Lattimore, P. (2018) "Creating transparency in B2B", *CIM Exchange*, 24th Aug, https://exchange.cim.co.uk/editorial/creating-transparency-in-b2b/

Lew, C. (2017) "Don't be transparent in your company unless you're considering these 2 things", *Inc.com*, 29th Nov, www.inc.com/claire-lew/how-transparent-should-you-be-in-your-company-consider-these-2-things-first.html\

Musk, E. (2014) "All our patent are belong to you", *Tesla*, www.tesla.com/en_GB/blog/all-our-patent-are-belong-you?redirect=no

Parris, D., Dapko, J., Arnold, R., & Arnold, D. (2016) "Exploring transparency: A new framework for responsible business management", *Management Decision*, 54(1), pp. 222–247, https://doi.org/10.1108/MD-07-2015-0279

Perez, T. (2018) "Open vs close work space environments", *The Perspective*, www.theperspective.com/debates/businessandtechnology/open-vs-closed-space-work-environments/

Thalbauer, H. (2019) "How a digital supply chain reduces volatility in a post brexit world", *Forbes*, 3rd Apr, www.forbes.com/sites/sap/2019/04/03/how-a-digital-supply-chain-reduces-volatility-in-a-post-brexit-world/#430f27bf759e

Wells, K. (2018) "8 reasons email is ineffective in the workplace", *Zinc*, 9th Feb, www.zinc.it/8-reasons-email-is-ineffective-in-workplace/

13 Overcoming the legacy of processes, systems and people

Gordon Fletcher and Marie Griffiths

Preface

Legacy in one form or another is a key barrier to change in many organisations. While the common legacy of 'old' IT systems is discussed in this chapter, consideration is also given to other forms of underlying complexity found within communications, data, processes and people. This chapter returns to the importance of strategic perspective and awareness of organisational qualities outlined in previous chapters to identify the key elements of success for shedding legacy in order to move towards creating a genuinely data-driven, people-focused organisation.

13.1 The burden of legacy

Every existing organisation has the burden of legacy. This burden takes a multitude of forms that prohibits any simple single solution to overcoming the challenge that legacy presents. Inevitably, organisations that recognise the impact that legacy is having on their organisational system and their business models has already made the first essential step towards addressing the challenge and implementing change.

Legacy can appear in any element of the organisational system; people, data, communication, processes, software or hardware. The more embedded the legacy, the greater the tendency that multiple elements of the system will be affected. As the people and data elements are at the core of becoming a data-driven, people-focused organisation, any legacy in these areas can also be the most challenging. For organisations that have had to deal with the GDPR (General Data Protection Regulations), much of their data legacy has been brought to the forefront through their efforts to become compliant. Although in theory this compliance activity may have already been undertaken and produced change, in practice data legacy is still a significant burden.

Legacy is any aspect of the organisational system that has not maintained pace with the current needs of the organisation and, as a result, is unlikely to be able to support future needs. This is a description that is overly mechanistic when applied to people within the organisation. Nonetheless, people within an organisation can be part of its legacy. Fortunately the legacy that is embedded within people is more readily retractable because it is attitude, skills and perspective that has not kept pace rather than being inherent within the person themselves. Attitudes can be changed through transformation, perspectives shifted with engagement and skills extended through training (see Chapter 6). But ultimately, and even after these interventions, if an individual and an organisation remain at loggerheads, there is the option of permanently parting company.

The legacy found embedded in other elements of the organisational system can be significantly more difficult to overcome. These structural and embedded elements are proxies to direct human action. By definition, this human influence on legacy elements is historical and not directly accessible. In other words, the people's decisions, thinking and actions that went into the creation of each legacy element happened at a point when they were regarded as the most appropriate or at least the most able to be implemented. As a legacy element of the organisational system, it means that these decisions, thinking and actions of people are now not the best fit for current needs. If the design of these elements was to be undertaken now afresh and without legacy, the resulting outcome would produce entirely different solutions.

The organisational system element that most precludes immediate change is data. A case study from the scientific world provides an indicative vignette of the potential extent to this challenge. Many of the radio astronomy telescopes around the world were built after the Second World War throughout the 1950s and 1960s. These projects at the time were an early vanguard for utilising computing technology. These radio telescopes captured space radio signals and converted them with these early computers into systematic data.

The Jodrell Bank World Heritage Site is one example of these early systems. To be consistent, the data at Jodrell Bank was recorded in specifically structured ways that were defined at the time that recording began. The telescope at Jodrell Bank continues to operate over half a century later, and while there have been significant and broadbased advances in computing technology, the telescopes continue to record the data in the same way as they did at the beginning of the project. The legacy format now appears antiquated and even limited in what is being recorded. The telescopes and their capabilities have been updated throughout their active service period, but astronomers and astrophysicists face losing an extremely large and comparable dataset if they alter the way that the data is collected or if they improve the fidelity of the recordings.

The best solution for the Jodrell Bank observatory is to maintain the same data structure for their earliest projects. New projects have been initiated since the initial establishment of the radio telescope. Each time new work commences it takes advantage of the best technology available at the time. The incremental approach being used in these radio telescopes is the best approach for this form of particular organisational system. The legacy is not so much a burden but an integral aspect of the activity, with new projects and experiments simply layered on top of the oldest and more established projects.

13.2   Preparation before transformation

The challenge for an organisation undergoing strategic digital transformation is to recognise which elements of the system contain legacy. The problem echoes the Rumsfeld event of acknowledging the presence of unknown unknowns or the self-awareness technique of the Johari Window (Luft & Ingham 1955). Each element of the organisation can be considered on a grid that assists the identification of potential legacy issues (Figure 13.1).

The individual variables to be considered are the expectations being placed on each element. The 4Vs (Volume, Veracity, Velocity, Variety) are indicative and useful starting points for identifying potential variables affecting each of the elements in the organisational system. The scale aspect in identifying legacy places also assists in ordering the degree of risk associated with the variable. The realisation, however, is that known variables and scale only occupy one quarter of the matrix. An unknown scale or variable or both represents

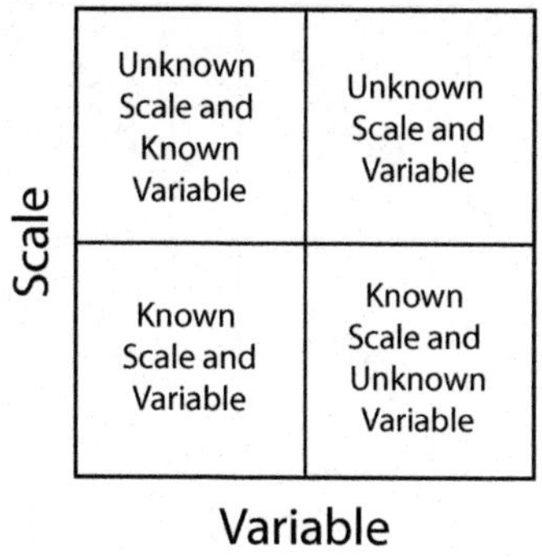

	Unknown Scale and Known Variable	Unknown Scale and Variable
Scale	Known Scale and Variable	Known Scale and Unknown Variable

Variable

Figure 13.1 Identifying legacy challenges

a double challenge, as some attempt at identification is needed before corrective decisions and actions can be undertaken.

At this point, indicative examples are useful. As a 'known known', a medium-sized business made an early decision to commit to a specific accounting software that has produced a legacy as the volume of data being processed has risen significantly as a result of the company's business model primarily using micro-transactions. The current software currently limits the ability of the organisation to grow. As a known variable with unknown scale, a business has a process for financial approval that requires agreement by three different role-holders. The process is primarily manual (or done through email attachments). There is awareness in the organisation that the current process is cumbersome and prevents everyone involved from focusing on other more valuable activities although there is still a need for the approvals. The variable is known, as it is an issue of variety (of individual approvals) although the scale of the problem is less clear.

'Unknown unknowns' are more difficult to describe as they can only be fully identified with hindsight. As an example, the story of the development of the light rail system in Greater Manchester provides insight. In 1992, the Manchester Metrolink began operating the first line of its new light rail system. The route took advantage of former mainline tracks and stations between Manchester and two of the ten borough town centres that encircle the city and make up Greater Manchester. As the network developed over twenty-five years, it has become the longest light rail system in the UK, with 43.7 million passenger journeys annually. As a result of its success, and with continuing expansion, an unexpected legacy has emerged. Initially using old mainline tracks and stations offered cost efficiencies and brought disused railway estate back into use. Low-floor urban-transport technology was also in its infancy in 1992, and this unknown is pivotal to the legacy that the system now faces. Since the first repurposed tracks the need to add new tracks has also brought the added cost of having to build raised platforms on these new lines and to modify the standard rolling stock to maintain the standard platform height of mainline train stations. Requiring a platform for passengers to access the trams also means that stops cannot be easily moved as demands change in the city and town centres. However, despite this legacy the network continues to grow and the number of passengers increases, which ensures that the Metrolink still achieves its initial purpose of relieving road congestion and improving commute times. With growing awareness around sustainability and creating

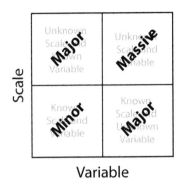

Figure 13.2 Prioritising legacy issues

zero-carbon transport solutions, an electrically powered mass transit system is an asset to the city-region.

The Metrolink example provides guidance regarding the management of legacy during transformation. In identifying the impact of potential legacy (Figure 13.1), these can be regarded as minor, major or massive. By tackling the minor issues, progress can be made as major issues become better understood in terms of variable and scale and hence become minor while massive issues are reduced to being 'only' major issues (Figure 13.2).

Within the minor issues, it is then possible to prioritise the impact of the legacy by the scale that it exerts an influence on the organisation. Legacy of low-scale impact will be easier to solve and may represent opportunities for quick wins. Tackling legacy issues with identifiable higher scale impact will represent a greater level of change within the organisation and will be more difficult to solve.

13.3   Interoperability

Legacy issues are often identified in relation to software. Very often, organisational decisions around software purchases are taken without wider consideration to its position as an integral element of the organisation. Software, its inputs and its outputs are also not neutral within the overall organisational system. The complaint regarding legacy is often articulated by frustrated people as the inability for the elements of the system to 'talk' to one another. These legacy issues can be labelled as a lack of interoperability. Some frustrations will relate to relatively low-level technical issues – such as the inability to open a spreadsheet containing macros on a mobile device. Other issues will be deeper and more strategic – for example, the lack of frictionless interchange about an individual customer across the entire organisation. Interoperability is a strong concept for understanding the depth of layers associated with any legacy issue across the organisational system – not solely software and data.

Interoperability is an organisational system quality (see Chapter 2). In a traditional technology sense, interoperability can be reduced to the ability of software packages to meaningfully exchange data between themselves. Put at the simplest level, the ability of a spreadsheet package to open different file formats other than the ones that it created is a low-level example of technical interoperability. Spreadsheet packages are a useful example because of their longevity and familiarity as a business technology and their massive penetration into organisation as an everyday tool. While other software exists that offers greater levels of interoperability at sophisticated levels, the practical reality is that many small organisations continue to use spreadsheets as a key tool for decision-making and planning. Highlighting the limitations of spreadsheet interoperability then also highlights the overall impact of this legacy on small- (and medium-) sized businesses.

However, while most spreadsheets can read and write a set of recognisable formats, giving them technical and syntactic interoperability there is much more that can be achieved in terms of interoperability. In a manner similar to digital maturity (see Chapter 3), there are higher levels of interoperability that relate to higher level understanding of the organisational system. The seven stage levels of conceptual interoperability model (LCIM) (Tolk & Muguira 2003) systematise the difference forms of interoperability. In the LCIM and the context of data exchange, these levels are described through progressively higher levels of sophistication as semantic, pragmatic, dynamic and conceptual interoperability.

Extending the spreadsheet example, having semantic interoperability would result in the meaning of the data also being retained when a sheet is shared. For a spreadsheet, this is not just the numbers and formulas that it contains but a representation of what these mean in an organisational sense. This is sometimes described as the meta-data of a file. But in the reality of current spreadsheet technology (and many other software), the meta-data sharing of meaning is reduced to defining a series of simple keywords, phrases or codes that describe the overall purpose of the contents of the file.

At a higher level of meaning, pragmatic interoperability brings greater depth and insight. This requires the unambiguous and systematic exchange of the intended meaning of the data contained in the spreadsheet. At this level, the current spreadsheet software start to reveal their limitations. The most effective way of getting this level of understanding with current spreadsheet formats is through more detailed notes and documentation. However, pragmatic meaning is not a systematic or embedded mechanism of current spreadsheet technology. To achieve this requires workarounds, for example an entirely separate sheet in the spreadsheet that explains the meaning of the data it contains, with descriptions of the columns and rows. Pragmatic interoperability in spreadsheet would require, for example, enforcement of systematic recording of the data context before the data could be successfully saved.

Progressing to the next level of interoperability reaches beyond the limits of current spreadsheet technology. Dynamic interoperability would enable spreadsheets to respond to changing context and circumstances in the organisation and externally that influence the data they contain. Possessing this capability would require spreadsheets to have continuous awareness of shifting organisational context. Popular spreadsheet software does offer the ability for creating dynamic linkage to external data sources; however, this is no more sophisticated than a technical interoperability. True dynamic interoperability would mean that the spreadsheet would have built-in capability to recognise a change to external context and the underlying assumptions under which the original spreadsheet was created. As a result of this awareness, a dynamically interoperable spreadsheet would also modify the data according to external changes or, at the very least, alert the people using the data to this change in synchronisation.

At the level of conceptual interoperability, the rationale and meaning of the system is fully captured. The system is not just documented but inherently defined to reflect its underlying purpose and meaning to the organisation irrespective of the specific technology being used. No spreadsheet software currently reaches this level of interoperability.

Table 13.1 Interoperability in the organisational system (using LCIM levels)

	Levels of Conceptual Interoperability Model	Interoperability of elements within the organisational system
Level 6	Conceptual	Strategic self-awareness of the element's relationship to the overall purpose of the organisational system and to other elements of the system
Level 5	Dynamic	Changeability and fluidity of the element in relation to alterations in the organisational system that may, in turn, be a result of a change in the external environment
Level 4	Pragmatic	Reusability and shareability of previous actions and outcomes that can be utilised usefully within other parts of the organisational system
Level 3	Semantic	Deliverability of individual outcomes and packages of outcomes from elements and combination of elements in ways that are consistent across the organisation
Level 2	Syntactic	The meaning of the terms being used is shared and consistent between elements of the organisational system
Level 1	Technical	The capability of an element to seamlessly interact with other elements of the organisational system as required and when required
Level 0	None	–

Conceptual or strategic interoperability should be the starting point for changes to the organisational system – irrespective of whether this is software, hardware, processes or people. This is in direct contrast to current practices regarding the organisational system which starts with technical capability and need rather than strategic purpose or fit. Inevitably, compromises must be made to identify a viable candidate element of the organisational system that is also technically interoperable.

The example of the spreadsheet is a necessarily limited discussion as it only considers what is one part of the overall software element of an organisational system. Taking the wider system view of the entire organisation, the issues of interoperability becomes even more acute (Table 13.1).

Using the LCIM hierarchy provides indicative guidance for the scale and nature of the action required to address identified legacy issues. If the challenge of legacy is presumed to be a lack (or low level) of interoperability, the first step is to position the legacy within the LCIM and to then determine what needs to change in order to move towards Levels 5 and 6 of the model. Returning to the acknowledged simplistic example of the spreadsheet, it is possible to identify that this legacy software element exists at Level 3 or 4 (if these are some additional workarounds). Improving the interoperability of this software points to acquiring pragmatic and dynamic interoperability capability. This awareness would then guide software procurement decisions that – given the current state of spreadsheet technology – would point to the adoption of entirely different types of software.

13.4   Persuading to change

The discussion of interoperability in identifying and tackling organisational legacy then returns to the importance of people. Overcoming legacy is inevitably a change programme. No matter how limiting the legacy element is for the organisation, there will inevitably be resistance.

The role of leaders within the organisation are key to driving the change needed to overcome existing legacy. As a leader, encouraging the organisational qualities of transparency, sharing, customisation, boldness and openness (see Chapter 12) in terms of the benefits that they bring to the organisation then links closely with the quality of interoperability. Having an organisation-wide aspiration to high-level interoperability supports pathways to change.

Identifying a balance of quick wins and longer term strategically relevant actions is the challenge for the leaders who are defining a programme of change. Recognising 'minor' legacy issues – where both the nature of the legacy and the scale of the legacy is known – is the starting point. The 'minor' issues with the greatest legacy are those high on the scale. However, persuading people to change and to support change in other elements of the organisational system also requires immediate success. These quicks wins are found with the small-scale specific legacy elements that bring immediate benefits to the people within the organisation. Initiating the transformation project through changes to small legacy elements before people are more widely engaged can provide tangible evidence for the benefits of a wider programme. Working with the most enthusiastic internal people (see Chapter 6) in the first stages will also help to enrol a wider level of grassroots support for the programme (Knight 2015).

The challenge in persuading people to change is tied to the routine and regularity that is provided by the existing legacy elements of the organisation. The current situation may seem unappealing when considered critically and externally, but considered from within it is comforting and endless. There has to be a great many pain points being created by the legacy element before some people will ever accept the risk of an unknown new element.

The lever for change comes with individual recognition that there is a "burning platform" (Kantor n.d.). The burning platform presents stark options that require urgent decisions. There is the choice to remain static, continue with the same practices and wait for the external forces to become more favourable. The other option is to be proactive and undertake radical risky change. Either decision is irreversible and neither choice guarantees success. The lesson from the burning platform – the Piper Alpha oil rig disaster – is to be proactive and take the risk rather than rely upon the ability or intervention of others to offer up a solution. For the leader introducing the change programme, it is a case of defining the burning platform and all of the burden of legacy that ties into it.

With supporters enrolled, quick wins identified and the burning platform defined, the leadership pressure is to then ensure that new elements of the organisational system become routine business as usual as rapidly as possible. This provides little opportunity for workarounds or resistance to develop and sets out the future immediately without any intermediate steps.

13.5 Direct substitution

A real temptation in addressing organisational legacy is to approach the challenge by seeking 'better' or 'newer' substitutes. In these circumstances each legacy is replaced directly by a more recent version of the same element. Returning to the spreadsheet example, the issues associated with this approach can be immediately realised.

An organisation may recognise the general limitations of spreadsheets to store all of its data without acknowledging the user convenience that spreadsheets offer. There is then a tendency to seek new software that will do more than the current software without considering the wider impact of this decision and the shared needs elsewhere in the organisation. Greater benefit and greater value may be realised for the organisation by combining or separating the existing ways in which spreadsheets are being used with the aspiration of reaching pragmatic and dynamic interoperability.

Examples of the greater benefits that can be achieved by avoiding simple direct substitution of legacy elements can be recognised throughout the organisational system. People's roles do not need to mirror those of the people they replace. Current discussions about the changing nature of work indicates that direct substitution of people roles would be ill-advised at best and, at its extreme, actively detrimental to the sustainability of the organisation (Vincent 2017).

Hardware elements including changes to the physical estate does not simply mirror the existing structures. Aiming for dynamic interoperability with a physical estate may push an organisation to explore a range of alternative. For example, a law firm may benefit from utilising agile working practices, and the shifting demands on office space may push the organisation to WeWork or a competitor. Processes can equally be substituted for their digital twin, but the reasons for a process needs to be critically assessed before being duplicated in a digital form. Changes in the organisational system – and improvements that come through greater transparency and sharing – may change or efface the need for the process.

Legacy is a challenge for any organisation with a history. Maintaining a strategic perspective, utilising technology to drive change and attending to the people elements of the organisation all support the necessary positive changes to the organisational system.

Key takeaways

- Legacy of all types is a significant barrier to successful digital transformation
- Different forms of legacy can be identified in every element of the organisational system
- Legacy can be defined as being minor, major or massive depending on what is unknown or known about the legacy
- Interoperability is an organisational quality
- An absence of interoperability (or low levels of interoperability) positions the extent that a legacy impacts upon the organisation
- Defining a burning platform and describing the irreversible options can persuade people to change and to support change (or to leave the organisation)
- Removing legacy from an organisation does not necessarily have to be done through direct like-for-like substitution with a 'better' version of the existing element

References

Kantor, R. (n.d.) "Create a burning platform", *Management Centre*, www.managementcentre.co.uk/create-a-burning-platform/

Knight, R. (2015) "Convincing skeptical employees to adopt new technology", *Harvard Business Review*, 29th Mar, https://hbr.org/2015/03/convincing-skeptical-employees-to-adopt-new-technology

Luft, J., & Ingham, H. (1955) "The Johari Window: A graphic model of interpersonal awareness", *Proceedings of the Western Training Laboratory in Group Development*. Los Angeles: UCLA, Extension Office.

Tolk, A., & Muguira, J. (2003) "The levels of conceptual interoperability model", *Fall Simulation Interoperability Workshop*, Sept, www.researchgate.net/publication/240319008_The_Levels_of_Conceptual_Interoperability_Model

Vincent, J. (2017) "Automation threatens 800 million jobs, but technology could still save us, says report", *The Verge*, 30th Nov, www.theverge.com/2017/11/30/16719092/automation-robots-jobs-global-800-million-forecast

Planning to change

Becoming a data-driven organisation

14 Tactics to build your digital strategy

Alex Fenton, Katrina Gallagher and Richard George

We have so far explored the importance of data to the sustained success of an organisation, what data is required and how it is used effectively. Does the organisation need to access external data? Will analysis of this data reshape their products or services? This understanding requires the gathering, analysis, storytelling and visualisation of data that may never have been dealt with before. This chapter focuses on the tools and processes that will support transformation into a data-driven and people-focused organisation. It also looks at the different types of data and considers the ethical and legal implications of personal data including the impact and opportunities of GDPR.

14.1   Selecting the tools for your organisation

Is it worth automating a process that already works? Is the cost of automation worth the investment for the improvements in productivity or the reduction in cost? This will often depend on the sector and the scale of the organisation. For example, AI-powered retailers grow 30% faster than the competition – with 50% higher profits. And AI adoption in retail is up 17% year-on-year. Contrast this to a statement that Elon Musk, a firm advocate of digitisation, made about production problems for the Model 3 electric-car – "Excessive automation at Tesla was a mistake" (Roof 2018) – when he found that, in practice, using a lot of automated tools made it harder to scale up than increasing human labour hours, and Tesla has struggled to meet demand.

Is digitisation an inevitable requirement in the future? Will the cost reduce as early adopters bear the brunt of trial, error and novelty premium? As competitors offer alternatives to the traditional product or service, it's difficult to predict whether this is destined to become the minimum people will accept or whether it's a short-term, costly gimmick. In earlier chapters there are examples of businesses that became quickly irrelevant as they failed to adapt to the expectations of their customers, for example Kodak, Blockbuster and the collective UK High Street (see Chapter 7). There are no shortages of progressive businesses that invested in new technology and did not survive.

What is the frequency of the task that you are considering digitising? How similar are the steps taken in each instance of a task? If your business offers a custom product or service, or produces a very small number of high-cost units, then digitisation may not result in a positive return on investment. But at the other end of the spectrum, businesses with very routine, high-volume tasks are prime candidates for automation.

What data is reused across the business? Can you improve customer satisfaction by streamlining data collection or using data to customise their experience? In almost all cases where duplicate data entry exists, it's worth looking at digital alternatives and integrations because every human data-input point is an opportunity for errors and inconsistencies, and customers on the whole will not appreciate being asked the same questions multiple times. There are a lot of free and low-cost options that should suit even the smallest of budgets to start building your digital strategy. To start answering some of these questions for your business in particular, you can use low-cost various techniques as a team. These activities can be scaled up to interactive virtual and physical events (Chapter 17). In addition, you may want to map out the estimated cost, output differences and other benefits/ drawbacks between your existing systems and alternative options.

14.2 Frame your design challenge

Figure 14.1 presents a low-cost technique which can be used to map out problems, potential solutions and new innovations to help build your digital strategy as an individual or a team. Start at question 1 with a specific problem within your organisation or a problem that you could solve through digital innovation. Work through each point on paper or digitally. Points 1–5 help you consider the problem and solution in order to complete point 6. This exercise can be undertaken with different groups within your organisation, customers or other stakeholders to help solve different issues or come up with different solutions.

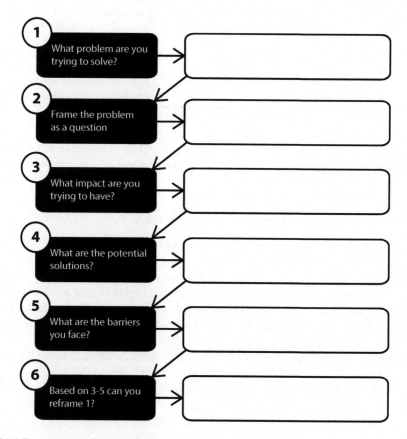

Figure 14.1 Framing your design challenge

Table 14.1 Framing your design challenge (example)

1. What is the problem you are trying to solve?	Targeting hard to reach populations through sport fandom to support the prevention agenda of tackling high levels of obesity and heart disease while supporting clubs to improve their means of communication with fans	**4. What are some potential solutions?**	Branded smartphone app which tracks fitness data to create a competition
2. Try to frame the problem as a question	How can we improve the health and wellbeing of fans while using digital technology to create a community?	**5. What are some of the barriers you face?**	App development is expensive and complex, fans may not want to use our solution, access to smartphones
3. What is the impact you are trying to have?	Trying to use technology to make our fans healthier while creating a digital supportive community	**6. Based on 3–5, how can you reframe 1?**	Can we use fans' smartphones and competitive spirit to improve health and wellbeing through visualising data and creating a digital fitness community?

Digital transformation is not always about increasing ROI, reducing costs, or improving output sometimes other measures such as health improvement or community engagement are prioritised (Table 14.1).

14.3   Evaluating the cost/benefit of digital tools

It is not always clear what the effects of digital transformation will be, and that can be a barrier that holds organisations back. To make a start on evaluating the costs and benefits of implementing digital tools, small steps such as speaking to other people in your niche, attending conferences or consulting with digital product owners who serve your industry can help bring the picture into focus. To refine your estimates, you might consider allocating a budget for small trials which are carefully measured to see how the transformation may play out if it was implemented on a bigger scale.

To illustrate how this might be approached, an indicative example is useful (Figure 14.2, 14.3, 14.4 and 14.5).

In a situation where the standard running costs are £7000/month, you've worked out an alternative solution with digital tools and reduced manual labour, which costs £20000 to initiate, then £2000/month thereafter (Table 14.2).

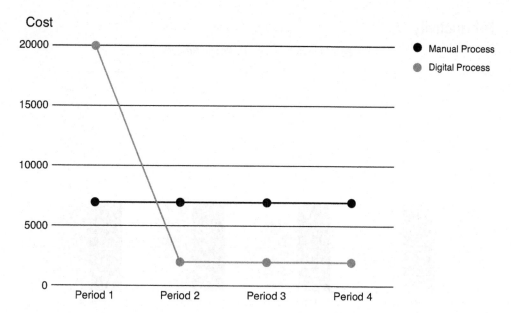

Figure 14.2 Visual example of running costs

Cumulative cost

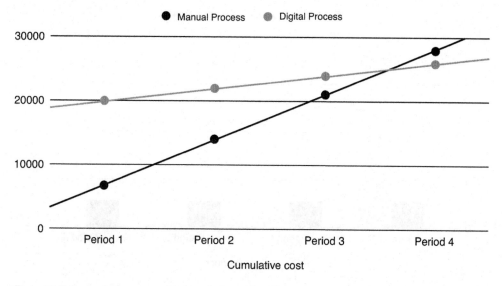

Cumulative cost

Figure 14.3 Example data now with cumulative projected costs

Productivity

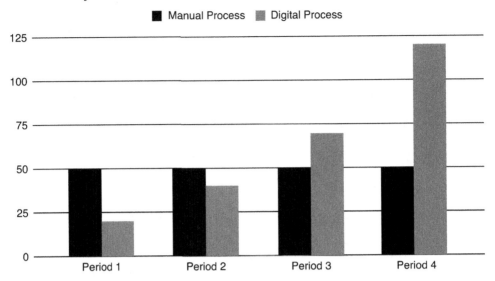

Figure 14.4 Visual example of productivity costs

Cost per product

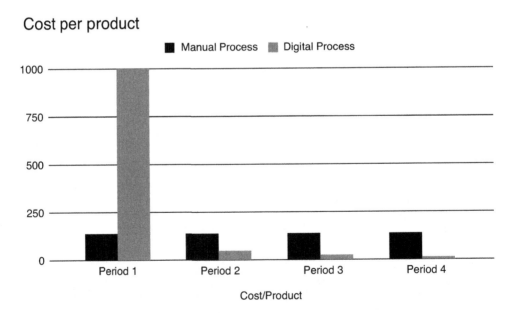

Figure 14.5 Visual example of cumulative costs/products

To compare like with like, and to clarify the point at which the digital process becomes more cost effective, use the cumulative projected costs.

You've also estimated that a digital upgrade could increase productivity after an initial learning curve (Table 14.3).

With this approximation, you can estimate the cost to produce each product and roughly the point at which the digital transformation pays off.

Where we refer to 'product', you can replace this with the unit of measure appropriate to the business (whether that's a billable hour, physical product, training session, subscription fee, donation or life changed).

Within a data-driven organisational environment it is also important to recognise that there are natural limitations to the data that can be accessed or interpreted (Table 14.4).

Table 14.2 Example running costs

Cost	Manual process	Digital process
Period 1	7000	20000
Period 2	7000	2000
Period 3	7000	2000
Period 4	7000	2000

Table 14.3 Example productivity costs

Productivity	Manual process	Digital process
Period 1	50	20
Period 2	50	40
Period 3	50	70
Period 4	50	120

Table 14.4 Natural limitation of data to consider

Limitation	Examples
Unconscious bias	Data managers need to be aware that they will be applying unconscious bias to the analysis and manipulation of data. For example, artificial intelligence and machine learning algorithms can often display some of the values, views and opinions of their developers. It's important to encourage diversity in teams
Conflict of interest	Some people are naturally averse to change and may highlight or exaggerate the negative consequences of a new system (and vice versa)
Tracking limitations	Multiple devices. Cookie blockers
Errors	Data input or validation errors.
What people do vs what people think they would do	An excellent example of this was a Sony focus group where customers were asked whether they would buy the black or yellow radio. The majority said yellow and justified their answer. As a reward for their participation, they were given a radio. They all left with a black radio (Natoli 2012)
Privacy	Some data may not be available for use other than that specified on collection

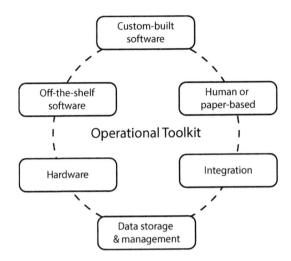

Figure 14.6 The operational toolkit

There are often unintended consequences to setting KPIs without wider consideration for the situation and the possibility that alternative and even negative actions could be deployed to produce success in these narrower definitions of performance (Barr 2017) (Figure 14.6). For example, if a rail company sets a KPI as the percentage of trains on time and the unintended consequence in some cases have been that late trains are cancelled to keep the figures looking positive.

Consider not only digital tools as part of your operational toolkit (Figure 14.6). When deciding on tools to use, your choices are abundant and vary widely for how tailored they can be – from a system that is custom built for your individual business to more generic 'off the shelf' solutions. Some software companies zoom in to service a certain industry so that the costs of a purpose-built system are spread across companies. Some software allows for integration with different tools, and others allow you to modify their systems to better suit your objectives. You will also have elements that need human management.

You will also need to evaluate the costs and price models for different options, such as software as a service (SaaS), open source, custom built or a combination of the three. Consider subscription fees, maintenance and hardware costs, as well as the skills required to maintain and use the systems. Consider the pros and cons of outsourcing versus training internal staff.

You may need to submit a request for proposal or you could consider partnering with technology companies who may help to customise to your requirements. Negotiating development time with a technology partner will be easier for larger organisations or when your chosen partner is in a research and development or startup phase. For some elements, a small pilot may be helpful to fully explore how a new tool might integrate with your business. You also may consider one system for the enterprise versus multiple systems for different departments or purposes. Some systems will integrate neatly with others, for example using APIs (application programming interface).

When planning a pilot, agree a use case, decide what the goal is, identify who will be involved and who will benefit from an improved system, and shortlist a selection of appropriate systems for the scale of the business.

14.4 People

People help with quality control and are often useful in unique or unusual situations. They can provide a necessary sanity check and safety net. We've probably all seen the results of clunky automation – for example, placeholder or poorly formatted data (Table 14.5):

Table 14.5 Poorly formatted email

"Dear ★ | FNAME | ★,
Welcome to your latest newsletter"

In some circumstances, it's cheaper and more productive to use people. We have discussed the link between people as a core part of the organisational system (Chapters 1 and 2). Checklists can sometimes be enough to help improve the efficiency and quality of tasks performed regularly by personnel. And checklists can also be used to help navigate between digitised systems, maintaining the best practice that was designed into the system.

Also bear in mind the people who will be impacted by any digital transformation process. Will your internal team need to change their day-to-day procedures, is any training required and will staff re-assignments or redundancies be required? Think about relevance and implications to customers, suppliers and wider stakeholders. For example, if you are considering digitising a customer-support system, how will they feel about it, and how can you make the transition easier for customers?

14.5 Timing and future proofing

The cost/benefit of replacing manual or paper-based tasks with digital systems will depend on the time period that you base your calculations on. Shorter term objectives will dictate lower investments in technology. Future incremental system upgrades may be a desirable strategy to balance efficiency and modernisation with profits and sustainable growth.

So when selecting systems and processes, keep in mind future opportunities and the longer term strategy of the organisation. It may be a wiser choice to use a system that is slightly less than optimal for the short term if it allows a more seamless transition or greater benefits in the next stage. Conversely, if it's likely that the available systems will be vastly improved by the next update, a more disposable short-term option could actually be more cost-effective in the long term. To map out the stages of digital transformation and aid your decision-making process, you can use a tool such as the maturity model (see Chapter 3) or HINGE (see Chapter 5).

In his original paper, Gordon E. Moore observed that the number of components in integrated circuits doubled every year (Moore 1964). Moore predicted that the trend would continue for at least ten years, and his prediction has continued to be accurate (Google AI Blog 2013). Whether this would have happened anyway or whether it is a self-fulfilling prophecy because his prediction has been used to set targets for development within the semiconductor industry, we will never know.

Moore's Law is often quoted when talking about technology in more general terms, for example with the improvements in processor speed, number of pixels, storage capacity or Internet speed (Figure 14.7).

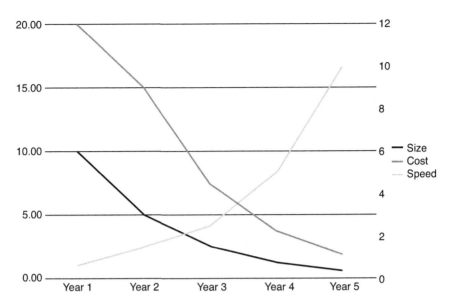

Figure 14.7 Example data showing Moore's Law

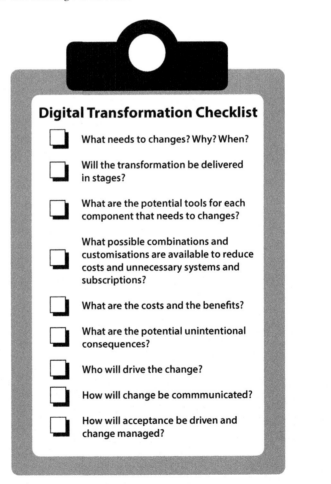

Figure 14.8 Digital transformation checklist

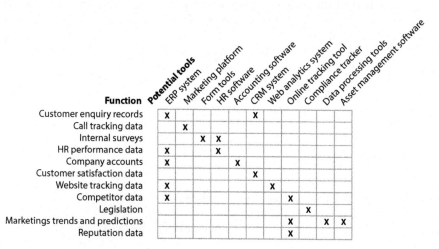

Function	Potential tools ERP system	Marketing platform	Form tools	HR software	Accounting software	CRM system	Web analytics system	Online tracking tool	Compliance tracker	Data processing tools	Asset management software
Customer enquiry records	X					X					
Call tracking data		X									
Internal surveys			X	X							
HR performance data	X			X							
Company accounts	X				X						
Customer satisfaction data						X					
Website tracking data	X						X				
Competitor data	X							X			
Legislation									X		
Marketings trends and predictions								X		X	X
Reputation data								X			

Figure 14.9 Data management mapping

14.6   Presenting your proposal

It's likely that you will need to get sign-off on the budget and resources to implement a digital transformation.

Use the digital transformation checklist (Figure 14.8) as a prompt for discussions and to help structure the final proposal.

14.7   Data management

Although there will be crossovers, different areas of the organisation will rely on different types of data and use different types of software to manipulate this data (Figure 14.9).

When building your digital strategy, find out what data is used for the different functions of the business and see where this data crosses over. During this exploration, you may find that two departments are entering and maintaining the same data or that customers fill in the same information multiple times because it's not stored effectively for later use.

14.8   Legal and ethical considerations

GDPR (General Data Protection Regulation) replaced the Data Protection Directive in 2018 to become the primary law regulating how organisations protect EU citizens' personal data. In some cases, GDPR has caused a number of problems for companies, such as "Opt in Fatigue" and excessive regulation and bureaucracy (Forbes Technology Council 2018).

There are also opportunities that have arisen from GDPR to consider as part of digital strategy. For example, the change has forced more organisations to think about why they are holding data and what data they are holding and to be more transparent about their storage of personal data and the rights of individuals control over their information. Building up more insightful, cleaner data is good for the organisation and its brand because the customer is less likely to receive irrelevant, erroneous or out-of-date communications. Prior to GDPR, organisations were able to purchase databases and use these to send unsolicited emails. While this practice may still happen, in principle, the change allows better, more targeted and creative ways to reach the end user, delivering more useful messages in a more ethical way.

It's important to include the person or people who are ultimately responsible for GDPR compliance in the selection and planning of digital transformation.

14.9   Case study: Hays recruitment

Hays have committed to digital transformation and have assigned their Marketing Director to evaluate and transform their business as an ongoing project. The transformation is not just about tools, it is also very much about the people using them. Hays underwent a restructure as part of their 2018 evolution and went from having one person to four people in data and business intelligence. They had to develop new skill sets via training their existing people, adding new people to their team or bringing in outside skills for certain specialist areas. They enlisted the help of KPMG to facilitate the digital transformation.

Note how there was an increase in their team. This change was contrary to the common perception that digitisation always means there will be less work available for people. Their objective was not to reduce staff and cut costs; they focused on improvements in efficiency, sales and customer retention.

The digital tools that they use now include Mya, LinkedIn, Google suite, WhatsApp Business, VideoMyJob, Salesforce Marketing Cloud and Go1, as well as internally developed custom tools for education, management, sales planning and timesheets.

Thea's belief is that "isolated processes do not serve the customer. The customer expects one picture."

But digital transformation isn't a new venture for Hays. In 2007, the group's CIO hired a former CEO of an IT outsourcing company to develop a programme of change. Together they worked to redesign the IT platform to structure their CV data and enhance search capabilities using open standards.

Digital transformation at Hays is an ongoing process, but so far, the results have been positive. Hays won the Glassdoor Employees' Choice Award for Best Places to Work in the UK in 2017 and the Compliance Register Platinum Awards for Most Effective Recruitment Team in Financial Services in 2016.

The story doesn't stop there. Hays is investing in the research and development of machine learning and artificial intelligence, which will, for example, help surface relevant applicants where they don't explicitly mention the required skills on their CVs.

Key takeaways

- As well as off-the-shelf digital tools, consider custom-built software, hardware, human/paper-based systems, hardware, integrations, data storage and management as part of an operational toolkit
- Think beyond typical key performance indicators such as speed and cost reduction
- Map out problems, potential solutions and new innovations to help build a digital transformation strategy
- Use data to work out the costs and benefits of different solutions and consider allocating a budget for small trials

- Evaluate how data will be managed and ensure it is used within compliant and efficient data management processes
- Consider future requirements. Transformation is a multi-stage and ongoing process

References

Barr, S. (2017) "When KPIs drive the wrong result", *Stacey Barr*, 13th June, www.staceybarr.com/measure-up/when-kpis-drive-the-wrong-result/

Forbes Technology Council (2018) "15 unexpected consequences of GDPR", *Forbes*, 15th Aug, www.forbes.com/sites/forbestechcouncil/2018/08/15/15-unexpected-consequences-of-gdpr/

Google AI Blog (2013) "Moore's Law, part 1: Brief history of Moore's Law and current state", https://ai.googleblog.com/2013/11/moores-law-part-1-brief-history-of.html

Moore, G. (1964) *The Future of Integrated Electronics*. Syosset, NY: Fairchild Semiconductor internal publication, Fairchild Camera & Instrument Corporation.

Natoli, J. (2012) "4 reasons focus groups don't work", *Give Good UX*, 18th June, www.givegoodux.com/4-reasons-focus-groups-dont-work/

Roof, K. (2018) "Elon Musk says 'humans are underrated,' calls Tesla's 'excessive automation' a 'mistake'", *TechCrunch*, https://techcrunch.com/2018/04/13/elon-musk-says-humans-are-underrated-calls-teslas-excessive-automation-a-mistake/

15 What to plan and when to make decisions with data

Gordon Fletcher, Marie Griffiths and Richard Dron

Preface

Existing organisations are often burdened with the legacy of out-of-date business models – an aspect of their existing complexity that prohibits obtaining the maximum benefit from being data-driven. Creating an alternative or reframing a business model may not require a radical shift in direction, but it does require a willingness to change, the integration of a coherent organisational vision and incorporating the beneficial qualities of digital technologies. The learning from previous chapters are brought together in this chapter to enable strategic decision-making.

15.1 Managing the complexity of transformation

The previous chapters have provided a depth of information on the multi-faceted nature of strategic digital transformation. The earlier discussions regarding digital maturity, competition, managing the process of transformation, the VUCA world and business modelling informs the leader with advice and guidelines on the *how*. In contrast, this chapter offers insight into the *what* and *when*.

It is essential to note that no two digital transformation projects are the same. Every organisation is unique as a consequence of, for example, their size, sector, drivers, leadership or customer base. Compounding this complexity still further, every organisation is at a different point in their journey towards digital transformation. For some SMEs it might only be an agenda item in meetings, for others their transformation is in the planning stage or already hitting key milestones that have been set. Transformation brings varying degrees of upheaval and may be a significant step change. What is certain is that there will be change, and all organisations will encounter complexities that must be managed.

Transformation is a continuous process of refinement and self-reflection as organisations navigate the VUCA world. This is not a new phenomenon. There has always been – to varying degrees – a continuous cycle of organisational change (Buckley & Perkins 1984). What differs now from the forms of organisational change described almost forty years ago is the current acceleration in the VUCA environment brought about in part by the exponential growth and use of digital technologies.

Buckley and Perkins (1984) use a seven-stage transition cycle for describing change (Table 15.1). This cycle provides demarcation of the many factors that define the change process. After forty years there have been major shifts in perspective that highlight the ways that leaders must now consider and address change. The key influence over the intervening years is primarily the increasing availability of data. While organisational data was

Table 15.1 The change cycle

Buckley and Perkins – 1984	Now	The major shift
Unconsciousness: Prelude to change but there is acceptance that change is building. Clues to this need are found within informal networks but through unconnected bits of information, sporadic symptoms and tentative new ideas.	**Conscious:** Aware that change is needed but unable or immobilised to enact immediate response. Uncertainty about how to move forward at an organisational level but increasing informal adoption of consumer digital technology.	Information overload with overwhelming external input from multiple channels, people and omnipresent consumer technologies (Chapter 2).
Awakening: Sudden awareness of the possibilities and problems facing the organisation. Little information available and heavy reliance on a few key people to articulate the vision. Broad anxiety about impending change.	**Awake:** Audits and analysis of internal and external forces driving the change together with horizon scanning support innovation and introduce possibilities (Chapter 7). *Start planning with data*	Recognition of the presence of the 4Vs of data and digital more generally. Understanding the untapped potential of data for the organisation.
Reordering: The process of analysing the existing situation and challenging the *status quo*. Reordering actions produces creative chaos with the belief that some turmoil is necessary to design for the future.	**Reviewing and restructure:** Developing and building on insight gained from previous stages (Chapter 16). *Data drives strategic thinking and decision making informing future and existing business models*	Technology has opened up the practice of business modeling. Business models are critical to move from the present to the future using data.
Translation: Formulating a vision of what the organisation wants to achieve – the desired future.	**Transforming:** Coherent organisational vision emerges through open and transparent actions. Strategic questions will emerge to be resolved by data (Chapter 6).	Strategy as well as overall vision and mission need to be kept within sight of the entire organisation. Operational activities then have clearer meaning.
Commitment: Implementation of the new vision. There is a commitment from across the people in the organisation.	**Commitment:** A willingness to change and an understanding across the people in the organisation of the new vision provides agreed momentum for change and a springboard for the transformational process (Chapter 1).	The complexities of the VUCA world coupled with the exponential growth of digital must be led and managed.
Embodiment: Brings the vision into daily operations. There is a shift from unconsciousness, structures are experimented with until they have the right fit and people develop new norms and behaviours.	**Implementation:** The range and combination of challenges that emerging technologies introduce requires development of a robust organisational system that aligns with leadership perspectives and overall vision and mission (Chapter 19).	Digital technologies influences and accelerates activities in every aspect of the organisation.
Integration: The necessary changes to both structural and behavioural are operational. Do not prolong stabilization or move too quickly – there is a return into unconsciousness stage.	**Iteration:** A structured and systematic approach to continuous organisational change is required. Managing digital transformation within an organisation is primarily a people challenge (Chapter 5).	There can be sharing of lessons learned as all organisations (micro- to multinational) are at a point on the transformation journey.

Source: Adapted from Buckley and Perkins 1984

present in the 1980s, it was not in a digital form and not readily accessible through consumer technologies. These two factors reflect the impact of the VUCA world since the cycle was originally developed.

15.2   Data-driven decision making

"If you can't measure it, you can't improve it" and "what gets measured gets managed" are statements often wrongly attributed to Drucker (Prusak 2010; Claulkin 2008). There are many critiques of these statements (Emiliani 2000) that resist the notion that management can be reduced to straightforward measuring. Irrespective of the value of solely quantitative management techniques, the prevalence of this type of thinking ensures that "what gets measured matters".

This series of quotes assists in critically positioning data within the context of becoming a data-driven, people-focused organisation. Measurement enables organisations to understand the consequences of previous actions and to establish a baseline for future comparisons. It is a critical necessity to recognise that what is being measured shapes perspective. Measuring what is simply easy to capture does not always capture what is strategically significant. Conversely, measurement that requires significant effort can become a burden without adding noticeable value to the organisation. There is clearly a thin gap between meaningless and laborious metrics that constantly risk invoking Goodhart's Law: "When a measure becomes a target, it ceases to be a good measure".

Measurement can only produce data. Having immediate access to the 'right' combinations of data is the key to becoming a data-driven organisation. What is done to turn that data into information and insight is the key to becoming a people-focused organisation. While some decisions can be driven directly by the 'right' data inputs, other decision-making processes may require 'gut reaction' or emotion. As more competitors become data-driven, it may even become a feature of organisations to take decisions that contradict the evidence provided by the data in order to deliver distinctive and unique value propositions. But even contrarian management decisions of this type are undertaken in light of the available evidence provided by the data.

A third aspect of being a data-driven organisation also necessitates a people focus. Organisations always function with incomplete data. Being data-driven better defines what or where these absences exists. In some cases corrective actions can be taken to acquire this data (but with conscious awareness of the risks of laborious measurement), and in other cases the data is impossible to obtain. A data-driven organisation will endeavour to identify proxy measurements to substitute for the impossible data. A people-focused organisation has the maturity and ability to conduct sustainable and defensible decisions made on the basis of imperfect data. A people-focused organisation understands the VUCA world through the lens of the 4Vs. The lack of data is seen as 'just' a lack of one or more of the 4Vs.

The opposite data circumstances is more commonly cited as a feature of the VUCA world. Ninety percent of data that is now in the world was generated in the past two years (Hale 2017). In the time it takes to read this sentence, up to 500,000 tweets have been added to Twitter and 50,000 images have been posted on Instagram. Access and the mature treatment of data is the enabler for all organisations to create more opportunities, optimise current processes and generate value (whether that is expressed as financial surplus, social benefit or both). The challenge for most leaders is understanding how to strategically invigorate their existing business models. This is increasingly only possible through the transformation into a data-driven organisation.

As with the accelerating 4Vs of data, the expectations of consumers and customers have increased through experiences with the nimble digital interfaces of social media and e-commerce. Significantly, among these experiences are those offered by the unicorns (businesses with valuation greater than $1bn) that fulfil a service or need that consumers hadn't even realised they needed so urgently ten years ago. Traditional consumer business models struggle to compete against a two-hour Amazon delivery turnaround, an endless volume and variety of stock or highly sophisticated mobile apps that appear, for example, to track the preparation and delivery of your pizza from order time to the knock on your door. However, even within the realm of consumer retail there are data-driven tactics that can be used to remain competitive and provide value to consumers and customers.

In the early stages of transformation an analysis of internal (Chapters 6 and 11) and external (Chapter 4) drivers together with horizon scanning (Chapter 7) shapes the planning for data-driven decision making. There is a strategic need to know what organisational data is currently being used and what data-driven decisions are currently being made. From the widespread use of tools such as enterprise resource planning (ERP) and customer relationship management (CRM) software down to the use of Google Analytics for analysing marketing channels, most organisations now employ some degree of data-driven decision making. Firms who adopt data-driven decision making have output and productivity that is 4% higher and profits that are 6% higher than can be explained by traditional inputs and IT usage (Brynjolfsson, E. & Steffenson McElheran 2017). The intelligence gained via horizon scanning, understanding future trends and identification of emerging technologies that may be disruptive brings insights into the organisation that is usable (Marr 2018). The insight gained from this type of research aligns data-driven decision making with key objectives that support strategic goals. An organisation's data is one of its most important assets. Jack Dorsey, founder of Twitter and Square, recounts that for the first two years of Twitter the company was "flying blind" with no idea what was going on with the platform or how people were using Twitter (Dorsey 2011). With imprecise and incomplete data, Twitter was making guesses and basing decisions solely on intuition. Learning from those early days of guesswork and mistakes, Twitter now treats the data and the analysis of that data as its product.

In an organisational environment full of uncertainty, change and imprecise data, knowing what to plan requires a firm strategic focus. It is an unexpected twist in the transformation from traditional practices to digital ones that some of the oldest and best documented techniques have become all the more significant. The importance of defining a genuine mission and vision for all organisations has become ever more acute in the digitally enabled VUCA world. The questions that emerge from asking how to achieve a vision are then what requires planning.

Airbnb's vision is "to help create a world where you can belong anywhere and where people can live in a place instead of just traveling to it". This vision raises immediate questions about to how to connect the people who want a different kind of travel experience with those who can provide those lived spaces. In many respects, this vision describes a traditional question of supply and demand. Irrespective of any decisions relating to the hardware or software of the organisational system that will be used to deliver this decision, what is key to bringing together these two sets of people and their needs is data. How that data is gathered, monitored and analysed to extract value, and how that value is turned into intelligence that is used to grow the organisation, are all key questions that come out of an examination of Airbnb's vision. With the important questions understood and an accounting of what data is needed to resolve them, more strategic and meaningful data collection can commence. In organisations with a legacy, some of the data of this type may have already been collected and stored internally. In some instances, the original purpose for collecting legacy data may be different from its newly realised application. Airbnb has no such legacy data, but it is instructive to consider the value of its earliest acquisitions of Accoleo in Germany and Crashpadder in the UK. Both companies were already established competitors, but what they brought to Airbnb was data that served its vision and helped to answer its question strategic questions.

The importance of data in realising organisation vision requires support and investment. Airbnb is large and, as a new business, is digitally focused, which means there is a large internal technology team. With sufficient resources employing in-house talent to interrogate and sense-make, data supports movement towards the organisational vision and answering its strategic questions. For smaller organisations, becoming data-driven may require working with key partners to bring the requisite people, software, hardware or even data itself. Data is a rich asset and a powerful resource that should be prioritised in the realisation of vision and mission. Internal organisational data may also be beneficial to other organisations. With the transformation of business models, placing data at the centre of organisations can create new thinking, new opportunities, new products, new services and new markets that align with the organisation's vision and mission.

15.3   When business models become obsolete

Discussions of innovation within organisations generally centres on creating new products and services. Increasingly, however, organisations are being more fundamentally challenged to reinvent their business models to address the central question of how they create value. A business model describes how an organisation creates and delivers its value proposition to consumers and customers. A business model also explains the mechanisms by which the organisation itself extracts value (profit or social value) from the delivery of that value proposition (Teece 1986, 2006). The acceleration of VUCA means that business models are simply less robust and less durable than they once were. Sector changes, technological disruption, consumer fickleness, global markets and, in some cases, structural obsolescence mean that any business model defined five or more years ago is in urgent need of reflection. In the smallest number of cases this action may reconfirm the ongoing validity of the model, but with the balance there will be a need for change.

The pressure on existing business models is also being driven by competitors. Previously, product innovation brought to market minimum viable products (Moogk 2012) that filled identified gaps in the market. Now, increasingly, entirely new startups evolve their business models in the same way. These new minimum viable business models allow firms to be freer and responsive to consumer demand and data (Teece 2010) – a general observation confirmed by Dorsey's comments about the earliest developments of Twitter. The minimum viable business model encourages organisations to be value-centric rather than product-centric. In this business model the organisation sells the benefits now and builds features later on while leveraging active co-creation with its end-users to create the products that address consumer needs (Hoyer et al. 2010).

A systematic approach to the transformation of business models coupled with an analytical process helps to mitigate risk and to maintain focus on the founding mission and vision (de Jong & van Dijk 2015).

1   **Outline the sector's current dominant business model** – an organisation must be able to question the fundamental core beliefs about how it creates value in order to make changes to that model (Amit & Zott 2012).

2   **Question important long-held beliefs** – identify tangible evidence that supports current internal organisational understanding of customer needs, interactions, technology, regulation, economics and ways of operating (Kirchmer 2017). The absence of evidence for existing beliefs is a key indicator of the need and scope of change required.

3   **Flip beliefs on their head** – organisations must be open to the reframing of existing beliefs through radical new hypotheses – ones that the current sector may be resistant to adopt (Trimi & Berbegal-Mirabent 2012). Apple, for example, realised that their customers would buy digital products online but wanted to buy their hardware instore. Dell, in contrast, had already moved their customer experience for hardware purchases online.

4   **Sanity-test the reframe** – entirely reframed beliefs may not actually be achievable or make sense. Applying reframes proven in other industries greatly improves the prospects of success (Doz & Kosonen 2010). Business model reframing, unlike product and service ones, have broad application across industries (Chesbrough 2010). Nominal evidence of this can be seen with the use of the term 'Uberisation' being applied to multiple transformation in the sector (Daidj 2019).

5   **Translate a reframed belief into your business model** – creating a reframe of the organisational mechanism for creating value requires management and leadership of the transformation, good timing and nerve (Markides & Oyon 2010).

15.4   The essentials of being a data-driven organisation

Start making data-driven decisions. It took two years for Jack Dorsey, the founder of Twitter, to realise the power of data and the pivotal role of data in the organisation.

Data should inform all strategic decision making, regardless of the size of the organisation. Having the 'right' data provides new insights that then can be converted into actions that enhance organisational performance. An example from material science is instructive (Hao 2019). By analysing journal articles from materials science journals over a nearly 100-year period, researchers were able to discover conceptual associations in the literature that can now be used to predict potential new materials with specific qualities.

Similarly, despite the leaking of the Panama Papers happening in 2016, there is now an awareness that still more revelations will be drawn out of the data through the use of artificial intelligence and machine learning (Guevara 2019). The original coverage of the tax haven resulted in bringing down two national governments and named 140 politicians from around the world. Yet the initial approach to the massive data set was primarily based on making everything searchable among a group of journalists – a form of private search engine. The analysis was then based on the journalists using the right combination of search keywords in order to unravel the network of personal and corporate connections. This original method has only scratched the surface of interlinkages and connection.

These dramatic examples of big data highlight that the first need of an organisation is to understand what data is needed to support the mission, vision and strategy. By focusing on this first need, there is a refining and restriction of choices of data rather than being overwhelmed by the 4Vs. Business models that support the strategy and vision then help focus actions into smaller achievable SMART objectives. Asking the right questions that are going to be answered by your data is the key. And knowing the right questions is a task for people within the organisation, not for the data itself.

The right questions contribute to achieving the strategic goals of the organisation. This mission-based approach empowers leadership to act strategically and gather key strategic data that supports the meeting of objectives. The next stage is to understand what data is now needed and where that data can be found, whether this is inside or outside the organisation. Often, much of the data that is required for the questions sits within your organisational system and is yet to be recognised. If there is data that needs to be collected, then additional activities needs to take place. Data gathering and collection is not an area of activity that you can neglect. For quick wins, and to help the change process, ask and answer those questions with data that you can access easily. Finding quick wins first is more productive and enables rapid learning from the process. Even these quick win activities will all require investment in terms of time, people and money. This strategic investment should have an agreed expected return and will provide justification for future data purchases that tackle the bigger and more complex challenges.

Data produces little value to the organisation without analysis, sense-making and translation to reveal insights and opportunities for the organisation. Reporting the insights in the right format for its intended audience is equally important and ensures that the data is represented in the 'right' meaningful way to inform the decision making-process.

As with so many aspects of strategic digital transformation, data gathering, data analysis, data representation and decision making is a continuous and iterative process.

Data is an asset, but it can be an expensive commitment of resources that requires visionary leadership to recognise the long-term benefits. Visionary leaders will be able to articulate the individual value of these benefits across all levels of the organisation.

Key takeaways

- Data should be at the heart of strategic decision making
- Make sure you ask the right questions so you get the right answers
- Ensure that you have in-house talent to interrogate and sense-make your data
- Foster a culture of innovation and experimenting with data
- Build trust and confidence with your customers as they are the holders of vital data
- Start making decisions with data as soon as you can

References

Amit, R., & Zott, C. (2012) "Creating value through business model innovation", *MIT Sloan Management Review*, 53(3), 41–49.

Buckley, K., & Perkins, D. (1984) "Managing the complexity of organizational transformation", in Adams, J.D. (ed.) *Transforming Work*. Alexandria, VA: Miles River Press.

Brynjolfsson, E., & Steffenson McElheran, K. (2017) "Data-driven decision making in action", *MIT IDE Research Brief*, http://ebusiness.mit.edu/research/papers/2011.12_Brynjolfsson_Hitt_Kim_Strength%20in%20Numbers_302.pdf

Claulkin, S. (2008) "The rule is simple: Be careful what you measure", *The Guardian*, www.theguardian.com/business/2008/feb/10/businesscomment1

Chesbrough, H. (2010) "Business model innovation: Opportunities and barriers", *Long Range Planning*, 43(2–3), 354–363.

Daidj, N. (2019) "Uberization (or uberification) of the economy", in *Advanced Methodologies and Technologies in Digital Marketing and Entrepreneurship*. Hershey: IGI Global.

De Jong, M., & van Dijk, M. (2015) "Disrupting beliefs: A new approach to business-model innovation", *McKinsey Quarterly*, 3, 66–75.

Dorsey, J. (2011) "A love for real-time data", *Stanford University*, https://ecorner.stanford.edu/in-brief/instrument-everything/

Doz, Y.L., & Kosonen, M. (2010) "Embedding strategic agility: A leadership agenda for accelerating business model renewal", *Long Range Planning*, 43(2–3), 370–382.

Emiliani, M. (2000) "The false promise of 'what gets measured gets managed'", *Management Decision*, 38(9), 612–615.

Guevara, M. (2019) "How artificial intelligence can help us crack more Panama Papers stories", *International Consortium of Investigative Journalists*, 25th Mar, www.icij.org/blog/2019/03/how-artificial-intelligence-can-help-us-crack-more-panama-papers-stories/

Hale, T. (2017) "How much data does the world generate every minute?", *IFL Science*, 26th July, www.iflscience.com/technology/how-much-data-does-the-world-generate-every-minute/

Hao, K. (2019) "AI analyzed 3.3 million scientific abstracts and discovered possible new materials", *MIT Technology Review*, 9th July, www.technologyreview.com/f/613933/ai-nlp-scientific-abstracts-material-science/

Hoyer, W., Chandy, R., Dorotic, M., Krafft, M., & Singh, S. (2010) "Consumer cocreation in new product development", *Journal of Service Research*, 13(3), 283–296.

Kirchmer, M. (2017) *High Performance Through Business Process Management*. Cham: Springer.

Markides, C., & Oyon, D. (2010) "What to do against disruptive business models (when and how to play two games at once)", *MIT Sloan Management Review*, 51(4), 25.

Marr, B. (2018) "How much data do we create every day? The mind-blowing stats everyone should read", *Forbes*, www.forbes.com/sites/bernardmarr/2018/05/21/how-much-data-do-we-create-every-day-the-mind-blowing-stats-everyone-should-read/

Moogk, D.R. (2012) "Minimum viable product and the importance of experimentation in technology startups", *Technology Innovation Management Review*, 2(3).

Prusak, L. (2010) "What can't be measured", *Harvard Business Review*, Oct, https://hbr.org/2010/10/what-cant-be-measured

Teece, D. (1986) "Profiting from technological innovation: Implications for integration, collaboration, licensing and public policy", *Research Policy*, 15(6), 285–305.

Teece, D. (2006) "Reflections on 'profiting from innovation'", *Research Policy*, 35(8), 1131–1146.

Teece, D. (2010) "Business models, business strategy and innovation", *Long Range Planning*, 43(2–3), 172–194.

Trimi, S., & Berbegal-Mirabent, J. (2012) "Business model innovation in entrepreneurship", *International Entrepreneurship and Management Journal*, 8(4), 449–465.

16 How to create responsive business models

Marie Griffiths and Gordon Fletcher

Preface

Eighty-two percent of leaders expect their organisations to be "digital" in some way within the next few years (Dell Technologies 2018). This indicates either a naivety regarding the scale of the task or a tsunami of digital strategies that are already under construction and progressing towards measurable success. Agility in terms of organisational qualities (and not just as a project management technique) is an essential hallmark of a data–driven, people-focused business strategy. The Sprint approach enables this type of working and represents part of the wider cultural change required to become sustainable, digitally enabled organisations that successfully deliver to its customers and consumers. Sprint is also (potentially) the means to deliver the vision and strategic objectives of an organisation. This chapter looks at the business models of the organisation as one of the key building blocks to support the delivery of an effective digital strategy and ways of prioritising the necessary actions for success.

16.1   The business model as a pivotal building block

The importance of digital transformation as a necessary aspect in all of an organisation's operations drives a need for usable and systematic approaches to understanding and defining the 'as is' situation and projecting forward to the 'will be' response. More specifically, the need for responsive change to the external VUCA world draws focus onto the most dynamic and most important aspect of the organisation: how it works with its customers and consumers to deliver a product or service.

The organisational system (Chapter 2) can be seen as the structural view of the organisation, but this type of artefact produces no value without a dynamic connection to at least one viable business model. Regularly reflecting upon the dynamic view of the organisation through its business models is crucial to the success of digital transformation. New business-model generation is also a pivotal aspect of the HINGE process (Chapter 5). This relationship between business models and organisational resources also links closely with existing academic literature regarding dynamic capabilities (Teece et al. 1997). The strategic challenge, drawing from this theory, is ensuring that the relationship between individual business models and the organisational system not only functions but is capable of changing (strategically pivoting) and re-prioritising as external conditions regularly shift and alter. Ensuring that a business model can remain 'fit for purpose' and continue to produce value for the defined group of consumers it addresses is premised upon the presence of an organisational system that can continue to appropriately resource and service the model.

The value and use of business models have enjoyed a renaissance with the publication of Osterwalder's co-created *Business Model Canvas* in 2010. The work was timely, in part, for its ability to support startups and technology-driven innovation and also because it offers a snapshot view of a business model in a single-page artefact that can be applied to any business in any sector. Osterwalder's canvas is not the only business model canvas, and the rising popularity of the work has produced a range of derivative new canvases for specific business niches as well as other purposes. Other canvases have also been developed that offer different approaches to representing a business model than that of Osterwalder. Two of these, the works of Mauruya (2012) and Stähler (2001), introduce additional considerations to business modelling that enrich the canvas while still remaining generic and a single-page artefact.

We introduce a hybrid of the three canvases from Maruya, Staehler and Osterwalder in this chapter as a working solution that connects the structural organisational system with the dynamic aspects of the organisation (Figure 16.1). The additional value of this hybrid canvas is the conscious awareness of its position within a wider strategic situation that may see one business model juxtaposed with another while also being more consciously people-focused. In this way an organisation's strategy is represented as a composition built out of its organisational system and the individual business model 'building blocks' with which it interacts.

The hybrid business model canvas consciously uses specific terms to emphasise its generalisable nature, the role of people, the complexity of different methods for monetisation

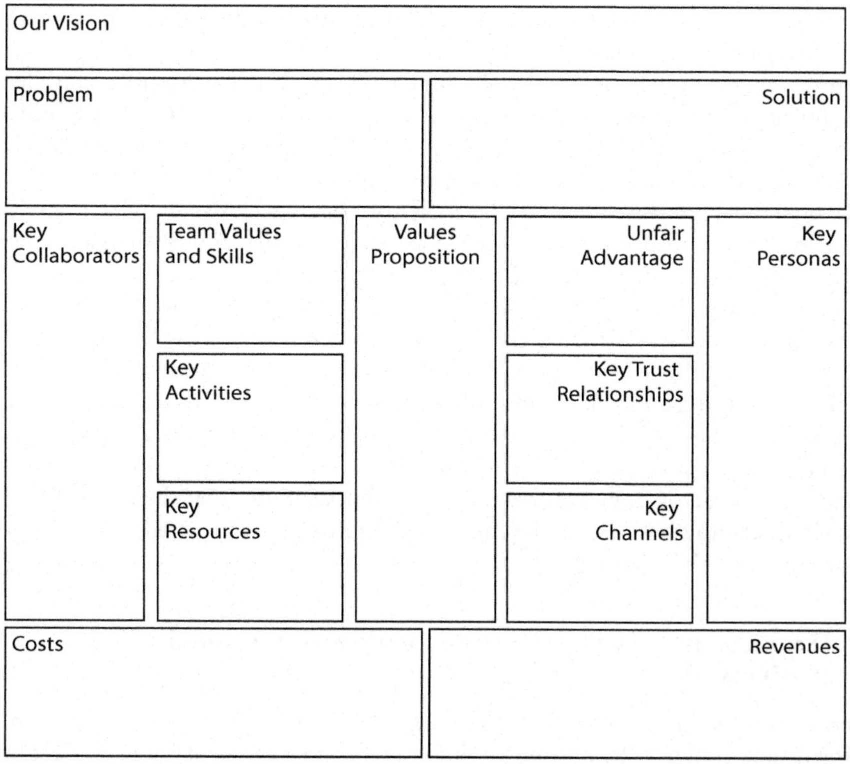

Figure 16.1 Hybrid business model canvas

and the relationship between consumers and buyers found with many products and services.

The business model canvas can be read in a variety of ways. As a series of layers, the canvas has a higher level strategic perspective connecting it to the organisational vision and a broad problem/solution statement. The centre layer of the canvas offers the operational aspects of the business model and the practical actions required to deliver the offering. At the base, and underpinning everything, is a relatively simple representation of the financial aspects of the model.

The centre layer of the canvas can also be read as being composed of three parts. In the centre are the elements of the business model that are the internal operations. The far left- and far right-hand sides of the model are the external aspects of operations of the model. In the very centre is the key value proposition. The value proposition captures the key ways in which the business model delivers some form of advantage, benefit, incentive and/or solution to its identified consumers. The value proposition is the pivot point for the entire business model that is reflected in its central position within the canvas.

The hybrid canvas encourages the business model to take advantage of the internal skills and values of its team as a separate section from the more expansive category of key resources. The skills of the team links the use of key resources with key activities to support the delivery of the overall business model. To the right of the value proposition, the key channels describe the way in which the value is delivered to the defined key personas. These persona may be buyer or user personas, or they may be both, but the value proposition should deliver for the personas that are defined in this box. The trust relationships describe the feedback loop for the business model and how the organisation will know it is delivering its value proposition successfully. In an environment of openness and transparency, this trust will in most circumstances be expressed in ways that are also visible to others.

A further aspect of the ways that the business connects with its personas is consideration of any unfair advantage that the organisation possesses and can exploit. The unfair advantage does not represent unethical activity but rather is a recognition that the organisation has something that is unique or distinctive that other competing organisations do not possess. In traditional businesses, this may be a territory or an exclusive supplier arrangement. In digitally mature organisations, this may be found in a particular user interface or experience. For example, among Amazon's early advantages was its 'one-click ordering' and the various ways in which it actively reduced the number of steps from initial product selection to the completion of an order, making it faster and more user friendly than competitors.

In combination, the hybrid canvas offers advantages over the three earlier canvases that it synthesises. An organisation could readily choose to use any of these canvases or create their own hybrid to develop a more focused (and consequently less generic) approach. However, the key recommendation is to use – as an organisation – a single canvas that is used consistently across the organisation. Consistency ensures that there is a shared language for describing business models, and the artefact can be discussed, shared and compared throughout the organisation.

16.2   From 'as is' to 'will be' – strategic direction through business models

The canvases for each business model create the visual building blocks for an organisation's transformation strategy. The starting point for all organisations is the 'as is' canvas for each business model that currently exists. This is a collective and inclusive activity for the entire organisation. For organisations that are small, have experienced rapid growth or are well established with significant legacy, documenting the 'as is' business models is always a valuable activity for identifying those pre-existing assumptions that cannot be supported by the evidence of data. Similarly, if the organisation cannot collectively define one or more of the elements of the canvas, there is a shortfall in understanding that requires further investigation and articulation through new (but potentially already existing) data.

Analysis of the 'as is' situation also encourages more precise identification of multiple business models that may exist when there is a collective organisational understanding that there are far fewer. 'As is' analysis also contributes to the prior internal audit step in the HINGE model for generating smart transformation actions (Chapter 5).

With the 'as is' situation defined, it is possible to move on to the 'will be' situation. As before, this should be a transparent activity for the entire organisation, and it is a task that cannot be completed in a single sitting. The 'will be' situation should be based on evidence and insight gained from, for example, the potential consumers (described as the key personas in the hybrid canvas). However, this is a caution embedded in weighting a new business model too heavily in any one direction. A 'will be' model derived entirely from this external input from the 'right hand' of the canvas is consumer focused and may require a more significant internal challenge and heavier investment in resources to deliver. A new model built from existing resources, people and activities will be more easily achieved and rapidly delivered but may be less likely to deliver a high-quality value proposition to consumers. These extreme situations highlight the value of the canvas as a one-page artefact. The 'will be' situation is a negotiated situation that necessarily represents a compromise based on the many intersecting elements of the business model. Bringing this level of strategic change to an organisation is continuously iterative. It may be necessary to progress through multiple cycles of change, moving repeatedly from 'as is' to 'will be' with an evolving business model in order to remain dynamic and responsive to the combined effects of a changing internal situation and the external VUCA world.

16.3   Agile approaches to strategy

The need to iterate rapidly and regularly through business models requires a delivery method that can keep pace with change without burdening the organisation with endless or repetitive strategising activities (see Chapter 17 for an innovation jam as an example). Similarly, there is a need to keep strategic thinking, as well as vision and mission, within the sight of the entire organisation. The agile movement within project management is relevant and provides guidance on how to balance relevance and responsiveness with day-to-day business.

Appropriately for the task of digital transformation, the principles of agile project management come from the software development industry. In this type of technical environment, short, iterative tasks are better suited for dealing with the complexities and interdependencies involved in creating robust software. The agile manifesto uses twelve principles that can be translated directly into the realm of digital transformation (Agile Alliance n.d.). The list presented below presents a generalised view of agile project management that can be applied to digital transformation and with the development of a 'will be' business model canvas.

1 Be customer focused – the customer's wants and needs are the priority
2 Change is inevitable – embrace and incorporate new inputs as soon as possible

3 Iterate rapidly on tasks – deliver quickly to improve quickly
4 Collaborate with many people who have different skill sets
5 Build tasks around teams – give them the environment and trust them to succeed (Chapter 6)
6 Prioritise meeting face to face over other methods of information-sharing
7 Good, well-received products and services are the best measures of progress and success
8 Being agile is sustainable – success and progress can be maintained indefinitely
9 Technical excellence and good design define being agile
10 Keep it simple
11 The best product and services emerge from self-organising teams
12 Teams collectively reflect and regularly tune, adjust and improve

Within Agile Project Management, two threads of thinking are currently predominant. Kanban uses a continuous delivery approach to delivery and focuses on shortening the overall time it takes to deliver the final project outcome. Scrum, in contrast, focuses on multiple quick iterations of activity to learn and to deliver the final outcome (in a manner similar to Gibbs Reflective Cycle – Chapter 10 and Action Research). Kanban and Scrum are not incompatible or necessarily set out in opposition to one another. Both threads of thinking are based on the core twelve principles but applied in a different way.

The iterative focus of Scrum introduces the concept of the Sprint (although it is sometimes introduced through Kanban as well), a tight cycle of activity that aims to produce outcomes and learning for the overall development process. Although the original focus of Agile methodologies was on software development, there are many other examples of sprints that have produced other types of outcomes. This includes book sprints developed during unconferences and innovation sprints that have been popularised by Google to design new products or services.

The use of the Sprint also echoes the iterative learning cycle defined by Kolb (1983). This model of learning continuously moves through the four stages of Plan, Do, Reflect, Conceptualise. Subsequent cycles learn from previous cycles. Folding Kolb's thinking into the use of Sprint also reinforces the digitally transformed organisation is not just technologically enabled – it is also a learning organisation. An organisation that learns from its past actions is less likely to repeat its mistakes and is more likely to develop rapidly. In this sense, Kolb and the use of Sprint places better explanation and context around the 'fail fast' mantra that is often associated with Silicon Valley startup culture and assists in explaining the perspective to other cultures where risk aversion can impede and even paralyse innovation and new ventures.

The sprint is the smallest unit of action in all transformational activity. Each of the five steps in the HINGE process can be delivered through one or more iterations of a sprint. Each iteration of a HINGE cycle feeds into a specific chosen change project, and these projects feed upwards in combination to produce strategic digital transformation.

At the same time, moving 'business as usual' activity towards sprint-based approaches and the associated principles of agile thinking changes the way the organisation itself functions. This constitutes every activity in the organisation as a project. Converging the ways that change activities and business as usual are conducted makes the organisation better able to deal with continuous change and reflects the sustainability principle of Agile Project Management.

What occurs in each sprint will vary by need and the task at hand. Sprint also employs roles and ceremonies to define proceedings. The roles of product owner, scrum master and the team can be readily unpicked and defined for any given task. The four scrum ceremonies, sprint planning meeting, daily scrum, sprint review meeting and sprint retrospective meeting closely echo the four stages of Kolb's learning cycle. Using this broader learning perspective, the purpose of these sprint meetings can also be adapted to any given task.

16.4 Connecting dynamic business models to organisational vision and strategy

With the generation of new business models at the heart of the HINGE process, there is a strong push for continuous systematic change of the organisation that responds dynamically and appropriately to external change – and particularly to changes relating to the buyer or user personas described in the canvas.

The relationship between the Sprint as the smallest focused unit of activity and all the levels of organisational management in terms of transformational change is highly iterative (Figure 16.2). The relationship between each layer is hierarchical, with mission and vision encompassing and representing the entirety of the organisation. Each layer of the organisation feeds into the next, down to the specific activities within individual sprints. Each layer of the organisation can be defined and reimagined through a sprint. Changes developed in this way at a 'higher' layer, e.g. Strategic Priorities, has consequences and requires re-examination at 'lower' layers, e.g. Organisational System. Similarly, changes at a lower layer may have consequences for higher layers. This upward change will be particularly true with the generation of new business models that may require changes to the organisational system in order to support its delivery.

The relationships between visionary and strategic management and the operational levels of management (Figure 16.2) do offer some indicative timeframes around their permanence. The visionary aspects of the organisation, even with the accelerating pressures of the VUCA world, should still provide a degree of certainty for the organisation and should last for 'years'. At the operational end of the organisation there will be more evidence of continuous change that can be recognised in terms of 'weeks and days'.

Figure 16.2 The relationship of Sprint to operational and strategic management activities

Key takeaways

- The business model is at the heart of the organisation's operations
- The business model canvas provides a single-page live document for sharing and comparing and communicating
- The Sprint enables tightly defined packages of work to be completed quickly that contribute to overall success
- All aspects of the organisation from the most visionary to the most operational can be undertaken through sprints
- Change at visionary and strategic levels of the organisation impact on the operational activities of the organisation

References

Agile Alliance (n.d.) "2 principles behind the agile manifesto", www.agilealliance.org/agile101/12-principles-behind-the-agile-manifesto/

Dell Technologies (2018) "New Dell Technologies research reveals a divided vision of the future", 30th Jan, www.delltechnologies.com/ar-sa/press/new-dell-technologies-research-reveals-divided-vision-of-the-future.htm

Kolb, D. (1983) "Problem management: Learning from experience", in Srivastva, S. (ed.) *The Executive Mind*. San Francisco, CA: Jossey Bass.

Mauruya, A. (2012) "Why Lean canvas vs business model canvas?", *Lean Stack*, 27th Feb, https://blog.leanstack.com/why-lean-canvas-vs-business-model-canvas-af62c0f250f0

Osterwalder, A., Pigneur, Y., Smith, A., & 470 practitioners from 45 countries (2010) *Business Model Generation: A Handbook for Visionaries, Game Changers, and Challengers*. Hoboken: John Wiley and Sons.

Stähler, P. (2001) *Geschäftsmodelle in der digitalen Ökonomie: Merkmale, Strategien und Auswirkungen*. Cologne-Lohmar: Josef Eul Verlag.

Teece, D., Pisano, G., & Shuen, A. (1997) "Dynamic capabilities and strategic management", *Strategic Management Journal*, 18(7), Aug, 509–533.

Part III

Making your plans happen

Acting and engaging

17 Visible change and inspiring others

Making events that challenge innovation

Alex Fenton, Naomi Timperley and Rosy Boardman

Preface

In the data-driven, people-focused organisation, there is a need to constantly test and sense-check new innovations. Virtual and physical events can be used to conceive, design and present these innovations. This can be for internal or external audiences and offers new opportunities for communication and engagement with colleagues, consumers and customers, encouraging sharing, co-creation, co-production and transparency. Actions that can bring about this organisational change in perspective include crowdsourcing, incubation and creation as well as the retention and recruiting of talent. These actions combine most effectively with an organisation capable of taking risks at all levels.

17.1 Events

Events are important to allow organisations to continually shape their digital transformation strategy. They support the creation of a people-focused organisation by offering tangible evidence that it is constantly outreaching to consumers and customers to sense-check its internal innovation. Effective events can be delivered either physically or virtually. Physical events include conferences, awards, trade shows, innovation jams, hackathons and networking meetings. It is also possible for an organisation to play a smaller part in a larger event such as having a presence at a trade stand or colleagues acting as expert panelists or speakers. Virtual events often mirror the format of physical events and can be in the form of an online convention, webinar or lecture. There is also the option of live streaming a physical event to allow for wider online participation. Technology makes all types of events more impactful, effective, engaging and inclusive. Events thrive on the "experience economy", but as virtual events and technologies become more commonplace, organisers look for ways to replicate or enhance the human to human (H2H) experience. Event attendees therefore want to feel unique and have a bespoke experience and technology offers potential to do this, carefully balanced with H2H.

Industry events and awards are an opportunity to bring organisations from a particular market sector together. Apart from the opportunities for raising a brand's image, awards nights also provide an opportunity to celebrate innovation with team members and build internal morale. Digital industry awards, in particular, are an opportunity to discover the latest innovators and innovations in technology, as successful innovations are often represented in at least one award category.

Maximising the organisational impact in all events requires foreknowledge of the format and require background research on the attendees and their organisations to make sure that all potential opportunities can be explored. It is easy to attend events or awards and come away with very little of value. Take note of the organisations, their innovations and the individuals who attended the event. Following up with some directed social media activity during or after an event can maximise these opportunities and realises additional benefit on top of the internal team building.

There is nothing new about using physical and corporate events to raise brand awareness and increase network size and opportunity. The change in the value of events that is brought by digital echoes the benefits of digital more generally. Each event is now heavily laden with a volume and variety of data that can be rapidly captured throughout the lifecycle of the event and pre- and post-event. The face-to-face aspect of physical events such as awards supports and reassures regarding the veracity of this data, leaving no doubt who you are contacting.

17.2   Events and co-creation

Events themselves can be used to showcase and discuss new innovations. Bringing together experts and customers to discuss new products and services captures key data that supports an organisation to horizon scan and test innovations. This purpose behind co-creation is the "the joint creation of value by the company and the customer; allowing the customer to co-construct the service experience to suit their context" (Prahalad & Ramaswamy 2004, 8). Events may be internal, external or a mix of both depending on the objectives.

"Innovation jams" are one form of co-creation (Evans 2017). This type of event involves bringing key stakeholders together at a time and location to innovate new products, services or ways of operating. These jam sessions can use a variety of techniques described by books such as *Gamestorming* (Gray et al. 2010) and *Thinkertoys* (Michalko 2006) as well as Lego Serious Play, art streaming and focus groups. The choice and combination of activities is determined by the objectives that are being set out to achieve. Irrespective of the specific activities, all of the activities should be captured (with the permission of all the participants) as fully as possible, including audio, video and the slides from the event organisers. It is common for organisations and participants to disregard specific aspects of activities as irrelevant during the event. This ad hoc decision makes it impossible to recover what are later revealed to be key thoughts and discussions when their value is realised.

Technology supports co-creation on all scales. Customer and stakeholder use of social media means that thoughts, ideas and innovations can be shared anywhere at any time. Social media and specific organisational platforms can be seen as streaming never-ending focus groups. Thinking of social media channels as focus groups also means that insight is not just received as text but also with video and pictures. The Github environment is not generally described as a social media channel, but it does highlight the potential in all sectors. Github, a shared space primarily for open source software projects, was recently bought Microsoft for £7.5 billion, giving an indication of the size of the software community on the platform. Anyone can make contributions to Github, and this supports the development of the stored projects. These contributions may not necessarily be code but come in a range of forms including translations, suggested improvements and contributed documentation.

Even without direct participation, the Internet of Things (IoT) enables the co-creation of innovation. For example, sensors set up by users such as environment-monitoring beacons allow organisations to capture a variety of data from multiple sources. This is effectively a form of technical co-creation. The concept is already well developed in the field of citizen science where joining up sensor data is seen as a key way to understand urban pollution at a very granular level (https://scistarter.org/air-quality-citizen-science). Citizen science and citizen health, which joins health monitors in a social network, are all seen as mechanisms for improving the delivery of personalised services as well as contributing to social wellbeing. The rise of 5G presents opportunities for further digital integration into events, including wearable technology and the increase of IoT-connected devices from sensors to screens and more.

As an indicative business case of technical co-creation, sensors can capture footfall and movements in and out of venues including large public areas such as airports or stadiums. The most popular and quickest routes can then be mapped out automatically, providing new insights into the ways in which consumers move around a physical space. This live and co-created data and the insight it creates is then returned to the individual consumers in the form of efficient route planning, accurate prediction of their journey time, time-limited offers and reward points that can be delivered through an app or wristband. The possibilities for co-created data to shape and personalise products and services are significant and offer consumers definite value in order to encourage participation. The individual's collected data can also be shared directly back with them, creating a transparent relationship with the organisation that is undertaking the collection. Being transparent is a relationship that is becoming increasingly important and expected by consumers. In this example, the transparency may not return anything of value to the individual, but it reveals openly the data that they are contributing to the overall project and shows that the organisation is acting ethically and consistently.

17.3 Social media and events

Social media is key to the delivery of successful events. The number of social media users worldwide reached 3.484 billion in 2019, which is an increase of 9% year-on-year (Chaffey 2019). The scale and continued growth of social media highlights the opportunities for organisations. Social media enhances live events and helps to create and sustain a meta-narrative during and after an individual event. "Keeping the story going" is the biggest challenge for event organisers and for organisations. Getting clearly defined medium- and long-term value from an individual event should be among its initial objectives. For example, hashtags and specific social media accounts that are created beforehand may evolve into specific avenues for innovations coming out of the event. Media prepared before the event, such as interviews with speakers and delegates, fuel these channels by raising awareness and starting interactions before the event starts. This content can also be extended and developed after the event.

Social media posts including tweets that are shown live on screens and woven into the event's narrative can become the basis of later conversations through retweeting and linking. Delegates who post pictures and videos become part of the captured story of the event while also enabling them to interact and meet each other virtually or face to face. Live streaming through social media also lets guests attend from anywhere and interact with the physically present participants and event organisers. User-generated content becomes part of the event's co-created narrative, with devices such as hashtags enabling ongoing event curation. Through co-creation, participants share ownership of the event's ongoing curation beyond its close, and this curation also helps to keep the story going.

All the data created by social media interaction before and during the event can be examined and analysed to inform future innovation and to reflect on current organisational strategy. A variety of qualitative and quantitative techniques can be deployed depending on the format of the event itself and what needs to be achieved. For example, qualitative social media comment analysis can be undertaken using a netnography approach (Kozinets et al. 2010) to reveal the connections and interactions between participants. Entry or exit surveys, social network analysis, registration and check-in software, website analytics and much more can be used in combination to gather, analyse and visualise the events impact. When conducted in real time, this form of analysis can allow event organisers to shape and pivot their activities during the event itself and can then be evaluated and refined for future events. Real-time analysis also allows the KPI outcomes of the event to be maximised which, in turn, creates more immediate and accurate reporting of return on investment metrics.

After an event, it is social media that becomes the channel for facilitating continued engagement. The event may be expressed as a form of nostalgia; "You missed EBIT20." The event may continue to be recognised for the role in defining thought leadership; "EBIT20 really clarified the concept for me". Or the event could become a reference point and marker for ongoing development in the field; "I first saw this demoed at EBIT20". As social media increasingly plays a key role in many organisations, it is also becoming a key contributor to their success or failure (Ramanathan et al. 2017). Previous studies have suggested that word of mouth about an organisation will amplify its marketing messages and disrupt the information gathered by consumers. With these influences, word of mouth has the ability to alter the information processing of consumers (Kozinets et al. 2010). A distinctive feature of digital word of mouth is its higher levels of credibility and its ability to better convince consumers in comparison with commercial messages (Sivadas & Jindal 2017). Understanding the extent of the power of social media confirms the important need for an event to leave a lasting positive impression on people's minds. A positive impression of an event means they are also more likely to post positive messages about the event and the organisation on their own social media (hopefully using the event hashtag). By building an event social media strategy with clear objectives, an organisation can maximise its visibility and improve its word of mouth reach while positively engaging the participants throughout.

Building the objectives for an event's social media strategy includes targeting the right channels. The most popular social media site worldwide is Facebook when measure through the metric of average daily users (Chaffey 2019). In the UK, three-quarters of Internet users have accessed Facebook in the last three months (Mintel Reports 2018). But popularity needs to be further explored. Facebook's core user base is 25–34 year olds, with 83% of people in that age group using it. The popularity of this channel "sticks" with this group as they age primarily because they were the main adopters from its launch in 2006 (Mintel Reports 2018). Targeting different age groups requires different channels. Instagram and Snapchat, for instance, have a younger user base and are popular during fashion events such as London Fashion Week. The nature of Instagram makes it a particularly useful social media channel for visually oriented events. This also aligns with organisations wanting to convey their brand image and personality in formats not easily captured with simple text. The careful selection of channels should be based around the preferences of the intended and expected audience, which can be refined using the data that comes back from these channels (Heinze et al. 2016).

17.4   Virtual events

Conferencing technology enables virtual events such as webinars that use 3D avatars and live video streaming with interactive tools and technologies. As Internet speeds increase and the capabilities of mobile technologies approach those of laptop and desktop devices, sophisticated virtual conferencing through virtual reality and the use of holograms at events will continue to grow (Thomas 2018). Lighter touch and more immediately deployable virtual events include promoting and using a social media hashtag at a particular time to enable wider interaction as a physical event.

Organisations are under increasing pressure to innovate and to provide exciting and engaging experiences for staff (including millennials) and externals such as existing or potential customers. The demand to further entertain people produces a pressure to introduce experiences driven by new technologies such as augmented reality (AR) and virtual reality (VR – entirely computer-generated reality such as the gameworld described in the film Tron). Augmented reality (AR) is an interactive technology that modifies the physical environment with superimposed virtual elements to create an immersive experience such as the Pokemon Go mobile game (Javornik 2016). These virtual technologies embedded into events enable the organisers to include something interactive, unique and memorable. Both AR and VR are now increasingly accessible through enterprise- and consumer-level technology that can support the creation of these environments by enthusiastic amateurs and individual organisations. Consumers are at a saturation point with existing mainstream consumer technology, resulting in a constant demand for innovation and spectacle in order to be entertained (Boardman et al. 2019). The need to continually move away from "normal" technology experiences forces organisations therefore to explore new technologies in order to keep attracting the attention of their consumers.

AR can put an organisation's information or images onto the world around its consumers, creating new business models and building new relationships with consumers (Javornik 2016). Already common examples of AR are smart mirrors and filters that can be imposed on a setting or person via a mobile app such as Snapchat (Boardman et al. 2019). Organisations use AR to create a filter conveying their brand image, and during events consumers can use these filters on their pictures before posting them on social media throughout the day. This creates a fun but clearly branded atmosphere and capitalises on the trend of people taking selfies and posting about their daily lives on social media platforms. Other early attempts to create a more in-depth and longer-term consumer AR experience can be recognised with smart-glass projects that are growing in popularity. Inspired by Google Glass, and with Apple rumored to be hitting the marketplace with a similar product, smart-glass wearers are given the tools to continually see the world through an augmented-reality lens.

Virtual reality (VR) is an immersive three-dimensional illusion that is entirely computer generated. VR worlds can be explored and interacted with through the use of special headsets (Virtual Reality Society 2017; Rubin 2018) or more completely immersive rooms. Organisations use VR during events to take complete control of a user's experience, immersing them in a different country, an entirely different world or in a new innovation in development such as a driverless car. The creation of VR experiences combined with the need for headsets makes the technology expensive and potentially beyond the reach of some events and organisations. At live events, immersive 360-degree video can also deliver the live experience to remote visitors. All of these additions to an event can make it more memorable and potentially increase positive word of mouth. However, the caveat for these specific examples is that as AR and VR technology becomes more commonplace and the associated technology occupies a lower price point, the interest expressed by consumers at an event will also decrease. The same effect can be seen with the decline of the video game arcade, which peaked in the 1980s. Interest then declined rapidly as home video game consoles matched and then surpassed coin-operated arcade video games.

17.5   The rise of the hackathon

Hackathons can be proving grounds for new ideas and innovation. These events are powerful tools to increase creativity and problem-solving among digital developers and innovators. "Hack days or hackathons are events where large numbers of people come together to collaboratively programme. Technology companies use them to generate new ideas and many events are open to non-programmers" (Rich 2013). At a hackathon, there is usually a low cost of failure, which reduces the risks associated with long-term projects for both the individuals attending and for the organisations involved.

Hackathons are time-limited events. Restricting the timeframe for development to often a few days of an event encourages quick thinking and forces participants to rapidly distil their ideas and concepts into actionable solutions. The risk is that the time constraint will produce outcomes that mirror existing solutions or developments. A key method to mitigate this risk is for the hackathon to be based around a carefully researched and defined objective that has been vetted prior to the event. Using a challenge-based hackathon minimises the chance of solutions that parallel or overlap with existing products. Outsiders bring a fresh perspective to internal challenges as well as an external perspective on existing products and the organisation itself. An organisation can get valuable instant feedback on existing products and how they can be improved or changed through a well-planned hackathon. Hackathons are also a great place for new ideas. For some organisations, new input can compensate for a lack of internal energy to innovate. It can stimulate employees within an organisation to start thinking again and challenge them to play by a new set of rules.

Internal hackathons display many of the same benefits as external competitions. Internal hackathons can unbind some of the corporate rules and processes that can hinder creative thought and help to build an acceptance of innovating behaviours within the organisation. Internal hackathons can solve all kinds of challenges that can range from day-to-day workflow issues, software solutions to manual processes, improving customer service or even the creation of new products. Internal hackathons give new energy to a company's innovation culture and capabilities. Fresh eyes (and heads) bring different perspectives and can offer creative, practical solutions more rapidly than conventional mechanisms for change. Hackathons come in many forms. A sports club for example, may want to develop new solutions for increasing fan participation or the competitive edge.

Hackathons are also a place to spot new talent for the organisation and its recruitment. By testing enthusiastic and capable consumers on real-world live problems, they help build a pipeline of talent. While hackathons have been primarily used by organisations to crowdsource new apps and solve pressing problems, they have also evolved into essential networking events and venues where talent and potential employers can meet.

17.6   Case study – creative entrepreneur

"Creative Entrepreneur", "Digital 4.0" and "Innovating Future Business" are a series of events started in 2014 by Salford Business School and staged at the University's technological campus at MediaCityUK. The events were co-created with business leaders, small- and medium-sized enterprises (SMEs) and students and staff of the University. The objectives were to educate, entertain and inform organisations and the next generation of business leaders about new technologies. The events were underpinned by a theme of innovation and digital technologies and utilised a variety of technologies and co-created expertise. Each event featured interactive workshops, VR/AR demonstrations, immersive video, master classes, expert keynote talks, film screenings, innovation jams, technology demonstrations and a pitching competition for new innovative ideas.

A website and social media channels on YouTube, Instagram, Twitter and Facebook were used for marketing the event to potential delegates as well as showcasing and archiving the speaker biographies and their recorded talks. Eventbrite was integrated into the website and used for data collection, registration and check in. Social media posts from attendees were encouraged some weeks before using the #CreativeEnt hashtag, and this was thoroughly integrated into the screens at the event to create an interactive experience for guests and further engagement. Data from exit surveys and interviews was also captured and reported as part of student projects. For each event, a complete impact report visualised this collected data including survey outcomes, netnography linkages, social network analysis and infographics for dissemination and sharing with attendees and key stakeholders. This use of data was acted upon to improve subsequent events. The event was run on a larger scale in some years and a smaller scale in the other years depending on the time, budget and the expected outcomes for each event.

The events were well received and assisted significantly in raising the public profile and awareness of the institution (Figure 17.1). Internally, the events helped to systematise the external offering of internal expertise and supported students to engage in industry competitions.

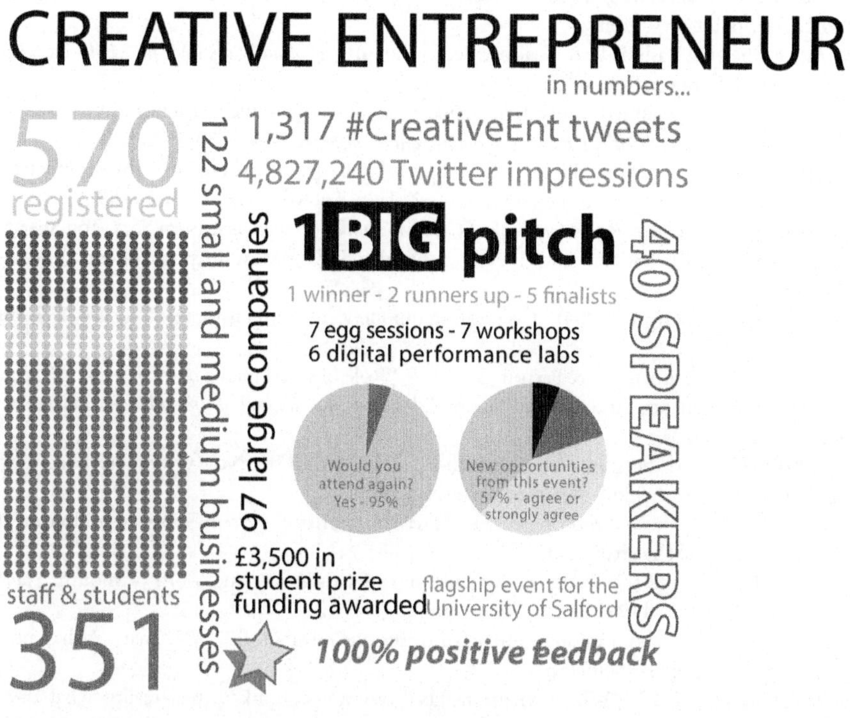

Figure 17.1 The Creative Entrepreneur event as an infographic

Key takeaways

- Events come in a range of forms to suit the specific objectives defined by the organisation
- Technology can enhance the engagement and experience at all events for participants
- Events should not be regarded as a one-off or isolated activity
- Events should be integrated with the strategic activities of the organisation, and the relationship of an individual event to overall strategic direction should be understood
- Hackathons and innovation jams can be designed to create new innovations, tackle real-world problems and identify new talented staff
- Events can contribute to positive organisational qualities including transparency and openness
- Events can be used to develop an organisation's co-creation and collaboration ambitions

References

Boardman, R., Henninger, C.E., & Zhu, A. (2019) "Augmented reality and virtual reality: New drivers for fashion retail?", in Vignali, G., Reid, L., Vignali, D., Henninger, C.E. (eds.) *Technology in Sustainable Product Development*. Cham: Palgrave Macmillan.

Chaffey, D. (2019) "Global social media research summary 2019", *Smart Insights*, www.smartinsights. com/social-media-marketing/social-media-strategy/new-global-social-media-research/

Evans, N. (2017) *Mastering Digital Business: How Powerful Combinations of Disruptive Technologies Are Enabling the Next Wave of Digital Transformation*. Swindon: BCS Learning & Development.

Gray, D., Brown, S., & Macanufo, J. (2010) *Gamestorming: A Playbook for Innovators Rulebreakers & Change-makers*. Sebastopol, CA: O'Reilly.

Heinze, A., Fletcher, G., Rashid, T., & Cruz, A. (eds.) (2016) *Digital and Social Media Marketing: A Results Driven Approach*. London: Routledge.

Javornik, A. (2016) "Augmented reality: Research agenda for studying the impact of its media characteristics on consumer behaviour", *Journal of Retailing and Consumer Services*, 30, 252–261.

Kozinets, R.V., De Valck, K., Wojnicki, A.C., & Wilner, S.J. (2010) "Networked narratives: Understanding word-of-mouth marketing in online communities", *Journal of Marketing*, 74(2), 71–89.

Michalko, M. (2006) *Thinkertoys: A Handbook of Creative-Thinking Techniques*. New York: Top Speed Press.

Mintel Reports (2018) "Social and media networks: UK", May, https://reports.mintel.com/display/859203/

Prahalad, C. & Ramaswamy, V. (2004) "Co creating unique value with customers", *Strategy & Leadership*, 32(3), 4–9.

Ramanathan, U., Subramanian, N., & Parrott, G. (2017) "Role of social media in retail network operations and marketing to enhance customer satisfaction", *International Journal of Operations & Production Management*, 37(1), 105–123.

Rich, L. (2013) "Behind the scenes at a hackathon", *BBC News*, 7th Nov, www.bbc.co.uk/news/av/technology-24825037/behind-the-scenes-at-a-hackathon

Rubin, P. (2018) "The wired guide to virtual reality', *Wired*, www.wired.com/story/wired-guide-to-virtual-reality/

Sivadas, E., & Jindal, R. (2017) "Alternative measures of satisfaction and word of mouth", *Journal of Services Marketing*, 31(2), 119–130.

Thomas, D. (2018) "Hologram phone calls: Sci-fi or serious possibility?", *BBC News*, 20th Sept, www.bbc.co.uk/news/business-45009458

Virtual Reality Society (2017) "What is virtual reality?", www.vrs.org.uk/virtual-reality/what-is-virtual-reality.html

18 Managing your human resources

Sequential-tasking and maker time

Alex Fenton and Jonathan Lord

Preface

This chapter focuses on the human resource issues faced in the 'always on' VUCA (Volatile, Uncertain, Complex and Ambiguous) world. With all of the benefits and flexibility of mobile digital working and data-driven management, this can also have negative consequences for organisations and their employees if not managed correctly. This chapter outlines a number of these issues and some potential ways to manage this. Aside from speeding up responses, 'always on' mobile communications could also create a superficial form of responsiveness. Responding to messages on a mobile could mean that workers react quickly but perhaps less accurately or in depth as when you have time to digest to create a more informed opinion. To drive internal innovation and encourage the greatest impact from face-to-face time, the 'always on' perspective must therefore be challenged. Sequential-tasking and maker time encourages focused activities around a single task that gets 'things' done and supports improved staff wellbeing.

18.1 Maker time

Some organisations already show some signs of this thinking with "email-free Fridays" or "maker days", but taking this further, some individuals, such as Jack Dorsey from Twitter, dedicate entire working days to a specific set of tasks so that, while Tuesday might be 'product day', Friday becomes 'people day'. This approach is compatible with the concept of the Sprint and Getting Things Done (GTD) (McGinn 2016) while also preventing burnout and the prospect of karoshi – or death by work. The 'right to disconnect' (Hesselberth 2018) from the workplace has been an informal right for centuries and has been governed by voluntary agreements between a tripartite arrangement consisting of employers, employees and trade unions. However, over the last couple of decades it is becoming increasingly necessary to incorporate this into organisational policy and procedures. The European Working Time Directive was conceived around 1993 to provide a legal framework for employers and employees to understand the boundaries of when they can and should have a rest from work.

With the advancement of technology, an increasing number of employees are required to permanently be on call through subtle obligations due to the normalisation of remote access within the workplace. This expectation can create pressure to be constantly accessible online or by phone, a tacit obligation that can be detrimental to employee mental health and wellbeing.

To build upon the legislative remit of the Working Time Directive, some governments are implementing contemporary legislation to combat the issue of employees being always 'switched on' and at the beck and call of their employees. For example, a legal case heard in France involved Rentokil Initial, who were ordered to compensate a former employee with a payment of 60,000 due to the company not respecting their 'right to disconnect' from their phone or computer outside of the normal working hours (Samuel 2018). French organisations are therefore legally obliged, under the so-called El Khomri law which is named after a former French labour minister, to negotiate with employees, or their representatives, on their rights to switch off and to implement monitoring processes to ensure this happens (King 2018). Specifically, the act also requires every French organisation with 50 or more employees to implement measures that regulate the use of electronic communication devices to maintain their employees' work-life balance.

As a large proportion of professional activities are now performed online, new digital rights are becoming more necessary to enable employees to exercise their fundamental rights. In 2018, Spanish law introduced a number of digital rights (Navarro 2019) which directly affected employees:

- the right to privacy in the use of technological devices at work
- the right to disconnect from work
- the right to privacy against the use of sound and video surveillance and geolocation technology

As well as the court's decision and subsequent legislation in France and Spain, the Labour Court in Ireland awarded €7,500 to a female employee who regularly had to reply to work-related emails outside normal working hours (Deegan 2018). The courts believed that sending and receiving emails outside of normal working hours exceeded her statutory maximum working hours. Therefore, the company had endorsed her working excessively as well as failing to monitor patterns of work and keeping proper records of excessive working hours.

Research in this area shows that, assisted by new technology, the inability to escape from work can have a damaging impact on people's health. A BUPA survey conducted in 2017 showed that over half (51%) of workers were kept awake at night by occupational stress (Scott 2017). Many employees who are working 'smarter' find themselves working for longer, and they are suffering from the consequences. Sixty percent check work emails outside of office hours, in particular on holidays (Waldersee 2018), and working smarter can mean 'always on'. The normalisation of bad habits and acceptance of the 'always on' culture can develop into a variety of issues, specifically stress, which can have a major impact on productivity and talent retention. In the UK, work-related stress, anxiety and depression accounted for 15.4 million working days lost in 2018 (HSE 2018).

18.2   Work/life management systems

18.2.1   *Getting things done*

Getting Things Done is a time management method devised by David Allen, who is a contemporary on the science of productivity (Duhigg 2016). The method is often referred to as GTD (Allen 2015). The GTD method centres on the moving of planned tasks and projects out of the mind by recording them externally and then breaking them into actionable work items. This allows the person to focus attention on taking action on tasks instead of recalling them.

What GTD gives you is a pragmatic system for keeping track of what you need to do, should do, or should consider doing. Therefore, when the system and your trust in the system is in place, the person's subconscious will stop keeping track of all the things they need to do and stop continually reminding them. This will then, theoretically, reduce stress and free up the mind to concentrate on more productive thinking rather than worrying about the process of organising the tasks. The concept is popular, and once users adapt their thinking strategy it has proven to be a key resource for all levels of employees.

The concept does, as with the other theories, need to be constantly updated to be attributed in the modern workplace, and the GTD concept was updated formally by Allen in 2015 to acknowledge the increasing embedment of information technology within individual working practices. However, the rapid development of Workplace 4.0, where technology will be seamless rather than manually instructed, would change the concept of GTD and how tasks can be automatically ordered. This is more of a development and recognition of how GTD can move with technology rather than making the system obsolete.

18.2.2   *The karoshi problem*

Japan's work culture is so intense that the phrase 'death by overwork' – karoshi – was coined and embedded into the culture of the country.

A 2016 report (Berke 2018) examining karoshi cases and their cause of death found that more than 20% of people in a survey of 10,000 Japanese workers said they worked at least 80 hours of overtime a month. Also, more than 20% work an average of 49 hours or longer each week, with half of all respondents stating they don't take paid holidays. This compares to the US, where only 16.4% of people work an average of 49 hours or longer each week. In the UK, a report by Jobrapido (Card 2019) found that over than half of UK workers (51%) who work additional hours outside their contract do not get paid overtime by their employer. The report also found that 60% of UK employees check their phone or email for work purposes at least once a day while on holiday, and 38 % of the UK admit to suffering from work-related stress. The problems of karoshi were placed under the spotlight even further when NHK, Japan's state-run news channel, admitted several years later that overwork had caused the death of a 31-year-old NHK female reporter in 2013 after an investigation by the Labour Standards Board. The employee, Miwa Sado, died of congestive heart failure and had been found to have worked 159 hours of overtime and taken only two days off in the month prior to her death.

Miwa Sado's death is only one of the suspected thousands of deaths from overwork each year. Matsuri Takahashi, a 24-year-old worker at advertising company Dentsu, took her own life in 2015. Takahashi was so overworked that she became clinically depressed and jumped to her death on Christmas Day in 2015. Dentsu was investigated and executives prosecuted for labour law violations after her suicide was ruled karoshi. The company was fined less than $5,000, although Dentsu's president, Tadashi Ishii, was forced to resign in the wake of the scandal.

As a result of the karoshi problem, Japan is trying to curtail the number of incidents through policies that allow employees more time off at work. The federal Japanese government also tried to address the problem by announcing its 'Premium Friday Plan', where workers would get the chance to leave at 3 pm on the last Friday of each month.

A year after the program was introduced, the government had not witnessed any fundamental reductions in incidents. The government discovered that many Japanese companies were organising their monthly finances and looking to achieve sales targets at the end of the month; thus, enforcing a shorter day has only increased the demands of staff at the end of the month.

Other companies have attempted to curtail karoshi cases by providing breakfast to those arriving early and dissuading them from staying too late. Others have enabled staff to take more time off as and when needed. Commentators on Japanese culture are cynical these measures will make a long-term impact, however. They believe Japan's true problem lies in its view of gender roles and the lack of protection for workers through labour law.

18.2.3   *The '996 system'*

In China, a system has unintendedly been adopted as the norm due to fierce competition in the tech sector. It's recognised that employees working for tech companies generally work longer compared to employees in other sectors. For a number of years, the '996 working time system' has become an implied routine for the industry where employees are required to work from 9 am to 9 pm every day for six days a week. What has made the situation even worse is that no overtime payments are made for these extended working hours. Some companies are now even including these within their HR policies.

Despite the increasing acceptance of the 996 system, Chinese tech employees are pushing back against the industry's notoriously long hours through innovative methods that could only be started in the tech sector. A group of developers started a project on the code-sharing platform Github called 996.icu – a reference to a comment by a programmer that working such a schedule could land an employee in the intensive care unit (Kuo 2019).

A prime example of the acceptance of a long hours working culture was the revelation in 2019 by Alibaba chairman Jack Ma, whose views on an optimal work system has come under scrutiny due to its promotion of an excessive overtime culture. Ma promoted the 996 system, stating it was key to an efficient and high-performing workforce which could support China's economy. While Ma believes that forcing employees to work punishing hours was inhumane, he also thinks that those who can "stick to a 996 schedule are those who have found their passion beyond monetary gains" (Chen 2019). This opinion was also supported by the founder of e-commerce giant JD.com, Richard Liu (Horwitz & Goh 2019), who, also commenting on his own work ethic, claimed that

> JD in the last four, five years has not made any eliminations, so the number of staff has expanded rapidly, the number of people giving orders has grown and grown, while those who are working have fallen. Instead, the number of slackers has rapidly grown. If this carries on, JD will have no hope and the company will only be heartlessly kicked out of the market. Slackers are not my brothers!
>
> (Horwitz & Goh 2019)

These are dangerous acceptances of a working culture that bypasses labour laws and best practice, as well as health and safety legislation, and 'encourages' employees to work long hours under the premise of the love of the job. In contrast, Germany has one of the highest productivity levels, and employees are 27% more productive than UK staff who work more hours per year according to a report by the Organisation for Economic Co-operation and Development (Chapman 2017), despite having the shortest working hours compared with all OECD member countries.

18.2.4 *Amazon Flex and Uber driving the way forward?*

Amazon Flex is the company's 'solution' to the perpetual complication of their drivers being classified as employees, which has major ramifications for the company. The system is similar to the Uber 'driver platform' system whereby drivers can claim delivery shifts which are labelled 'blocks' via an app. They drive their own cars to an Amazon warehouse, collect packages which they deliver in their own vehicles and are paid directly. As a result of this system, Flex drivers are not Amazon employees and therefore accrue no benefits or pay for their own car maintenance and other costs and have no real employment rights or influence over their own working conditions.

A number of investigations into the Flex system by financial analysts at Bernstein have uncovered regressive working conditions, with drivers often receiving pay below the minimum wage once they have factored in all of their expenses and illegal working hours (Zaleski 2018). As with the996 system being promoted as being good for employees, Amazon has made much of the fact that the company provides a flexible working option that suits workers who are interested in a work–life balance, so they can pick and choose when they work. Amazon also publicly promotes their guaranteed hourly rates for Flex. These subtle tactics by companies like Amazon result in workers having to work longer hours over protracted periods, which can affect their physical and mental wellbeing. It has also created a second-tier worker system whereby Flex drivers in reality are paid less than the guaranteed hourly rates and have little employment protection.

In the UK, companies such as Uber, Pimlico Plumbers and Deliveroo have been challenged in the law courts around the status of their drivers, with Uber and Pimlico Plumbers currently having their drivers labelled as employees rather than self-employed workers due to the arrangements between the two parties. The case initially commenced when two drivers, on behalf of a group of 19 others, took legal action against Uber, arguing that they were employed by the company rather than working for themselves, therefore gaining them access to rights such as minimum wage and paid holidays.

As with the 996 system, Uber's Flex scheme does have its advantages for workers, mainly due to the flexible working patterns; however, trade unions have argued that workers are being tricked into accepting precarious work by global corporations who have adopted these types of employment arrangements to save as well as make more money.

Although Amazon and Uber are well known for their impressive systems, business models and use of data to build large empires, they have both experienced a range of issues regarding their human resources. In the warehouse, Amazon has been accused of creating intolerable conditions with "allegations that workers have been penalised for sick days and that some are camping near one of its warehouses to save money commuting to work" (Osborne 2016). Similarly, Uber has been involved in a number of high-profile HR cases of bullying and sexism, creating a toxic working environment (Isaac 2017). This bad press can ultimately lead to drops in share prices and make it harder to recruit staff, particularly into specialist roles.

Considering the increasing precarious working arrangements used by Uber and Amazon, there is a risk that companies do not retain the knowledge and skills required for consistently performing at a high level or are unable to instantly utilise their current workforce. Therefore, a system of seamless knowledge needs to be incorporated into the organisation as a golden thread. The next section will highlight the strategies that can be adopted to achieve this status.

18.3   Managing internal and external staff and knowledge transfer

For organisations large and small, there are staff undertaking a range of core functions. In a smaller company, staff may be performing multiple functions. A good example is a marketer in an SME. They are often responsible for traditional marketing (print), digital marketing (social media and SEO), representing the organisation at trade shows, updating the website and internal communications (newsletters, intranets and more). Digital transformation in many ways has added additional responsibilities to these roles. Managers have always taken responsibility for remaining competitive, but this has taken on a new and more complex dimension in the volatile VUCA world (Chapter 1). What this means in practise is that, where there is a knowledge gap in these areas, training, development, systems and knowledge transfer is required from external organisations (large organisations, SMEs and micro companies/freelancers).

Knowledge transfer can be defined as a way for a specialist organisation to work with another to effectively solve a problem while embedding the skills and capability into that organisation to solve a problem on a more permanent basis. Training may be part of this solution, but knowledge transfer usually involves working more closely between two or more organisations to form a partnership. In the next chapter, we also discuss ways to embed innovation on a more permanent basis. The diagram below represents your organisation with these external organisations feeding in specialist knowledge in order to 'plug the gap'.

In the short term, when a technology or digital transformation is new, organisations cannot take the risk of employing someone to plug this gap. The solution therefore is to employ an external agency to provide a system, software, hardware, service, training or knowledge transfer. As the digital transformations grow, however, and move up the levels of the digital maturity model, your organisation may outgrow the concept of outsourcing services to external organisations. It may become more of an embedded core function of your organisation, and therefore training and knowledge transfer for existing or new staff will replace some of the functions of outside suppliers.

This can be a painful experience or transition. For example, the wrong external organisations, software or employees may be put in place. This can be a costly and time-consuming process to fix so it is important to get this right. Only sometimes through painful and costly experience will an organisation progress. Training and knowledge transfer from reputable and well-rated providers for existing competent and willing staff is often a more long-term and sustainable option in order to embed digital transformation into the organisation more permanently, embedding this knowledge and capability into the company. In the 2019 PwC internal audit report (PWC 2019), out of 2,500 organisations surveyed, 73% were investing in technology training and 66% had employees with advanced technology skills. These figures are likely to grow.

Knowledge transfer is highlighted using the dotted lines in Figure 18.1. A particular employee (or employees) may be the recipient of this knowledge transfer from an external organisation, but it is then crucial that this knowledge is embedded more permanently in the systems, data and other relevant employees on an ongoing basis. From an HR perspective, therefore, it is crucial to use the data available to make the right appointments of staff with the correct skills and mentality to fulfil functions. From a managerial perspective, it is also crucial to appoint the correct external organisations and to also consider knowledge transfer. Ultimately, the goal here is to avoid single points of failure (SPF) and frustrating bottle necks.

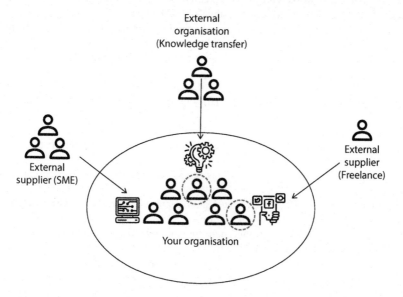

Figure 18.1 Your organisation and interactions with external organisations and knowledge transfer for digital transformation

These are all too common when it comes to digital transformation strategy. For example, one employee in the organisation (internal or external) may be able to perform a specific function such as setting up new company email addresses or managing social media accounts. This situation needs to be avoided so that there is cover and mitigation if this person is not available or leaves the organisation. Ongoing knowledge transfer therefore can offer one solution from a people perspective. In Chapter 2, we outlined the six interacting elements of People, Data, Software, Hardware, Processes and Communications. The diagram above further explores and reinforces the importance of these elements working strategically in harmony.

Key takeaways

- All staff members should have the right to time away from work
- All staff members should be encouraged to disconnect from the workplace
- A positive work/life balance can actually improve performance
- HR should encourage a culture that promotes positive work/life balance
- Technology has to be managed in the workplace to prevent the proliferation of an 'always on' culture

References

Allen, D. (2015) *Getting Things Done: The Art of Stress-Free Productivity.* London: Little Brown Book Company.

Berke, J. (2018) "Japan is facing a 'death by overwork' problem", *Business Insider*, www.businessinsider.com/japan-is-facing-a-death-by-overwork-problem-2018-3

Card, K. (2019) "Majority of workers do not get paid overtime", *The Briti*, 4th Jan, http://thebriti.co.uk/majority-of-uk-workers-do-not-get-paid-overtime-p212-184.htm

Chapman, B. (2017) "UK workers are 27% less productive than German counterparts, say British business leaders", *The Independent*, www.independent.co.uk/news/business/news/uk-workers-less-productive-germany-business-france-american-sir-charlie-mayfield-john-lewis-be-the-a7834921.html

Chen, L. (2019) "Jack Ma again endorses extreme overtime as furor rages on", *Bloomberg*, www.bloomberg.com/news/articles/2019-04-15/jack-ma-again-endorses-extreme-overtime-as-online-furor-rages-on

Deegan, G. (2018) "Executive awarded €7,500 for having to deal with late night emails", *Irish Times*, www.irishtimes.com/business/economy/executive-awarded-7-500-for-having-to-deal-with-late-night-emails-1.3584537

Duhigg, C. (2016) *Smarter Faster Better: The Secrets of Being Productive in Life and Business*. Chicago: Random House.

Health and Safety Executive (2018) "Work related stress, depression or anxiety in Great Britain, 2018", www.hse.gov.uk/statistics/causdis/stress/index.htm

Hesselberth, P. (2018) "Discourses on disconnectivity and the right to disconnect", *New Media & Society*, 20(5), 1994–2010, https://doi.org/10.1177/1461444817711449

Horwitz, J., & Goh, B. (2019) "China's JD.com boss criticises 'slackers' as company makes cuts", *Reuters*, https://uk.reuters.com/article/uk-jd-com-labour/chinas-jd-com-boss-criticises-slackers-as-company-makes-cuts-idUKKCN1RP05U

Isaac, M. (2017) "Inside Uber's aggressive, unrestrained workplace culture", *The New York Times*, www.nytimes.com/2017/02/22/technology/uber-workplace-culture.html

King, S. (2018) "Should there be a 'right to disconnect' for UK employees?", *The HR Director*, www.thehrdirector.com/features/holiday/right-disconnect-uk-employees/

Kuo, L. (2019) "Working 9 to 9: Chinese tech workers push back against long hours", *The Guardian*, www.theguardian.com/world/2019/apr/15/china-tech-employees-push-back-against-long-hours-996-alibaba-huawei

McGinn, D. (2016) "Still trying to get more done", *Harvard Business Review*, https://hbr.org/2016/04/still-trying-to-get-more-done

Navarro, C. (2019) "New data protection act introduces digital rights for employees", *Lexology*, www.lexology.com/library/detail.aspx?g=b27b2fb6-7d77-4b6f-bc3d-6a251a9e1471

Osborne, H. (2016) "Amazon accused of 'intolerable conditions' at Scottish warehouse", *The Guardian*, www.theguardian.com/technology/2016/dec/11/amazon-accused-of-intolerable-conditions-at-scottish-warehouse

PWC (2019) "State of the internal audit profession study 2019", www.pwc.com/us/en/services/risk-assurance/library/internal-audit-transformation-study.html

Samuel, H. (2018) "British firm ordered to pay €60,000 by French court for breaching employee's 'right to disconnect' from work", *The Telegraph*, www.telegraph.co.uk/news/2018/08/01/british-firm-ordered-pay-60000-french-court-breaching-employees/

Scott, K. (2017) "73% believe employers should do more to support employee health", www.employee-benefits.co.uk/issues/january-online-2017/73-believe-employers-should-do-more-to-support-health-of-staff/

Waldersee, V. (2018) "The majority of employees check work emails while on holiday", *YouGov*, https://yougov.co.uk/topics/economy/articles-reports/2018/08/15/majority-employees-check-work-emails-while-holiday

Zaleski, O. (2018) "Amazon Flex workers are left out of minimum pay raises", *Bloomberg*, www.bloomberg.com/news/features/2018-11-01/amazon-flex-workers-are-left-out-of-minimum-pay-raises

19 Enabling organisational change

Co-creation, co-production and co-consumption

Marie Griffiths and Richard Dron

Preface

With greater transparency and engagement, the opportunities to build trust with customers and clients also increases. The collaborative combination of co-creation, co-production and co-consumption provide mechanisms for a data-driven, people-focused organisation to engage with customers and supply chains in ways that increase levels of trust and build lasting social capital. These actions build strong external relationships and support the achievement of an organisation's vision. To illustrate the value of collaboration in digital transformation, a series of international case studies are used to reveal the patterns of success that exemplify leading practice.

19.1 Collaboration

In traditional organisational innovation paradigms, an organisation identifies user needs, developing products and services at private expense and profiting through their protection and sales. That said, more and more organisations are increasingly engaging in collaborative mechanisms and network structures. These mechanisms and structures can provide a competitive advantage through the combining of skills, competencies and resources of connected organisations as well as (Figure 19.1) leveraging their end-consumer knowledge of products and services to co-create more compelling and relevant value propositions (Lee et al. 2012).

Traditional concepts of value creation based on sequential value chains (Porter 2011) have evolved; in modern organisation, networked organisations (Santos et al. 2018) redesign values and shuffle structural, technological, financial and human capital, responding to their business' opportunities (Fine et al. 2002). Such organisations evolve their structures to maximise value-chain capabilities so as to respond to industry dynamics (Fine et al. 2002) and customer preference (Prahalad & Ramaswamy 2004). As such, collaboratively networked organisations, like Airbnb, or Ovo Energy, have increased agility in dynamic markets (Romero & Molina 2011). Enabling co-creative environments enhances organisational innovation processes (Nambisan 2002) and unlocks competitive advantage sources (Prahalad & Ramaswamy 2004).

For customers, interaction with an organisation co-creates consumption experience (O'Cass & Ngo 2011), enhancing brand experiences (Nysveen et al. 2013) and strengthening end-user relationships (Payne & Holt 2001). There are yet further added benefits: employee engagement (Hatch & Schultz 2010); improved supply chains (Jüttner et al. 2010); shareholder commitment (Madden et al. 2006); and, occasionally, beneficial

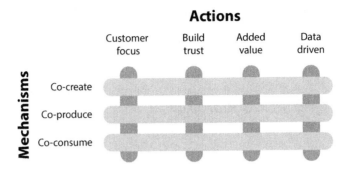

Figure 19.1 Mechanisms of collaborations for digital transformation
Source: Adapted from Fletcher et al. 2016

knowledge sharing with competitors (Kohlbacher 2007), with associated potential benefits and risks (Ilvonen & Vuor 2013).

The other collaboration practices alongside co-creation that we suggest as being mechanisms for organisation to adopt are co-consumption and co-production (Figure 19.1). We look to Heinonen et al. (2019) in their work on how online communities create value, as they take an alternative viewpoint o whether value is formed in the customer domain or the providers and whether the value is viewed as with the individual or collectively. Traditionally, value is viewed as an interaction between a customer and a provider, a 'trade-off' between what has to be given up or traded in order to receive a benefit or gain back. Transactional activities become less viable as a sustainable part of a business model when value formation occurs within collaborative environments and at multiple points along the customer journey. The presence of co-creation and co-consumption activities across multiply actors also problematises the idea of a transaction itself as a discrete manageable event. We have identified a number of 'actions' that organisations are utilising to engage with their customers and clients.

19.2   Co-creation

Perhaps the seminal voices in relation to co-creation as a research paradigm are Prahalad and Ramaswamy (2000) in their article "Co-Opting Customer Competence". More recent scholarship by Ramaswamy and Gouillart (2010) can be considered a key text in the discussion of how co-creation can enable and support organisational change. Co-creation shifts emphasis away from traditional organisation-centric perspectives that consider consumers as passive outsiders who are transacted with at point of purchase. Instead, within the co-creation paradigm, consumers are integral to value creation and can do so at multiple points of the value chain (Ng & Briscoe 2012).

Organisations that co-create unlock consumer intellectual capital and feed this forward into developing products offering superior user experiences. Furthermore, enthusiastic end-users (or customers) prove to be willing collaborators in ideating, designing and marketing their co-created products, increasing their brand loyalty and readiness to pay a premium.

19.3   Embedding organisational co-creation

Co-creational organisations requires an enabling platform as driver no matter whether interactions are formal or informal, online or offline.

- Online co-creation platforms can be used to engage end-users and employees of an organisation in change – online connectivity and mobile and social media driven by Web 2.0 technologies enable organisations to leverage online co-creation. Such online platforms make co-creation with potentially infinite participants globally and simultaneously possible, and while these are powerful tools, on a technical level they are simple applications to implement.
- Personal interaction as a co-creation platform – design sprint techniques (Knapp et al. 2016) include activities such as brainstorming, prototyping, simulation, or interviewing with a focus on interactivity between actors. Meetings are enabling platforms for co-creativity through facilitation (Konsti-Laakso et al. 2012).
- Digital embeddedness of dialog into processes; co-creation as routine interactions with end-users (Furner et al. 2014) – creating feedback loops through surveying the team have proven value (Harter et al. 2002), yet co-creative organisations create opportunity for user interaction through rating systems, comments, chat functionality and short user surveys (Fink 2015) that stimulates internal organisational improvement. Furthermore, employee-facing processes like training completion, recruitment or performance management can benefit from embedding processes to understanding how experience may be improved.

These platforms can enable co-creation to become an embedded and habitual approach to transforming organisational change.

19.4   The co-creation and co-production of organisational change

In traditional management models, processes such as ideation are seen as a higher management and consultancy role (Todnem 2005), with employee involvement only at implementation phase. This may result in untapped business value because employees will have insight into organisational improvement (Benson et al. 2013) and will champion these ideas more passionately than those they are less connected to. Co-creation enables environments that co-produce organisational change and support transformation objectives by engaging employees through a sense of ownership of activities such as implementing new technology, post-merger integration, restructuring or transformation of work culture (Lee et al. 2012). Such approaches have many benefits.

Ideation generates ideas that improve organisational operations; ideas that emerge enable underlying connections or themes to be uncovered, grouped into meaningful clusters and metricised for their value (Shah et al. 2003). As a human-centred approach, this produces effective designs supporting behaviours and reflecting needs and aspirations of the team (Khosla et al. 2003) by enabling co-design organisations to better identify their team needs. Interaction through co-creation develops stronger social-capital relationships amongst participants (Storbacka et al. 2012); in turn, this creates loyalty through interaction and workplace experiences which are more reflective of employee needs. Furthermore, co-creative processes affirm employee agency (Leavy 2014; Ramaswamy & Ozcan 2016) proactively, enabling them to be a part of organisational improvement.

LEGO can be considered as pioneering in its approach to co-created product design, evidenced through the Lego's IDEAS co-creation platform. Their website enables LEGO end-users to post set designs within an online community who can vote and feedback on these. Projects receiving over 10,000 votes enter a review phase where LEGO set designers and marketing decide on the viability of the product. Voting motivates design creators to leverage social networks to drive engagement with their submission, which in turn places the user centrally within brand promotion activities. When designs are realised, the user co-creators are credited on packaging materials and receives royalties worth 1% of net sales (LEGO IDEAS 2018). LEGO also organisationally engages with IDEAS through blog posts where they present end-user projects and interview the designers (LEGO IDEAS 2014). This longstanding approach to co-creation has permitted Lego to make rapid advances in innovative products starting in 1988 when their Mindstorm robot kit became successful by opening boundaries and allowing committed users to independently develop the range of Mindstorm products (Hatch & Schultz 2010).

LEGO Mindstorm communities grew rapidly without company involvement, and within a month end-users had significantly improved the product through adapting the LEGO firmware (Von Hippel 2005) to increase functionality. Connectivity in online communities accelerated purchasing, and LEGO was unable to keep up with demand, selling out two weeks before Christmas that year. This led to a market segment change: 70% of customers for Mindstorms were over age 18, and the product became a craze amongst technical adults, leading to some Silicon Valley firms banning LEGO Mindstorms kits at work. The popularly of LEGO as an ideation tool has also been realised though LEGO products created for use in education including universities, such as MIT (MIT Technology Review 2017). From the core of LEGO Mindstorms products curriculums were created for the MIT engineering department where the hacking of :LEGO software by students enabled the creation of advanced robotics functionalities.

19.5   Co-production

Co-production has become a buzzword in public service provision, where

> Co-production means delivering public services in an equal and reciprocal relationship between professionals, people using services, their families and their neighbours. Where activities are co-produced in this way, both services and neighbourhoods become far more effective agents of change.
>
> (Boyle & Harris 2009, 11)

It is grounded in the theory that it is possible to achieve better outcomes, synergies and public engagement when public services, service users and communities combine strengths and capacities (Loeffler & Bovaird 2016). For organisations it represents an emergent hybrid, drawing on the legacies of 'bottom up' community activism that focused on campaigning for rights and social justice and 'top-down', new, austerity-driven public management aligned to the country's welfare discourse which emphasises the values of active citizenship and involvement of citizens as co-producers, not simply consumers (Durose et al. 2009). Such co-production focuses on community development through individuals and groups that are creative resources and experts in their own social situation

(Freire 1972). This community development is value-based approaches which harness participatory processes that validate and empower individuals, groups and communities involved; furthermore, they have proven effective in creating long-term change (Seebohm et al. 2012; Shaw & Mayo 2016).

The National Health Service (NHS) is increasingly leveraging value through co-production of services and tasking their management to do so, as evidenced in their model for co-production (Coalition for Collaborative Care 2017). NHS co-production shifts assumptions that their service users are passive recipients of care to recognise their contribution in the delivery of services (Cahn 2000) while empowering front-line staff (Needham & Carr 2009). The King's Fund is an example of an NHS initiative designed to enable disruption of "the 'them and us' relationship dynamic in health and care systems" (Seale 2016), acknowledging how

> Achieving a more collaborative dynamic will require a change in the way that all of us work. The ability to adapt, communicate and shift between roles will be important for all who seek to establish a new, collaborative relationship that puts safety and quality at the heart of health and care in our communities.
>
> (Trimble 2015)

As such, the NHS continually encourages "patients, service users and carers who work with [them] . . . to influence decision-making at a strategic level" (Centre for Patient Leadership 2013, 4).

With time, co-production of many health-related resources and services has moved into the domain of those most connected to them, the end-user (Von Hippel 2005). Platforms enabling end-users to share and create solutions are increasingly common and take various forms; these can be through the supporting of specific communities (GMKIN 2019) or as crowdsourcing platforms for health solutions (Patient Innovation 2019). Such platforms have grown through community-crowdsourcing engagement and creating social business models around them (Disrupt Disability 2019; Be My Eyes 2019).

19.6 Co-production driven by experiential desires of the consumer

The need for digital transformation is being driven by consumers, users, customers. As the instigators for change that are also a valuable source of knowledge for the products, services and experiences that they desire (Yachin 2018). Historically, organisations have sourced knowledge from and listened to their customers; this has been through traditional routes such as surveys, customer feedback and market research with focus groups. Digital technologies are enabling alternative routes in which to capture this knowledge source, and there has been a massive shift in the relationship to customers.

Organisations are can now capture complete digital portraits of their customers' wants, desires and interests. As customers have become disenchanted with traditional brands and indifferent to their unwanted attention a shift in power has occurred that enables customer-driven innovation. When this innovation is coupled with the need for organisations to be creative and resourceful new ways of interacting with customers become clearly mutually beneficial. Additionally, different business models have emerged, and the consumers have (sometimes unwittingly) become co-producers in the supply chain. Many of us have self-delivered flat-packed furniture to our spaces from warehouses in

IKEA stores and then self-assembled the products. The added value in this co-produced mechanism is access to affordable designer furniture, but this value must then compensate the resources of the consumer's time and labour. There is also the element of built-in trust of the customer's experience of the IKEA brand in this co-production mechanism (see Figure 19.1).

The co-production mechanism in some sectors has been driven by certain demographics that are valuing experiences rather than possessions (O'Lenski 2017). Organisations wanting to invest in attracting this demographic need to offer interesting events that build in activities that add brand value, and engage the customer. Classes and workshops are a growing experience, with Lululemon, a Canada-based retailer, offering a range of community-based exercise classes, festivals and retreats for their customers to interact with the brand (O'Lenski 2017). Though these activities might not be directly related to products or services being sold, the message and brand are being reinforced.

More locally, many organisations are using co-production mechanisms, opening their doors at alternative hours to host cooking classes and bread-baking classes. One award-winning restaurant, The Allotment in Manchester, offers vegan cooking classes and makes the claim that there is such a shortage of vegan chefs they are using these classes to recruit from. Similarly, there are opportunities to co-produce different gin and vodka flavours in many distilleries, as organisations look to offer experiential events to attract consumers into their physical spaces. They are multi-purposing their spaces during potential quiet periods, and they offer an experience to co-produce a product. Additional value added for organisations offering these co-production sessions are an opportunity for in-depth consumer feedback, brand building and consumer purchase of add-on products, and many return as consumers of the main business purpose. Business owners can then capture these experiential activities for marketing purposes, and they can be shared across social media channels.

19.7   Co-consumption

Conventional consumption can be viewed as the exchange of goods or services for a payment. In this transaction there is no opportunity or expectation that the consumer will be involved in any part of creations, development or production processes outside of traditional marketing engagements. However, Botsman (2018) identifies a "reinvention of traditional market behaviors – renting, lending, swapping, sharing, bartering, gifting – through technology, taking place in ways and on a scale not possible before the internet". This definition does, however, miss the detail that co-consumption sits firmly in a middle ground between sharing and commerce (Belk 2014), providing access to goods and service rather than a direct ownership model. The co-operative models of business that are encouraged by sharing through social networks is increasingly now more typically a process of sharing with strangers Sholar (2014). These new arrangements fully challenge the transactional model of business – which could be characterised in contrast as being transacting with strangers.

Other monikers of co-consumption are the sharing economy, peer-to-economy or P2P (peer-to-peer) services, but typically providers on either side of the transaction can provide a rating and a review to build trust and demonstrate trust for future consumers. Typically co-consumption is often linked with large-tech enterprises such as Airbnb (accommodation rentals), eBay (auction platform) and Uber (ride sharing) that have disrupted traditional sectors. However there are many such co-consumption initiatives, such as charity shops and car sharing like BlaBlaCar (BlaBlaCar 2019). Rowe (2017) observes that much research has focused upon the economic and market orientation, ignoring the social aspects, non-economic value that the author argued is necessary to construct a complete understanding of the co-consumption mechanism. In the case of Parkrun this model for co-consuming sports is now a global event. Generally offered in local parks for free, these 5km weekly timed runs are open to everyone. The emphasis is not just on running for health or a good race time but also on the contribution that can be made through volunteering as a course Marshall or other roles on race day. As it is based on a voluntary model for running races, Parkrun relies entirely upon a co-consumption mechanism to exist.

19.8   Opportunities

With greater transparency and engagement, opportunities to build trust with customers and clients also increases. The collaborative combination of co-creation, co-production and co-consumption provides mechanisms for a data-driven, people-focused organisation to engage with customers and supply chains in ways that increase levels of trust and build lasting social capital. These actions build strong external relationships and support the achievement of an organisation's vision. To illustrate the value of collaboration in digital transformation, a series of international case studies are used to reveal the patterns of success that exemplify leading practice.

Key takeaways

- Organisations need to make data-driven decisions in embedding co-consumption mechanisms opportunities
- Build trust by embedding a culture of transparency across all touch points and through the provision of mechanisms for review and feedback
- Add value by providing intermediary platforms where customers can come together and share, build and enhance products and services
- Plan events that actively engage your customers in innovative ways
- The traditional retail model is broken. Be creative to get customers into your physical spaces so that these activities can be reported on digital channels
- Ensure that any activity, workshop or experience is meaningful for the consumer rather than just an alternative form of advertising
- Ensure that any data of the experience is captured, measured and responded upon

References

Belk, R. (2014) "You are what you can access: Sharing and collaborative consumption online", *Journal of Business Research*, 67, 1595–1600.

Be My Eyes (2019) "Be My Eyes: Bringing sight to blind and low vision people", www.bemyeyes.com

Benson, G., Kimmel, M., & Lawler III, E. (2013) "Adoption of employee involvement practices: Organizational change issues and insights", *Research in Organizational Change and Development*, 21, 233–257.

BlaBlaCar (2019) "Share your journey with BlaBlaCar: Trusted carpooling", *BlaBlaCar*, www.blablacar.co.uk

Botsman, R. (2018) "Thinking", https://rachelbotsman.com/thinking/

Boyle, D., & Harris, M. (2009) *The Challenges of Co-Production: How Equal Partnerships between Professionals and the Public Are Crucial to Improving Public Services*. London: Nesta.

Cahn, E.S. (2000) *No More Throw-Away people: The Co-Production Imperative*. Washington DC: Edgar Cahn.

Centre for Patient Leadership (2013) "Bring it on: 40 ways to support patient leadership", http://engagementcycle.org/wp-content/uploads/2013/03/Bring-it-on-40-ways-to-support-Patient-Leadership-FINAL-V-APRIL-2013.pdf

Coalition for Collaborative Care (2017) "A co-production model: Five values and seven steps to making this happen", http://coalitionforcollaborativecare.org.uk/a-co-production-model/

Disrupt Disability (2019) "Disrupt disability", www.disruptdisability.org

Durose, C., Mangan, C., Needham, C., & Rees, J. (2009) *Evaluating Co-Production: Pragmatic Approaches to Building the Evidence Base* (Vol. 4). London: Institute for Excellence (SCIE).

Fine, C., Vardan, R., Pethick, R., & El-Hout, J. (2002) "Rapid-response capability in value-chain design", *MIT Sloan Management Review*, 43(2), 23–24.

Fink, A. (2015) *How to Conduct Surveys: A Step-By-Step Guide*. Thousand Oaks, CA: Sage Publications.

Fletcher, G., Greenhill, A., Griffiths, M., & McLean, R. (2016) "The social supply chain and the future high street", *Supply Chain Management*, 21(1), 78–91.

Freire, P. (1972) *Pedagogy of the Oppressed*. Myra Bergman Ramos (trs). New York: Herder.

Furner, C., Racherla, P., & Babb, J. (2014) "Mobile app stickiness (MASS) and mobile interactivity: A conceptual model", *The Marketing Review*, 14(2), Summer, 163–188.

GMKIN (2019) "About us", http://gmkin.org.uk/about-us/

Harter, J.K., Schmidt, F.L., & Hayes, T.L. (2002) "Business-unit-level relationship between employee satisfaction, employee engagement, and business outcomes: A meta-analysis", *Journal of Applied Psychology*, 87(2), 268.

Hatch, M.J., & Schultz, M. (2010) "Toward a theory of brand co-creation with implications for brand governance", *Journal of Brand Management*, 17(8), 590–604.

Heinonen, K., Campbell, C., & Ferguson, S. (2019) "Strategies for creating value through individual and collective customer experiences", *Business Horizons*, 62(1), Jan–Feb, 95–104.

Ilvonen, I., & Vuori, V. (2013) "Risks and benefits of knowledge sharing in co-operative knowledge networks", *International Journal of Networking and Virtual Organisations*, 13(3), 209–223.

Jüttner, U., Christopher, M., & Godsell, J. (2010) "A strategic framework for integrating marketing and supply chain strategies", *The International Journal of Logistics Management*, 21(1), 104–126.

Khosla, R., Damiani, E., & Grosky, W. (2003) *Human-Centered e-Business*. Boston: Springer.

Knapp, J., Zeratsky, J., & Kowitz, B. (2016) *Sprint: How to Solve Big Problems and Test New Ideas in Just Five Days*. New York: Simon and Schuster.

Kohlbacher, F. (2007) *International Marketing in the Network Economy: A Knowledge-Based Approach*. Basingstoke: Palgrave MacMillan.

Konsti Laakso, S., Pihkala, T., & Kraus, S. (2012) "Facilitating SME innovation capability through business networking", *Creativity and Innovation Management*, 21(1), 93–105.

Leavy, B. (2014) "Venkat Ramaswamy: How value co-creation with stakeholders is transformative for producers, consumers and society", *Strategy & Leadership*, 42(1), 9–16.

Lee, S.M., Olson, D.L., & Trimi, S. (2012) "Co-innovation: Convergenomics, collaboration, and co-creation for organizational values", *Management Decision*, 50(5), 817–831.

LEGO IDEAS (2014) "Interview with Tom Poulsom, and a first look at Birds", https://ideas.lego.com/blogs/a4ae09b6-0d4c-4307-9da8-3ee9f3d368d6/post/1d54e054-0437-42ae-a7c5-20dddc8cf879

LEGO IDEAS (2018) "Product idea guidelines", https://ideas.lego.com/guidelines

Loeffler, E., & Bovaird, T. (2016) "User and community co-production of public services: What does the evidence tell us?", *International Journal of Public Administration*, 39(13), 1006–1019.

Madden, T.J., Fehle, F., & Fournier, S. (2006) "Brands matter: An empirical demonstration of the creation of shareholder value through branding", *Journal of the Academy of Marketing Science*, 34(2), 224–235.

MIT Technology Review (2017) "MIT's Lego Legacy: Iconic toy maker supports learning through play", www.technologyreview.com/s/609588/mits-lego-legacy/

Nambisan, S. (2002) "Designing virtual customer environments for new product development: Toward a theory", *Academy of Management Review*, 27(3), 392–413.

Needham, C., & Carr, S. (2009) *Co-Production-an Emerging Evidence Base for Adult Social Care Transformation: Research Briefing*. London: Social Care Institute for Excellence.

Ng, I., & Briscoe, G.(2012) "Value, variety and viability: New business models for co-creation in out-come-based contracts" Working Paper. Coventry: Warwick Manufacturing Group. Service Systems Research Group Working Paper Series (Number 06/12).

Nysveen, H., Pedersen, P.E., & Skard, S. (2013) "Brand experiences in service organizations: Exploring the individual effects of brand experience dimensions", *Journal of Brand Management*, 20(5), 404–423.

O'Cass, A., & Ngo, L.V. (2011) "Examining the firm's value creation process: A managerial perspective of the firm's value offering strategy and performance", *British Journal of Management*, 22(4), 646–671.

O'Lenski, S. (2017) "Top alternative forms of experiential marketing that drive engagement", *Forbes*, 14th Dec, www.forbes.com/sites/steveolenski/2017/12/14/top-alternative-forms-of-experiential-marketing-that-drive-engagement/#d66563059175

Patient Innovation (2019) "Patient innovation, sharing solutions, improving life", https://patient-innovation.com

Payne, A., & Holt, S. (2001) "Diagnosing customer value: Integrating the value process and relationship marketing", *British Journal of Management*, 12(2), 159–182.

Porter, M. (2011) *Competitive Advantage of Nations: Creating and Sustaining Superior Performance* (Vol. 2). New York: The Free Press.

Prahalad, C.K., & Ramaswamy, V. (2000) "Co-opting customer competence", *Harvard Business Review*, 78(1), 79–90.

Prahalad, C.K., & Ramaswamy, V. (2004) "Co-creating unique value with customers", *Strategy & Leadership*, 32(3), 4–9.

Ramaswamy, V., & Gouillart, F.J. (2010) *The Power of Co-Creation: Build It with Them to Boost Growth, Productivity, and Profits*. New York: Simon and Schuster.

Ramaswamy, V., & Ozcan, K. (2016) "Brand value co-creation in a digitalized world: An integrative framework and research implications", *International Journal of Research in Marketing*, 33(1), 93–106.

Romero, D., & Molina, A. (2011) "Collaborative networked organisations and customer communities: Value co-creation and co-innovation in the networking era", *Production Planning & Control*, 22(5–6), 447–472.

Rowe, P. (2017) "Beyond Uber and Airbnb: The social economy of collaborative consumption", *Social Media and Society*, 3(2), https://journals.sagepub.com/doi/full/10.1177/2056305117706784

Santos, G., Murmura, F., & Bravi, L. (2018) "Fabrication laboratories: The development of new business models with new digital technologies", *Journal of Manufacturing Technology Management*, 29(8), 1332–1357.

Seale, B. (2016) "Patients as partners: Building collaborative relationships among professionals, patients, carers and communities", www.kingsfund.org.uk/publications/patients-partners

Seebohm, P., Gilchrist, A., & Morris, D. (2012) "Bold but balanced: How community development contributes to mental health and inclusion", *Community Development Journal*, 47(4), 473–490.

Shah, J., Smith, S., & Vargas-Hernandez, N. (2003) "Metrics for measuring ideation effectiveness", *Design Studies*, 24(2), 111–134.

Shaw, M., & Mayo, M. (eds.) (2016) *Class, Inequality and Community Development*. Bristol: Policy Press.

Sholar, J. (2014) "Debating the sharing economy", www.tellus.org/pub/Schor_Debating_the_Sharing_Economy.pdf

Storbacka, K., Frow, P., Nenonen, S., & Payne, A. (2012) "Designing business models for value co-creation", in *Toward a Better Understanding of the Role of Value in Markets and Marketing*, Review of Marketing Research, Vol. 9, pp. 51–78. Bingley: Emerald Group Publishing.

Todnem By, R. (2005) "Organisational change management: A critical review", *Journal of Change Management*, 5(4), 369–380.

Trimble, A. (2015) "A new relationship with patients and communities?", www.kingsfund.org.uk/blog/2015/03/new-relationship-patients-and-communities

Yachin, J. (2018) "The 'customer journey': Learning from customers in tourism experience encounters", *Tourism Management Perspectives*, 28, 210–210.

Von Hippel, E. (2005) *Democratizing Innovation*. Cambridge, MA: MIT Press.

20 Service innovation and transformation

The case of WeChat

Yun Chen and Wu Zhao

Preface

Business innovation is closely associated with the enterprise boundary, focusing on internal control to carry out innovation activities and use internal innovation resources. But this format faces the challenge of knowledge dispersion, information dissemination, personnel mobility, product/service commercialisation acceleration etc. So, breaking the closed innovation paradigm and changing the way business value grows has gradually become one of the most important issues across the world. Innovation research direction has changed internationally to globalisation, popularisation, R&D outsourcing, user innovation etc. (Herstad et al. 2014). These have gradually become important driving forces for future enterprise development and economic growth.

20.1 Innovation and transformation

There has been much research relating to open innovation, most of it focusing on the strategic level (Curley & Salmelin 2018; Enkel et al. 2010; Goldman & Gabriel 2005; Kim & Kim 2018). In this chapter we transform this perspective by conducting an in-depth analysis of Tencent's WeChat business open service innovation practice case from a micro perspective. Through nearly 10 years of development, WeChat has evolved from a simple instant text and voice messaging software to a multi-agent participating multilateral platform and now towards a business ecosystem (Sun & Niu 2016). In the transition from communications platform to business ecosystem, open innovation has been a key enabling factor. This chapter walks through the different strategies WeChat adopted at different stages for its successful evolution into an innovative organisation ecosystem. The chapter also looks at the synergy mechanism in the ecosystem that positively supports the sustainable growth of WeChat.

Tencent CEO Huateng Ma emphasised the concept of "connection", connecting people, people and equipment, equipment and equipment, services and services, and people and services. Through this extensive and extensive "connection" in many fields, WeChat has realised new business models from various channels, products, marketing, services and processes and has built a new open service innovation platform. Tencent's development process reveals the process of enterprise open service innovation and opens up the black box of an enterprise's open service innovation process. This development reveals how organisations can better utilise a platform's advantages, innovate resources from users inside and outside the enterprise, and achieve allocative efficiency. WeChat open service

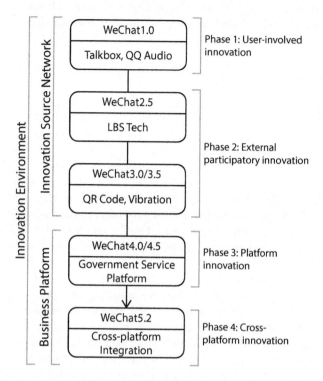

Figure 20.1 WeChat innovation evolution process and synergy mechanism

innovation involves four phases with support for three synergy mechanisms – innovation environment, innovation-source interactive network and business platform (Figure 20.1).

20.2   Case study – Tencent's WeChat

Tencent, founded in 1998, is an Internet-based technology and cultural enterprise based in Shenzhen, China. Its mission is to "improve the quality of life through internet value-added services that connect everything". Guided by its "user oriented" business philosophy, Tencent achieves its mission via the delivery of integrated Internet solutions to over one billion people. WeChat, one of Tencent's core platform services, officially launched on January 18, 2011. It has been in a leading position in the domestic development and is very representative of the industry. According to "WeChat User Data Statistics Report 2015", WeChat monthly active users (MAU) reached 549 million on more than 90% of smartphones in more than 200 countries around the world.

20.2.1   Dynamic evolution analysis of WeChat open service innovation

Tencent WeChat products have been different during different periods of their development. From the initial product prototype to the mature product service, in-depth understanding of its dynamic evolution process provides a realistic reference for enterprises.

Based on case study analysis, the evolution process is defined as having four stages: user-involved innovation, external participatory innovation, platform innovation and cross-platform innovation.

Phase 1: User-involved innovation

In this phase, the WeChat team focused on user management, based on product-design concepts, to carry out small-scale auxiliary innovation so that user knowledge leads innovation. This phase also lays the foundation for open service innovation.

User involvement in the innovation can improve the quality of service development by reducing uncertainty in innovation (Bosch-Sijtsema & Bosch 2015). The concept of "prosumer" refers to the dual role of producer and user (Ritzer et al. 2012). Many large organisations have adopted this concept and integrated it into their strategy; for example, Nokia established interactive relationships with users to promote the development of Symbian's ICT ecosystem, while "Customer – First" is emphasised in Alibaba. Innovating by working with customers not only deepens customer relationships but also advances early product innovation (Chapter 19).

The development of WeChat at this stage was mainly focused on the instant messaging function. Since its original version had no unique selling point and was similar to other products on the market, it was not successful. As a result, the WeChat team changed its thinking and paid attention to their early users (or lead users). Understanding lead users can help enterprises better grasp potential demand and development trends. The WeChat team cooperated with lead users through its community to optimise product performance. Through this form of user participation, the WeChat team extended its knowledge about the communications market, products and services, as well as the precise communication needs of users. In early 2011, TalkBox (WeChat 1.1) was released with instant voice messaging. This version was the outcome of user innovation. Drawing on user feedback, adjustments were made to the voice intercom function from its original version. The voice intercom function uses distance-sensing tech to turn the speaker on or off according to the distance between people's ear and the phone. This function change improved user experience.

Phase 2: External participatory innovation

During this phase the WeChat team relied on the "outside-in" innovation paradigm, participating with external innovation sources and drawing external thoughts inwards to integrate with the internal technology development. This phase facilitated the development of new markets with technology spillover. This phase also provides the foundation to further future platform innovation.

External participation occurs when external ideas break through the boundaries of the organisation and enables absorption and integration with internal sources to achieve innovation. On 3 August 2011, WeChat team released WeChat 2.5. The main feature of this version was the implementation of the distance social mode based on location-based service (LBS). The innovation source was the Korean EL software. With the support of LBS technology, the EL system can list the geographical location of users. Inspired by this idea, WeChat 2.5 also breaks through the acquaintance social model and uses LBS technology to realize the combination of location socialisation and stranger social interaction. On 1 October 2011, WeChat 3.0 was released, adding the "shake" feature. This function is the expansion and deepening of stranger social interaction, which allows random socialisation and further enriches the user experience and enhances the entertainment elements of the system. At the end of 2011, WeChat3.5 added a QR-code function to expand social circles through the scanning of a QR code card. These two functions draw on SHAKE IT and QR codes from Japanese LINE software. At the same time, the WeChat team focused on sound and visual design in order to bring it in line with the user's social interests in the context of Chinese culture.

All these three functions are popular functions of WeChat and reveal the successful integration of internal and external ideas and resources to promote innovation.

Phase 3: Platform innovation

The WeChat team established a new platform for government services. Collaborating with government, which faces the ever-increasing and rapidly growing demand for online services, this phase did not just promote service innovation in the WeChat platform but also facilitated the construction of a smart city and the improvement of government service quality and efficiency.

Establishing a platform on which other sectors rely is critical to integrating external strengths and transforming the business model of open service innovation (Chesbrough & Crowther 2010). When a platform has user stickiness, it will attract more investment and enhance the value of the platform which produces a virtuous circle (Yun et al. 2017). The business platform can be understood in terms of both the scale and scope of the economy:

- Economic scale: The growth of transactions and the increase of data will improve the scale of the economy. Based on huge amounts of user data, important information such as user preferences, user types and user purchasing patterns can be analysed. This provides the possibility for personalised services and targeted advertising. These advantages also facilitate the development of other business functions within the enterprise
- Economic scope: Having diversity of services reduces costs and increases revenue. When services meet the diverse needs of users, they also create more benefits for the enterprise. This attracts the participation of other organisations and directly expands the platform

WeChat 4.0 and 5.0 reflects its extension to becoming a one-stop platform for other services (e.g. city-wide services) and goes beyond simple social-networking capability. Services provided on the WeChat platform include medical care, household administration, immigration, taxation, vehicle services, tourism and transportation. The platform was first released in Guangzhou Province in December 2014. At the end of 2015, it had been launched in 72 provinces and 14 cities with more than 3,000 services providing 27 types of services involving public security, traffic control, medical care etc., with over 150 million users. Platform innovation has had a significant impact on WeChat.

Phase 4: Cross-platform innovation

At this phase, the WeChat team took advantage of specialisation and platformisation to collaborate more broadly. This widening out of participation has had a positive effect on the development of the business platform and continues to create and deliver more commercial value.

The essence of cross-platform innovation is to achieve platform agglomeration and value expansion by connecting with external platforms through an existing platform. Based on WeChat's large user base and social network, WeChat Wallet (included in WeChat 5.2) has expanded the Chinese e-payment market. In 2015, WeChat adopted a cross-platform model, combining the WeChat red envelope (one of the core Wallet system functions) with the Spring Festival Evening platform. This new service experience did not just provide support for WeChat Wallet promotion but also enhanced interaction with the audiences for the Spring Festival Gala through the WeChat platform. The per capita viewing time during the Spring Festival Gala extended from 149 minutes in 2014 to 155.5 minutes in 2015. The audience also participated with more depth during the Spring Festival Evening. During New Year's Eve 2015, the total number of WeChat red envelopes sent and received exceeded one billion. At this stage, WeChat broke the boundaries of its own platform and realised cross-platform integration. After that, on Chinese White Valentine's Day, 400 million WeChat red envelopes were sent and received; on Children's Day the figure totalled 500 million, and during the Mid-Autumn Festival the number reached 2.2 billion. On New Year's Eve 2016, the peak of the WeChat red envelopes was at 12:05 am, when 2.4 million red envelopes were issued and 6.2 million red envelopes were opened in this single minute. The total number of WeChat red envelopes sent during the day was 2.31 billion.

The establishment of cross-platform cooperation has injected significant value into WeChat. A large number of users participating in the WeChat red envelope activity cooperated with various aspects of the platform. This has promoted the WeChat platform, which also has had a profound impact on the development of Tencent's mobile payment business.

WeChat's dynamic evolution highlights the essence of different innovation stages to produce a successful transformation. However, the innovation cannot be successfully implemented without a suitable environment.

20.3   The synergistic mechanism of WeChat's open service innovation

Macdonald-Smith et al. (2017) see service innovation as involving multi-stakeholders and joint interactions to form a service innovation network that promote innovation. The synergy mechanism is to study how each subsystem achieves synergy. The synergy mechanism of WeChat includes three aspects: Innovation Environment, Business Platform and Innovation-Source Interactive Network (Figure 20.1). The innovation environment promotes the development and improvement of innovation activities and provides basic support for innovation activities. The business platform is a redefinition and innovation of the business model by the organisation, extending the business value by establishing a platform that other sectors rely on. The innovation-source network is a mix of internal and external innovation sources that breaks the organisational boundaries for new interactions and cooperation.

WeChat innovation environment

The WeChat business group is one of Tencent's headquarters business and is within the policy circle of Guangzhou and Shenzhen. Assessed by the Institute of Finance and

Economics of the Chinese Academy of Social Sciences, Shenzhen ranked first in China's urban comprehensive economic competitiveness index, and Guangzhou ranked fifth. The two regions not only have high economic output per unit area but also have the lowest energy consumption. This demonstrates their innovative entrepreneurship and ecological sustainability. In addition, neighbouring Hong Kong, Macao and Taiwan have provided greater support for the transformation rate from the perspective of its geographical advantages. In addition, Shenzhen and Guangzhou are both immigrant cities, and the population is multi-dimensioned. This has fostered its inclusive, open and cultural urban character, which has a potential positive impact on the formation of an innovative atmosphere. Its diverse population promotes tolerance and understanding among people, and it also fosters an innovative and healthy ecosystem. The innovation environment provides the necessary policy support, institutional guarantee, cultural atmosphere and technical conditions for WeChat team innovation.

WeChat innovation-source network

The innovation-source network is the core of the WeChat team, including users, internal and external organisations. From the perspective of internal organization structure, the WeChat team is divided into product operation group, development group, client UI group and marketing expansion group. All of their members are involved in innovation: for example, the product operation group is mainly responsible for the overall planning and basic operation of WeChat products, thinking and optimization; the development team covers both internal and external technologies in the terms of the research environment; the client UI group focuses on the visual and interactive design of WeChat products; and the marketing development group selects the appropriate cooperation mode and channel development and gathers market information and user needs. The interaction network with external parties is mainly reflected in the fact that the WeChat team actively extracts external innovation sources from users and other organisations to enhance the innovation of products, which is mainly reflected in the user-involved innovation stage and external participation.

WeChat business platform

The business platform reflects innovation at a micro level and is the basic mechanism for innovation value creation. WeChat has worked with various platforms to establish multi-industry cooperation in different fields such as finance, city services and games. The huge user base and gradually expanding platform prove the success of the WeChat platform business model. First, as the user base increases, it will help users get a better social experience. Therefore, the increase of their own network nodes and the expansion of network scale will enhance the effectiveness of each user. Second, as the number of users increases, the service providers will be improved. These benefits attract more suppliers who, in turn, provide users with more diversified services and improve user effectiveness. The gathering of friends in WeChat has generated platform dependence, which makes the user have certain stickiness. Therefore, the WeChat platform has attracted more and more users to use the platform by providing free basic communication services, and in return, the increase in the user base has promoted the efficiency of the platform. In addition, at the other end of the WeChat platform, a large number of third-party service providers offer users a diverse range of products and services because of the strong stickiness of the WeChat business platform. With the increase of suppliers, the breadth and commercial value of WeChat platform services have also been gradually expanded.

Based on the analysis of the innovation synergy mechanism, it can be seen that having full interaction between internal teams, users and many external organisations is at the core of successful open service innovation.

20.4   Lessons from WeChat

This chapter discussed the open service platform innovation, using Tencent's WeChat business as a case study. It has provided the deep insight of its digital transformation process in terms of phrases and synergy mechanism. Based on the analysis of the case study, it can be seen that open service platform innovation and transformation is a dynamic evolution process that benefits from a synergistic support mechanism. The interaction between users, internal teams and external organisations is essential to the success of this kind of digital transformation. On the other hand, both business platforms and innovation-source networks need to be developed and matched with policy support, technical conditions and cultural atmosphere in the innovation environment. The development of the innovation-source network directly affects the realisation and improvement of the business platform, while, in return, the business platform has essentially affected the evolution and development of the innovation-source interactive network.

Key takeaways

- Innovation requires a combination of optimal internal and external circumstances
- Inside the organisation, policy support, technical conditions and the right cultural environment are required
- Incremental innovation provides opportunities for review and for user engagement
- External innovations must be managed but can provide significant benefit

References

Bosch-Sijtsema, P., & Bosch, J. (2015) "User Involvement throughout the Innovation Process in High-Tech Industries: User Involvement in Innovation Process", *Journal of Product Innovation Management*, 32(5), 793–807.

Chesbrough, H., & Crowther, A.K. (2010) "Beyond high tech: Early adopters of open innovation in other industries", *R & D Management*, 36(3), 229–236.

Curley, M., & Salmelin, B. (2018) *Open Innovation 2.0 the New Mode of Digital Innovation for Prosperity and Sustainability*. Cham: Springer.

Enkel, E., Gassmann, O., & Chesbrough, H. (2010) "Open R&D and open innovation: Exploring the phenomenon", *R & D Management*, 39(4), 311–316.

Goldman, R., & Gabriel, R. (2005) *Innovation Happens Elsewhere Open Source as Business Strategy*. Boston: Morgan Kaufmann.

Herstad, S., Aslesen, H., & Ebersberger, B. (2014) "On industrial knowledge bases, commercial opportunities and global innovation network linkages", *Research Policy*, 43(3), 495–504.

Kim, H., & Kim, E. (2018) "How an open innovation strategy for commercialization affects the firm performance of Korean healthcare IT SMEs", *Sustainability*, 10(7), 2476.

Macdonald-Smith, C., Price, A., Holch, P., & Watson, E. (2017) "Service innovation symposium", *Psycho-Oncology*, 26(S2), 29.

Ritzer, G., Dean, P., & Jurgenson, N. (2012) "The coming of age of the prosumer", *American Behavioral Scientist*, 56(4), 379–398.

Sun, B., & Niu, C. (2016) "Design and implementation of property management system based on WeChat public platform", *Wireless Internet Technology*, http://en.cnki.com.cn/Article_en/CJFDTotal-WXHK201619059.htm

Yun, J., Won, D., Park, K., Yang, J., & Zhao, X. (2017) "Growth of a platform business model as an entrepreneurial ecosystem and its effects on regional development", *European Planning Studies*, 25(5), 805–826.

Part IV

Assessing your success

21 Permanently embed innovation into your organisation

Always interconnected

Alex Fenton and Naomi Timperley

Preface

Innovation is a pivotal ingredient for the successful digitally enabled, data-driven, people-focused organisation. An innovation ecosystem must be ever-present in ways that echo the demands of continuous external and internal change. Building a sustainable innovation ecosystem within the organisation is central to its long-term success and the realisation of its vision.

21.1 The innovation ecosystem

Strategic digital transformation is not directly about digital technology but about the way in which digital technology allows organisations to solve problems and improve. Strategic digital transformation involves permanently and sustainably embedding an environment that is conducive to innovation by having a positive impact on the organisational system to fully leverage change. It takes advantage of the opportunities derived from the speed of interconnected digital technology and its accelerating impact across society in a strategic, prioritised way and with self-awareness of present and future shifts. Digital transformation has impacts across all organisations including governments, public-sector agencies and organisations that are involved in tackling social challenges such as pollution or aging populations. For example, "In some countries, such as Japan, digital transformation aims to impact all aspects of life with the country's Society 5.0 initiative, which goes far beyond the limited Industry 4.0 vision in other countries" (iScoop n.d.).

Creating a data-driven, people-focused organisation is key to creating an innovative environment that is flexible enough to meet the challenges of the always changing VUCA world. This chapter focuses on how to create a sustainable innovation ecosystem that brings long-term organisational success and supports the realisation of its vision. We present a prototype model for any organisational innovation ecosystem. The prototype system contains the elements of colleges and universities, industry, non-government organisations and government as well as investment and funding (Figure 21.1). Deploying constant iterations and revisions of these elements is crucial to the ongoing sustainability of the innovation environment in the organisation.

For example, universities and colleges provide access to new generations of talent through student projects, graduate placements and other focused and programme-specific features. Research intensive organisations, including universities, offer expertise in particular areas of knowledge. This embedded expertise can be exchanged and expressed in many forms, including bespoke and collaborative research. Industry engagement has never been

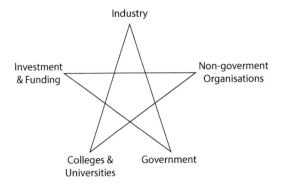

Figure 21.1 The innovation ecosystem

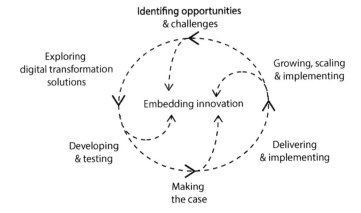

Figure 21.2 The process of embedding innovation, adapted from seven stages of innovation
Source: After Nesta 2019

more important to higher education institutions. Institutions are working with industry to (re)design programmes of study to ensure they are producing capable and employable graduates and to incorporate engaging real-world learning experiences. Impactful and industry-meaningful research is also increasingly important to academic researchers, with funding and performance measurement being assessed on these criteria. This means that universities are keen and willing to work with individual organisations to support the development of their innovation ecosystem.

21.2   Embedding innovation

Embedding innovation is a continuous and ongoing activity, but the process will most usually begin with the identification of opportunities or specific problems that require a solution (Figure 21.2). Undertaking research (Chapters 4, 6 and 9) to identify potential candidate solutions and opportunities progresses the activity. From here, a specific solution can be trialled, developed, tested and compared with benchmarks or previous performance. Once a solution is in trial and producing positive results, the case can be made for the commitment of further resources and upscaling the innovation so that it can be delivered across the organisation and permanently embedded. During each of these increments, elements of innovative thinking patterns are also being introduced and embedded into the organisation. By embedding the drive and mindset to innovate, each future cycle of delivering an innovative solution into the organisation becomes marginally easier and normalised.

21.3   Funding

Digital transformation and innovation requires funding. Although the situation will vary between individual countries, there are generally pools of funding available through innovation schemes that encourage industry and research organisations to work more closely together in order to extract maximum value from the research organisations and release the beneficial outcomes of research into the commercial world. A combination of organisational and external funding streams can be used to support innovation. The involvement of funding bodies often brings the additional benefit of knowledgeable and experienced people who assist to ensure that the external funding is applied to maximum effect and that the support delivers the intended outcomes. Universities also have access to funds (unavailable to commercial organisations directly) that enable the support of innovative projects.

In the UK, Innovate UK provides funding ranging in scale and funding from small short-term activities to significant projects that attempt to tackle common and 'big' societal issues. Often, these projects require match funding depending on the size of the company and depending on the required funding amount. This approach on occasion requires a consortium of multiple partners to support the planned innovation. A longstanding and successful example of this funding approach are KTPs (Knowledge Transfer Partnerships) (Gov.UK 2017). The scheme started in 1975 as the Teaching Company Scheme (TCS) and was rebranded as KTPs in 2003. To unlock KTP funding, a business contributes 33% – 50% per cent of the project cost and through Innovate UK the government funds the remainder. It is a well-established way for a university, organisation and a recent graduate to come together on a specific project that is the catalyst for an innovative product or service based on a new business model. Working with research organisations and drawing on support through schemes such as KTP is regarded as a vital component of the UK's current industrial strategy (Figure 21.3). At an organisational level, the KTP scheme is a successful and well-trodden way to innovate in all sectors.

Figure 21.3 Word cloud generated from the UK Government green paper "Building our industrial strategy"
Source: Gov.UK 2017

21.4 Innovative digital technologies and how to embed them

Strategic digital transformation strategy and innovation is about much more than just using specific technologies or a digital marketing plan. It is important to horizon scan and assess current trends in order to keep a focus on the future (Chapter 7). Mature digital organisations focus on integrating technologies to transform how they function overall, while less digitally mature ones will use individual technologies to solve discrete problems as they arise or as they reach a level of pain that necessitates a solution. Strategy drives innovation, not technology.

To reinforce this perspective of strategically driven transformation, it is appropriate to position current technologies within the innovation ecosystem for the value they can bring to a strategy. This perspective is in direct contrast to simply listing the functions of current technologies and then endeavouring to determine a meaningful organisational use case for them. Any list of technologies is inevitably already out-of-date, and there are undoubtedly now newer technologies that could be added to this list. As two examples of technology that may justify inclusion here, blockchain technology and cryptocurrencies promise to have a major impact on payments, and trust relationships are already deployed in applications for specific sectors and have proven to bring additional capability with the right use case. However, while AI and machine learning have matured rapidly to become accessible in directly useful ways for SMEs and other organisations, there is currently less evidence of the immediately useful and strategic value of blockchain. It is an exercise for the reader to create and maintain a more up-to-date list featuring the technologies that are strategically relevant to your own organisation.

21.4.1 *Social media*

Most organisations are familiar with the value of social media channels such as Facebook, Twitter and Instagram. Beyond this 'normal' list, though, there are many niche social media channels. Social media can be used in many different ways that go beyond straight advertising. Social media can be used to reach out to any audience in highly targeted groups or individually; it can be also used to horizon scan, for internal communication and to co-create. The selection of an appropriate combination of channels will depend upon available resources, objectives, location and target audiences.

For example, China has an entirely separate social media ecosystem with different channels than those used elsewhere. The starting point for social media is to start with a small number of channels, focusing on relevant content that interacts with the right audience, build up the organisation's social capital and then grow the activity outwards to other relevant channels. Social media is also used to effectively interconnect with people within the organisation. Using a familiar consumer-friendly interface reduces friction in an organisational context and gains all the advantages of social media without the need to reinvent or introduce an entirely new channel (that may be met with resistance). Social media channels also offer up additional data to channel owners that can be analysed to gain insight about the organisation and its offerings.

21.4.2 *AI and machine learning*

Artificial intelligence and machine learning use computing power and algorithms to mimic the cognitive functions of humans. When machines carry out tasks that are based on algorithms that 'learn' in an 'intelligent' autonomous manner, that is AI. AI is often presented in fiction as being in direct opposition to the human race, and these is some evidence for this criticism. *Home Deus* (Harari 2016) documents the way in which global finance is largely controlled by AI, and this control will eventually result in many existing jobs being lost. Elon Musk too has been a critic of the increasing over-reliance on automation and AI in particular (Martin 2019)

However, in contrast to the sensational extrapolations, many observers are moving their expectations from a situation of massive job loss to significant job evolution as organisations find better ways for people to work in conjunction with these technologies. In many ways, AI and machine learning is at its most effective when combined with the higher level analytical skills and decision making. "Given the likelihood that many jobs will change rather than disappear, organisations need to understand the new skills required. In a recent McKinsey survey of executives at companies with revenues of more than $100 million, 66% of respondents said "addressing potential skills gaps related to automation & digitisation"" (Barro & Davenport 2019).

21.4.3 Internet of Things

The term Internet of Things (IoT) dates back to 1999 and has become more popular as the volume and variety of the various devices connected to the Internet continues to increase. A poll by Consumer Affairs shows that although 70% of people owned an IoT device, only 20% had a firm grasp of the meaning of IoT. "The internet is no longer a web [of computers] that we connect to. Instead, it's a computerised, networked, and interconnected world that we live in. This is the future, and what we're calling the Internet of Things" (Schneier 2017).

IoT devices are made 'smart' by their connectedness and noisy output of data. An increasing number of diverse devices are now connected. These include smartphones, laptops, vehicles, wristbands, cameras, light bulbs, Alexa and Google Home devices and smart appliances such as microwaves and fridges. In fact, in 2015, there were 15.4 billion devices estimated to be part of the IoT, and this number is forecast to grow to 75.4 billion by 2025 (*ACHR News* 2016).

The deployment of high-speed 5G services will also play a major role in the continued growth of IoT. As well as increasing Internet speeds, 5G also increases the quantity of IoT devices that can be connected in one area, which provides new opportunities for retail, smart cities, driverless cars and supporting the IoT ecosystem. IoT can be embedded into organisations in a variety of ways. Using wristbands to aid internal people communication, creating a community by measuring fitness levels or developing entirely new IoT products could form part of the innovation in a digital transformation strategy.

21.4.4 Smartphone and apps

Ownership of 'smart' mobile phones continues to grow on a global scale. The number of mobile app downloads in 2017 was 178.1 billion and is forecast to be 258.2 billion by 2020. Revenue-wise, this will equate to 188.9 billion dollars in revenue in 2020 (Clement 2017). Apps (or smartphone applications) are programs that run on the smartphone and can take advantage of the capabilities of the phone such as the camera, GPS positioning, microphone or accelerometer. These are often known as native apps. In contrast, web apps are actually mobile friendly or responsive websites that run through a browser interface on the mobile. While web apps are typically quicker, cheaper to develop and easier to maintain than native apps, they are less capable of using the built-in capabilities of the phone. The choice of native app, web app or a combination (a hybrid app) should be based on the goals and budget of the specific project. It may be that a web app or mobile-friendly website is a good starting place to introduce the objectives of a digital transformation project.

21.4.5 *Virtual and augmented reality*

Virtual reality (VR) relies upon immersing people into a simulated world. The other related technology of Augmented reality (AR) uses devices such as smartphones and tablets to overlay graphics into the real world, creating a combined hybrid interactive 'augmented reality' experience. The growth of these technologies has created a new wave of interest in VR and AR. The overall market in the US alone grew from $6.1 billion in 2016 to $27 billion in 2018. By 2022, it is predicted to be worth $209.2 billion, as these technologies move from being for niche audiences such as gamers to the mainstream (Liu 2019). AR's rise has been driven by the attention given to it through the success of games such as *Pokemon Go*. Meanwhile, VR has been given a boost with improved technologies from suppliers such as Playstation 4. Facebook also purchased the originally crowdfunded Oculus Rift platform and, alongside improving the hardware, have also developed Facebook Spaces. Although rendered virtual worlds such as Second Life have existed since 2003, mainstream social networks such as Facebook are now evolving their 2D 'flatland' experience into 3D social media. Existing examples and case studies around existing niche applications coupled with low cost VR or AR equipment show how these technologies will become relevant to a wider range of organisation in the future.

21.5   The internal incubator

Accelerators and incubators bring together and support aspiring entrepreneurs and fledgling business ideas. They have become synonymous with, and symbols for, the growth in the number of startups and of startup 'culture', development and innovation. Both concepts incorporate the objective of rapidly growing startups but are often misinterpreted as synonyms. 'Innovation labs' are also seen as being a source for startup development and growth but are distinct from accelerators and incubators, as they tend to be delivered by larger corporations and have a more inward-looking focus.

The incubator is a space for ideas and innovation that drives innovation. The presence of incubators is becoming increasingly common within organisations of all sizes. Finding the strengths of people inside and outside and surfacing their passions and motivations is beneficial for the organisation and supports staff retention and development (Chapter 6). The internal incubator is a key mechanism for becoming more people-focused in this way while also producing intrapreneurs and new ideas and motivating people to take responsibility. Entrepreneurial leadership practices enables people to achieve more and increases their satisfaction.

Great moments of innovation can happen with relatively few resources. People with your organisation know who the customers are, they know what questions to ask and to solve existing issues with products or services. People within the organisation can put themselves in the shoes of the customer – often because they are also customers. Innovating organisations understand the importance of moving with responsive agility, and remaining aware of emerging trends, competitors and new opportunities is all first nature.

By treating every interaction as an opportunity to grow insight, an innovating organisation is also a learning organisation. Take what has been learned – through observation, interacting with extremes, interviewing and listening – is all fuel for innovation.

Ideas remain ideas until they become actions. The design thinking skills of ideation, prototyping and rapid iteration all enable actions to be drawn out of ideas. Using experimentation to learn from failure and moving from incremental to radical innovation approaches can all quickly transform an idea into a new product or service. Using rapid prototyping and getting tangible output from ideas help to work through the kinks and get to better usable solutions faster. Design thinking isn't just a method but can fundamentally change the fabric of an organisation.

21.6   Why collaboration is important

Collaboration leads to many new opportunities that enable goals to be achieved more rapidly and encourages growth within the organisation. Collaboration is also about bringing organisations together. Working with people from different sectors and different backgrounds broadens perspectives and extends the reach of the organisation while also boosting credibility. External investors consider the partnerships that an organisation makes as a tangible measure of credibility and standing. The choice of collaborator can be important too. Funders consider this factor too. Collaborations should reflect the organisational brand sentiments, ethos and goals. In other words, partner with people that bring a positive impact to the organisation.

Successful collaboration starts with good networking, and while 'natural' networkers may regard what they do as common sense, there are nine broad principles for working with the right people (Table 21.1)

Do not be afraid. Startups are often reluctant to talk about their own business. The result is a lack of open conversations, information sharing and learning. As a result, 'shy' organisations miss out on making valuable connections or the prospect of creating lasting partnerships. Don't hide behind concerns over intellectual property; a networking conversation does not need to become some form of full disclosure. Take advantage of natural partnerships. Often the obvious connections are the closest and easiest collaborations to broker. Getting involved with the local communities, schools, colleges or universities is the best starting points for the longest lasting relationships.

Consider the key target market. If other organisations from other sectors are targeting the same audience, there are potentials for unusual but mutually beneficial partnerships. Collaboration of this type helps everyone involved to achieve their goals.

As an organisation, be open to having conversations and openly asking for help. This form of openness and boldness is rare in British culture and across much of the English-speaking world. However, innovation works best if it is not conducted in remote isolation; reach across existing networks and ask people if they can help.

Get a mentor. Mentoring can make a real difference. Mentoring advice and support is especially good for learning how to build good connections and how to collaborate, both internally and externally.

Get positive reinforcement. Build an organisation with people who support one another and lift each other up. Working with like-minded people builds a mutually supportive drive and ambition to achieve that cannot be artificially created.

Table 21.1 The nine principles of collaboration success

1. Be transparent	There is a difference between telling the truth and being transparent. Transparency is about telling the truth before you're asked and divulging important information along the way. Transparency builds and encourages trust (Chapter 12).
2. Say what you are going to do and follow through	No one wants to collaborate with someone who drops the ball. Good collaborators know how long it will take them to get something done and then deliver on time. They can be counted on and because of that, people love working with them.
3. Allow for a little give and take	Collaboration isn't about getting what you want all the time. People will be more likely to collaborate to help you if you collaborate when they need help as well.
4. Listen to understand, not to respond	People like to be heard and know their ideas and thoughts are being taken into consideration. Effective collaborators ensure they are listening (truly listening) to their partners and change direction when it makes sense based on this feedback.
5. Stick to your beliefs	Great collaborators are passionate about their work and know what success looks like. They have high standards and morals. Both of these attributes make them exciting to work with. When something needs to be done, or a moral decision needs to be made, there is no compromise or easy way out. Good collaboration is about doing what is right.
6. Know which battles to fight	Life isn't about being right all of the time. Effective collaborators know this and will let go when they could 'take it or leave it'. Good collaborators know when others are being passionate and compromise where possible.
7. Be authentic	People expect to work with the real person. Being an effective collaborator means knowing yourself, what you stand for and how your talents, beliefs and values benefit the challenge at hand. Others will appreciate and trust that you will always give honest feedback.
8. Be kind	There's a lot to be done. Everybody is busy. Remember that there is a way to get things done without making enemies along the way. People work harder, smarter and faster when they like who they are working with. Kindness goes a long way.
9. Step up	Collaboration is about occasionally going above and beyond in unexpected ways. When people know you will step up when needed, the collaboration is much easier.

Key takeaways

- Digital transformation requires the permanent embedding of innovation
- An innovating environment acts positively on the organisational system
- The wider innovation ecosystem is a collaborative environment drawing on multiple organisations and support
- Organisations working with research institutions can collaborate to unlock funding for innovation
- Various technologies exist that support digital transformations with the most important criteria being the capacity to solve a problem

References

ACHR News (2016) "75 Billion IoT Devices Predicted by 2025", 22nd April, www.achrnews.com/articles/132303-billion-iot-devices-predicted-by--

Barro, S., & Davenport, T. (2019) "People and Machines: Partners in Innovation", *Sloan Management Review*, Summer, 11th June, https://sloanreview.mit.edu/article/people-and-machines-partners-in-innovation/

Clement, J. (2017) "Mobile app usage: Statistics & facts", *Statista*, www.statista.com/topics/1002/mobile-app-usage/

Gov.UK (2017) *Building Our Industrial Strategy*, UK Government, https://assets.publishing.service.gov.uk/government/uploads/system/uploads/attachment_data/file/611705/building-our-industrial-strategy-green-paper.pdf

Harari, Y. (2016) *Homo Deus: A Brief History of Tomorrow*. London: Harvill Secker.

iScoop (n.d.) "Digital transformation: Online guide to digital business transformation", www.i-scoop.eu/digital-transformation/

Liu, S. (2019) "Forecast augmented (AR) and virtual reality (VR) market size worldwide from 2016 to 2023", *Statista*, www.statista.com/statistics/591181/global-augmented-virtual-reality-market-size/

Martin, S. (2019) "Elon Musk WARNING: Artificial Intelligence could be an 'IMMORTAL DICTATOR'", *The Express*, www.express.co.uk/news/science/1112515/elon-musk-artificial-intelligence-ai-news-google-deepmind

Nesta (2019) "Innovation Methods", www.nesta.org.uk/feature/innovation-methods/

Schneier, B. (2017) "Click here to kill everyone", *NY Mag*, http://nymag.com/intelligencer/2017/01/the-internet-of-things-dangerous-future-bruce-schneier.html

22 Measuring the digital transformation in an organisation

Audit to discover what value was added

Alex Fenton, Wasim Ahmed and Mick Hides

Preface

Reactive organisations move through different strategies and business models with surprising regularity. A mature business with visionary management pauses and reflects to critically assess what has changed and what additional value has been created as a result of their strategic change. Data-driven, people-focused organisations do this with increasing ease and at the same time also rapidly identify new and emerging opportunities. Becoming a self-reflective and self-critical organisation requires a change in collective behaviour that must become an habitual part of "business as usual".

22.1 Avoiding the reactive

In earlier chapters, we explored how the use of data gives better insight into the market, the competition and internal processes. This chapter is a deeper exploration of what it means to be a proactive and digitally mature organisation. This examination is focused through the lens of measuring change and auditing the organisation to determine what value has been added. Any exploration of value must first define what is meant by the term and how this relates to the core mission and vision of the business. In effect, the units of measurement must be defined with an acknowledgement of organisational context. In this way, the meaning of value is a subjective assessment found within the relationship between the customer/consumer and the organisation.

For the customer or consumer, the value is the relationship of perceived benefits set against investment in a product or functionality. In simpler terms, value represents the extent to which they are willing to invest time, effort or money. Even more concisely but more theoretically, it is the use-value of a product or service. Value has a much wider meaning than direct financial investment or financial capital – an important consideration when optimal price points are reaching zero, combined with the rise of free and freemium business models. In addition, raising brand awareness and building social capital are also valid areas to add value to an organisation. Nonetheless, this meaning of value, its exchange value or money-price, is the form of the concept that is most commonly recognised by consumers. A consumer's investment, as opposed to the narrower meanings of payment, cost, money-price or exchange value, is a measure of how much of their time they will commit to the acquisition of an item.

For the organisation, the meaning of value is closely linked with that of the customer/consumer. The link to economic value and the labour theory of value remain influential in shaping organisational perspectives on value creation. These perspectives are also the heritage for the argument made throughout this book regarding people-focused digital transformation. It is through people's labour that value is created, and the measurement of value directly equates to the quantity of labour that has been applied to the creation of the commodity. In a post-industrial sense, this equation can still be evidenced through the application of devices that act as a proxy for the direct labour of people, including technologies such as software and robotics. What becomes more problematic is the question of whether digital technologies are solely a conduit for human labour or whether they act as an amplification device for that labour. Put in another way, do digital technologies create additional value over that of human labour alone? How this relationship between digital technology and labour is understood then becomes a key question for defining the value that is being created by the organisation.

Understanding existing and prospective customer/consumer needs and desires is a significant step in determining use-value (Table 22.1). For any digitally transformed business this means spending time getting to know their customers, understanding what they want and building social capital. Understanding this use-value relates then to organisational determination of the labour expenditure both directly by their people and indirectly through their technology that is required. This direct relationship explains many of the sector-wide disruptions that are the result of new business models where digital technologies have displaced direct human labour and, in doing so, have created additional use-value. Examples of these sectorial disruptions include accommodation sharing, price comparison, social media and ride hailing.

The Uber ride-hailing app mediates direct consumer and driver interactions through their own access to mobile consumer technology with the resulting offer of on-demand transport (for the consumer) and on-demand riders (for the driver). Uber and other

Table 22.1 Examples of creating use-value

Company	What do they do	Use-value example
Uber	Ride-hailing app launched in 2009	Ease of use Lower fares
Liftshare.com	Liftshare.com is a UK-based app extending the same idea to match members looking to car share to save money and reduce environmental impact.	Save money Reduce environmental impact Speed of response
Fitbit Care	Fitbit Care combines wearables, digital interventions and health coaching through the new Fitbit Plus app to deliver a more personalised healthcare experience and better health outcomes through employers, health plans or health systems.	Outsourced health care Centralised expertise
Cybertill Ltd	Cloud-based EPoS system and retail management software for retailers, brands, visitor attractions and charity retailers.	Gift Aid streamlining HMRC compliance
Netflix	Netflix is the world's leading internet entertainment service, with 130 million memberships in over 190 countries enjoying TV series, documentaries and feature films across a wide variety of genres.	Ability to create own viewing schedules Immediate access Multiple devices

ride-hailing apps maximise the productive labour of the driver by reducing waiting time and minimising movement between locations with no riders while simultaneously increasing the use-value to riders by supplying transport more rapidly. Exchange value, the price that the rider pays, is less significant in this perspective than an initial cursory observation might suggest. Pricing is reduced to being a calculated algorithmic outcome determined from this wider assessment of labour and use-value (or supply and demand).

In contrast, the traditional taxi business model involves a human dispatcher manually tracking the location of drivers in relation to the location of waiting riders. The additional human labour required by the traditional model was borne by the dispatcher whose role was to link all the variables of the system together as well as the driver and rider who had to accurately inform the dispatcher of their locations for the system to function correctly. Displacement of this labour with a data-driven solution changes the value relationships in ride-hailing. The displacement of labour is pivoted around the shifting need for robust software development rather than experienced dispatchers.

Uber and other organisations recognise that there is opportunity for further change in the relationship of labour and value within the ride-hailing business. The other key labour displacement in the transport sector will come with the introduction of autonomous vehicles. With the removal of drivers from the value chain, labour is again displaced in favour of sensor and artificial intelligence development.

22.2   Performance assessment

Determining the use-value of a product or service and how this will be perceived by the customer/consumer provides the unit of assessment for measuring the performance of a particular business model. By identifying the primary parameter of customer/consumer time, the 4Vs can then be used to understand each of these four different dimensions of beneficial use-value. Velocity is the most evident dimension of benefit with a product or service enabling user actions to be completed more rapidly and directly marketed as a time-saving device. A product or service could just as readily enable greater volume of action through parallel actions, automation or process reduction. In combination, greater velocity and volume changes a user's time-based actions by making them more productive. Any increases in veracity and variety that a product or service can bring to a user's time can then be regarded as an efficiency advantage (Table 22.2).

Equally important is examination of the organisational structure that supports individual business models. Internal examinations of this type also tend to be reduced to the labour-oriented measures of productivity and efficiency. However, digital transformation and its wider impact on the organisation justifies a further parameter in form of innovation as an equally important consideration. Where efficiency and productivity are generally regarded as measurements of the quality and quantity of an organisation's internal activities, innovation can be seen as the measure of its rate of change. This refers back

Table 22.2 Use-value in terms of efficiency and productivity and the parameters of the 4Vs

Use-Value	Quantity	Quality
Productivity	Volume	Velocity
Efficiency	Variety	Veracity

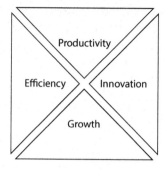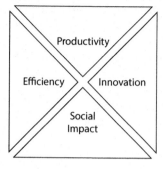

Figure 22.1 Organisational measures of success with growth-oriented or social-impact-oriented strategies

to the importance of the need for organisations to recognise change as a constant in the activities, that digital transformation itself is never a completed project and that one of the key aims for digital transformation is the creation of an innovating internal environment.

A further measure of the organisation's success is the extent to which it achieves its overall goals. This is a consideration of the extent to which an organisation's own activities are in alignment with supporting its mission and vision (Figure 22.1). Public and third-sector organisations will most likely focus on an assessment of the social impact that their work has achieved, whereas a commercial organisation may be focused on some form of growth and often financial growth at its heart. These four variables are considered in combination with the acknowledgement that there is a degree of tension in equally achieving high-quality outcomes among all of these variables simultaneously.

A further challenge to assessing the extent to which an organisation is innovative and has progressed towards achievement of its goals are the ways in which this can be compara-tively measured.

22.3   Being data-driven

Value streaming, a key component of lean management, looks to remove or reduce waste within a process. The availability of data within a digital business enables a more meaning-ful evaluation of the value stream.

The relevance of the data being captured should be clarified at this point. Identifying what data is being captured and how this relates to the value stream is a key element, as it is very easy to be seduced into assessing meaningless data leading to the wrong conclusions.

Prior to implementing a change it is vital to determine the current situation or "as is" status. Knowing the current situation enables the target performance to be determined; this is the "to be" goal. Once the change is underway the data will provide evidence of a successful change as well as demonstrating the stability of the system.

Further examples can be seen in professional and semi-professional sports clubs. Data and change measurement is becoming increasingly critical to achieve competitive advan-tages on and off the pitch. They may employ social listening services to rapidly monitor launches of kits and/or particular services. This insight should then be acted upon; for instance, if a new service receives a particularly negative press then remedial action may be put into place.

Recent years have seen a more sophisticated use of data such as machine learning and artificial intelligence which can be used to predict and extrapolate rich information from data. Sports clubs draw upon millions of data points from players such as diet, training routine and physical activity over previous games in order to predict the possibility of a player becoming injured. Sports clubs often also use data in the player recruitment process. Mistakes in employing the wrong players or team tactics can be costly. Therefore, having the correct systems in place to measure change in complex and shifting landscape internally and externally is fundamental to maintaining the competitive edge.

There are also questionable uses of using digital data within organisations, such as snooping on employees, utilising algorithms to predict employee departure, monitoring web traffic and crawling the Internet to find employee-related information. The methods of monitoring employees for audit purposes is going to increase (Wartzman 2019). They mention controversy over Amazon winning a patent for a wristband that allows for the ultrasonic tracking of an employee's hands in order to monitor the performance of an employee on assigned tasks.

Measuring the right things is far more important than measuring efficiently. The volume of data present within a digital system can be overwhelming, and it is important to identify which data to concentrate on. Multiple customers within a process mean competing values, and any business needs to determine which have priority.

The volume of data being presented needs to be managed to ensure effective assessment. Data analysis involves inspecting, cleansing, transforming and modelling data to allow interpretation and inform decision making. Increasing data-processing capacity and capability transforms the handling of large data sets into instantaneous results. Especially where the results are being viewed by an unskilled audience, any data needs to be translated into a usable form. The simplest version of this involves the use of data visualisations, such as graphs, which can also extend to identifying trends to become a predictive tool in real-time.

A wide range of data-visualisation tools exist and continues to grow, meaning all organisations have access to powerful data-analysis tools. Translating data therefore into visual forms allows a wider range of people to be able to make judgements as well as more skilled data analysts to reveal further details especially around outliers that otherwise may be dismissed as noise. Knowing the location and density of existing members of a service might persuade new users to join or not. Extending the ability to analyse large data sets opens the potential for artificial intelligence in learning characteristics of the process (Ismail 2018).

22.4 Becoming a self-critical organisation

The 2018 PwC annual report on internal audit reports surveyed 2,500 organisations. It found that 75% of internal audit functions that use advanced technology with the correct blend of employee skills and knowledge contribute significant value back to the organisations. The report also found that more advanced internal audits were creating departments with a cohesive technology and talent strategy (PwC 2018).

The use of data to audit continually and measure change is therefore crucial to delivering value. It allows organisations to better understand the role and impact of new technologies and innovations. Management expects that decision makers and external consultants such as internal auditors understand the potential of new technologies and can provide data-backed advice on how to capitalise on the opportunity but also to manage any risks associated. This is the key to becoming a self-critical organisation. Utilising data analytics, monitoring and intelligent automation were also key to enhancing productivity and thriving. Self-critical organisations are therefore taking calculated risks to invest in technology, tools and training based on evidence from audits.

A truly self-critical organisation is one in which the cycle of audits and review is embedded throughout the culture of the organisation, extending the learning organisation concept (Garvin 1993). This extends to all parts of the organisation, and it will fail (or at best be constrained) where this thinking is limited to a small group.

Auditing best practice is a proactive, risk-based approach undertaken by the organisation analysing and assessing data and business processes.

Risks can be determined using the digital business model with specific emphasis on VUCA and 4Vs. Specifically, an external review of the business can determine the VUCA challenges as discussed in Chapter 2. Digital businesses tend to have a higher risk appetite than more traditional counterparts, and as such the management of risk must adapt accordingly to align with the strategic objectives. The 4Vs can be translated into key performance indicators enabling continual monitoring of business health between predetermined tolerances. Indicative (trending) or actual breaching of these tolerances flag issues which prompt automatic and/or manual responses. Further exploration of the business model determines the ability of the business to consistently add value for evolving and expanding customer' expectations. Audits should cover not only the individual business model elements but also interactions between elements as a whole business system.

The implementation of live data and continual monitoring only reinforces the need for periodic audits to review measures and ensure VUCA and 4V decisions are still valid. The rapidly changing environments in which digital businesses thrive mean assumptions made at the commencement of the audit cycle are potentially no longer relevant or accurate (Veracity).

The audit need not be restricted to just looking within an organisation but where comparable data exists benchmarking against competitors or market leaders in similar organisations or situations.

Key takeaways

- Organisations are increasingly becoming proactive and digitally mature, and therefore it has become important to develop an understanding of the uses of data in organisations
- Digital organisations that gain popularity among consumers offer and create value through the use of digital technologies
- Cross-sector digital disruptions have occurred in digitally mature and proactive organisations who have created additional "use-value" for consumers
- A wide range of organisations, including accommodation sharing, price comparison, social media and ride-hailing services, have created new value for consumers
- Use-value can be evaluated in terms of efficiency and productivity and the parameters of the 4Vs
- Organisations should understand the concepts of becoming "data-driven" and what it takes to be a self-critical organisation

References

Garvin, D.A. (1993) "Building a learning organisation", *Harvard Business Review*, July–Aug, https://hbr.org/1993/07/building-a-learning-organization

Ismail, N. (2018) "The customer journey: What it takes to add value in the digital era", www.informa-tion-age.com/customer-journey-value-digital-era-123470510/

PWC (2018) "Moving at the speed of innovation: The foundational tools and talents of technology-enabled Internal Audit", www.pwc.com/sg/en/publications/assets/state-of-the-internal-audit-2018.pdf

Wartzman, R. (2019) "Workplace tracking is growing fast: Most workers don't seem very concerned", *Fast Company*, 20th Mar, www.fastcompany.com/90318167/workplace-tracking-is-growing-fast-most-workers-dont-seem-very-concerned

23 Read me first

The importance of continuous change

Marie Griffiths, Gordon Fletcher and Alex Fenton

Preface

During the preparation of this book we have spoken to many people about the project and its purpose. The audience for our conversations has ranged from small-business owners and C-suite people to public servants and third-sector leaders. We have talked to developers, marketers and entrepreneurs. It became evident very quickly that there are many different ways to tackle digital transformation, and there is definitely no single right way. However, there is one consistent message that comes out of every conversation. Once started, digital transformation is a continuous process.

23.1 New ideas need old buildings

Jane Jacobs' aphorism "new ideas need old buildings" is particularly evocative for discussing digital transformation. The statement functions on three levels. As part of the hardware of the organisational system, the old buildings are required as the incubation spaces for new ideas. In the old buildings, risky new ideas can hide in the shadows to grow and be nurtured without immediate high pressure for return on investment or the expectations of conformity that might be required in newer buildings. This is the meaning that Jacobs originally intended.

Taking this statement still further down a resources path: investing in people and their new ideas requires a short-term balancing of resources. Other resources will have to receive less immediate attention in order to realise a benefit in the long run. These resources might include the "old buildings" as well as other parts of the organisation.

This book has drawn on the third and final possible level of interpretation to Jacobs observation. While digital technology brings new ideas and new ways of doing things, coming to terms with these perspectives is sometimes best achieved with older concepts and theories that provide a sound home for our understanding. Throughout the book, a range of concepts and theories with extensive and long heritages provide the tools to gain a robust and consistent understanding of the current situation.

This observation returns us to the previous observation made in the preface of the chapter. There is no "right" way to do digital transformation, and there is no "right" concept or theory for understanding the impact of digital transformation. The only truism that can be consistently applied to digital transformation is that it is a continuous process. This makes it doubly important to take a theorised approach to the constantly changing digital landscape, as it is through theory that a consistent viewport on the VUCA world can be maintained.

23.2   The "read me" anti-anti-pattern

The final chapter of this book is entitled "Read me first" as tacit recognition that most organisations find themselves in a process of digital transformation without any forward planning or strategic understanding of what they want out of the process or how they have arrived at the current situation. The prevalence of fast, exciting and permanently beta consumer technology arriving into the workplace has slowly eroded the previously high wall that separated slower but more robust and secure enterprise technology. Employee demands for better technology (in their terms) and workarounds using their own devices has forced transformation onto organisations almost through a process of stealth. Just like a consumer clicking "Accept" on a software license they have downloaded without reading it first, organisations have initiated digital transformation before reading any form of manual.

Although there are many ways of undertaking strategic digital transformation, advocating the reading of a manual after the process has started may appear to be of minimal value, but this could not be further from the case. This is when the anti-anti-pattern becomes relevant. A pattern is a repeatable form of thinking that supports consistent good practice. Patterns are particularly common in architecture (Alexander et al. 1977) and software engineering (Gamma et al. 1994). It is easier to develop new solutions within these sectors, as the accumulated knowledge embedded within patterns can be rapidly joined together to address different combinations of issues and provide a solution. However, this ease of use can generally only be realised if patterns are applied at the beginning of the design process. The discussions and approaches described throughout this book cannot be seen as a set of patterns – a digital transformation process has already begun in most organisations in some way.

An anti-pattern is an action or behaviour that responds to a situation in a way that appears to be a solution in the short term but is revealed to be counter-productive in the longer term. Not reading a manual when a new item is purchased and before it is used is an example of an anti-pattern. Because a piece of software, flat pack furniture or a kitchen appliance appears to be immediately easy to use, there is little appeal in investing additional time to read the manual. In the beginning, reading the manual appears to be an unnecessary time-consuming distraction. The realisation of this oversight only comes later when something isn't working correctly.

Once the opportunity to apply a pattern has been lost and an anti-pattern has been deployed as a makeshift workaround, the only opportunity that remains is to take remedial action by applying an anti-anti-pattern. This action then can effectively be seen as a post hoc pattern. This book presents a series of anti-anti-patterns for digital transformation. With digital transformation already commenced in some form, then consideration is needed within the organisation for post hoc patterns.

23.3   Alternative routes through this book

With so many ways to do digital transformation, and with different organisations already having varying priorities and divergent levels of maturity, there is a need for individualised roadmaps. To avoid an unnecessarily prescriptive reading – in chapter order – individuals and organisations are encouraged to consider their own best route through this book. The density of keywords across the book provides an initial indication of what threads could be followed (Figure 23.1). People and data figure heavily, while some phrases can also be

Figure 23.1 Word cloud overview of the keywords used throughout the book

spotted as smaller sub-threads, such as "VUCA world". Looking at the contextual link-ages between the keywords, a different insight is revealed, including Chapter 20's in-depth case study of WeChat (Figure 23.2). Some potential routes through the book include a people thread (Figure 23.3) that would focus attention on Chapters 2, 6, 11, 13, 14, 15 and 21. A data thread takes the reader through Chapters 2, 9, 14, 15 and 22 (Figure 23.4). A combined change and transformation thread (Figure 23.5) offers the reader a different route through Chapters 1, 5, 8, 13, 15 and 16.

23.4   Executive summary

The final way of reading this book is to take the executive summary approach. Remove the narrative and explanation, excise the rationales and justification for each step and con-sideration and just go straight to the summary information. Throughout the book each chapter has presented a "Key Takeaways" section. Compiled into a single list this forms a useful executive summary.

Chapter 1

- The external environment is volatile, uncertain, complex and ambiguous – the VUCA world
- The VUCA world cannot be managed
- The VUCA world continuously challenges the organisation
- Digital transformation is the strategic response to VUCA and its challenges
- The goal of strategic digital transformation is to produce a data-driven people-focused organisation

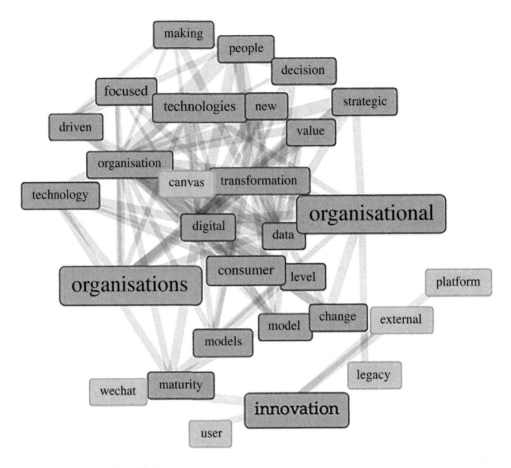

Figure 23.2 Keywords and linkages

Chapter 2

- The digital difference is not a binary relationship with the physical world
- The digital difference labels all the benefits that strategic digital transformation can bring to any organisation's structure and its business models
- An organisation's structure includes the aspects largely hidden from consumers
- The business models used by an organisation describes its visible consumer aspects
- The 4Vs assist in defining VUCA challenges to the organisation and the ways that they can be managed
- Systems qualities – or non-functional requirements – define what the organisation does well in responding to the VUCA world

Chapter 3

- Digital maturity labels an organisation's current situation in relation to digital technology and is not an organisational goal in its own right
- Digital maturity is a continuum of organisational experience

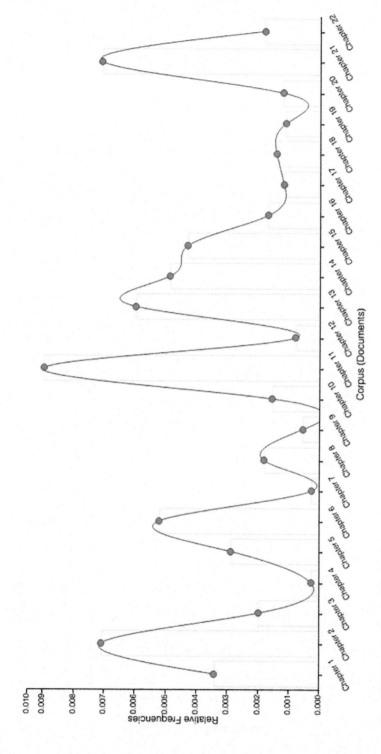

Figure 23.3 People thread of the book

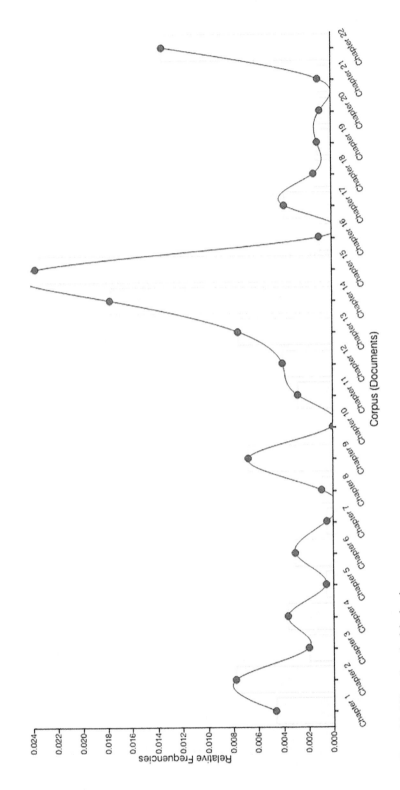

Figure 23.4 Data thread of the book

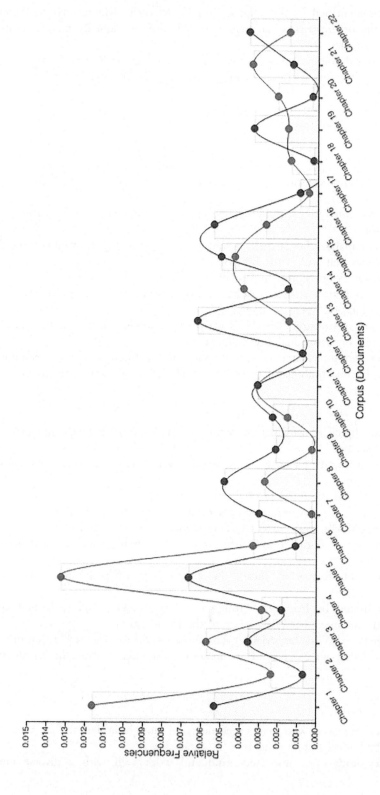

Figure 23.5 Change and transformation thread of the book

- The levels identified by the Digital Business Maturity Model refer to the overall state of the organisation – an organisation is only as digitally mature as its least mature element
- Consumer technology and operational activities at the lower levels of maturity must eventually give way to strategic perspectives and the deployment of organisational technologies
- Transformation actions being undertaken within an organisation are indicative of its current levels of maturity

Chapter 4

- Competitor analysis should be a sustainable, systematic strategic organisational activity
- Competitor analysis should look beyond immediate threats and current competitors
- Competitor analysis should include scanning of close partners as well as more distant opportunities that are on the horizon
- At its widest extent, competitor analysis is global in its scope
- Strategic competitor analysis requires an organisation to be self-aware, critical of its own situation and open to change
- An outcome of strategic competitor analysis is to develop an innovating organisation and internal organisational environment
- Analogies and storytelling techniques such as the braided river can support and contextualise the findings of competitor analysis for the entire organisation

Chapter 5

- Managing digital transformation within an organisation is firstly and primarily a people challenge
- Multiple push and pull factors exist within every sector for doing strategic digital transformation
- Communicating the purpose of the transformation is key to its success
- The messages being communicated should vary between audiences
- Do not transform your current business processes, look forward
- A shared vision: digital transformation must be strategic and aligned across the organisation
- Grassroots transformation should be encouraged when it aligns with overall strategy
- Projects should be managed through short cycles with highly defined, quickly delivered outcomes that bring value to the organisation
- Consider the "A" in the SMART acronym to stand for "agreed" to ensure a harmonised shared agreement and organisational alignment within the transformation project.

Chapter 6

- Visionary leaders are knowledge specialists and thought leaders and are able to pivot
- Visionary leaders inspire others
- Visionary leaders are respected, kind and work well with a diverse range of people

- Visionary leaders take responsibility for failures and share successes
- Visionary leaders build trust across the organisation
- Visionary leaders encourage a positive work/life balance
- Visionary leaders are flexible and know how to manage in different situations
- Visionary leaders can help shape the company vision and mission and get buy in from the entire organisation

Chapter 7

- Don't bring your current situation into the future – the actions of your people and the use of your data is what makes you distinctive
- Ask questions, don't restrict yourself to solving current or immediate problems
- Horizon scanning process should be a catalyst to challenge static thinking
- There is no definitive methodology or template for horizon scanning – but it is not just a checklist of competing products
- Horizon scanning has to be viewed as a credible process by all key stakeholders
- Horizon scanning should support (the creation of) an internal culture of innovation
- Horizon scanning should be reported in a format for communicating internally, it should be written in plain language and in a style that focuses on the results
- Horizon scanning requires justification of the findings if they are to challenge the status quo

Chapter 8

- Critically and systematically assess new technologies and trends
- Embed a process for sharing trends and future insights that are happening in your sector with your teams
- Aspire to become the "unshockable" organisation that is up-to-date and informed
- Introduce initiatives to stem talent flight
- Encourage a happy and diverse workforce that knows they are listened to
- Adopt a new vantage position for your organisation
- Investigate the "zoom in, zoom out" approach to take a more dynamic approach to strategy
- Constantly connect with people outside the organisation
- Place customers at the heart of your organisation

Chapter 9

- Competitor analysis is an important ongoing process.
- Do not take data at face value
- We have now more information on our competitors than ever before
- It is important to note who your competitors are in the digital space
- Your customers are the ultimate source for meaningful benchmarks

Chapter 10

- Understanding how others view your organisation includes knowing why skilled individuals would choose to work for your organisation rather than another
- Chief decision makers must recognise that successful digital transformation cannot be piecemeal and substantial support may be required in their own ranks

- "Not doing digital" is no longer an option for organisations of any size, and "doing digital" is dependent on human ingenuity
- It is the people who populate the workforce that will make your organisation digital; for long-term sustainability and competitive advantage you require the most appropriate workforce
- Digital transformation in organisations is here to stay – it isn't a threat, it's just the new normal

Chapter 11

- An internal audit of the organisation reveals it complexity, legacies and potential points of resistance to change
- The audit focuses on capturing and documenting the organisational system in detail
- Using the organisational system as a focus for the audit encourages a new perspective on existing functional structures
- Emphasis is on identifying the critical interactions in the organisation with focus on the most distinctive aspects of the organisation: its people and its data
- Cultural and infrastructural considerations can then be connected with these interactions

Chapter 12

- Transparency, Openness, Sharing, Boldness and Customisation as five hallmark organisational qualities are indicators of progress towards strategic digital transformation
- Each of the five qualities interact together
- Emphasis on any single quality potentially impedes the development of the others
- Delivering these qualities within the organisation will be a challenge to the internal culture
- The five qualities are enabled and delivered by digital technologies
- The presence of consumer digital technology in the VUCA world creates much of the imperative to have these five organisational qualities

Chapter 13

- Legacy of all types is a significant barrier to successful digital transformation
- Different forms of legacy can be identified in every element of the organisational system
- Legacy can be defined as being minor, major or massive depending on what is unknown or known about the legacy
- Interoperability is an organisational quality
- An absence of interoperability (or low levels of interoperability) positions the extent that a legacy impacts upon the organisation
- Defining a burning platform and describing the irreversible options can persuade people to change and to support change (or to leave the organisation)
- Removing legacy from an organisation does not necessarily have to be done through direct like-for-like substitution with a "better" version of the existing element

Chapter 14

- As well as off-the-shelf digital tools, consider custom-built software, hardware, human/paper-based systems, hardware, integrations, data storage and management as part of an operational toolkit
- Think beyond typical key performance indicators such as speed and cost reduction
- Map out problems, potential solutions and new innovations to help build a digital transformation strategy
- Use data to work out the costs and benefits of different solutions and consider allocating a budget for small trials
- Evaluate how data will be managed and ensure it is used within compliant and efficient data management processes
- Consider future requirements. Transformation is a multi-stage and ongoing process

Chapter 15

- Data should be at the heart of strategic decision making
- Make sure you ask the right questions so you get the right answers
- Ensure that you have in-house talent to interrogate and sense-make your data.
- Foster a culture of innovation and experimenting with data
- Build trust and confidence with your customers as they are the holders of vital data
- In asking the question "when to make decisions with data", the response is now, today, as soon as you can!

Chapter 16

- The business model is at the heart of the organisation's operations
- The business model canvas provides a single-page artefact for sharing and comparing
- The Sprint enables tightly defined packages of work to be completed quickly that contribute to overall success
- All aspects of the organisation, from the most visionary to the most operational, can be undertaken through sprints
- Change at visionary and strategic levels of the organisation impact on the operational activities of the organisation

Chapter 17

- Events come in a range of forms to suit the specific objectives defined by the organisation
- Technology can enhance the engagement and experience at all events for participants
- Events should not be regarded as a one-off or isolated activity
- Events should be integrated with the strategic activities of the organisation, and the relationship of an individual event to overall strategic direction should be understood

- Hackathons and innovation jams can be designed to create new innovations, tackle real world problems and identify new talented staff
- Events can contribute to positive organisational qualities including transparency and openness
- Events can be used to develop an organisation's co-creation and collaboration ambitions

Chapter 18

- All staff members should have the right to time away from work
- All staff members should be encouraged to disconnect from the workplace
- A positive work/life balance can actually improve performance
- HR should encourage a culture that promotes positive work/life balance
- Technology has to be managed in the workplace to prevent the proliferation of an "always on" culture

Chapter 19

- Organisations need to make data-driven decisions in embedding co-consumption mechanism opportunities
- Build trust by embedding a culture of transparency across all touch points and through the provision of mechanisms for review and feedback
- Add value by providing intermediary platforms where customers can come together and share, build and enhance products and services
- Plan events that actively engage your customers in innovative ways
- The traditional retail model is broken. Be creative to get customers into your physical spaces so that these activities can be reported on digital channels
- Ensure that any activity, workshop or experience is meaningful for the consumer rather than just an alternative form of advertising
- Ensure that any data of the experience is captured, measured and responded upon

Chapter 20

- Innovation requires a combination of optimal internal and external circumstances
- Inside the organisation policy, support, technical conditions and the right cultural environment is required
- Incremental innovation provides opportunities for review and for user engagement
- External innovations must be managed but can provide significant benefit

Chapter 21

- Digital transformation requires the permanent embedding of innovation
- An innovating environment acts positively on the organisational system
- The wider innovation ecosystem is a collaborative environment drawing on multiple organisations and support
- Organisations working with research institutions can collaborate to unlock funding for innovation
- Various technologies exist that support digital transformations, with the most important criteria being the capacity to solve a problem

Chapter 22

- Organisations are increasingly becoming proactive and digitally mature, and therefore it has become important to develop an understanding of the uses of data in organisations
- Digital organisations that gain popularity among consumers offer and create value through the use of digital technologies
- Cross-sector digital disruptions have occurred in digitally mature and proactive organisations who have created additional "use-value" for consumers
- A wide range of organisations, including accommodation sharing, price comparison, social media and ride-hailing services have created new value for consumers
- Use-value can be evaluated in terms of efficiency and productivity and the parameters of the 4Vs
- Organisations should understand the concepts of becoming "data-driven" and what it takes to be a self-critical organisation.

References

Alexander, C., Ishikawa, S., & Silverstein, M. (1977) *A Pattern Language*. Oxford: Oxford University Press.

Gamma, E., Vlissides, J., Johnson, R., & Helm, R. (1994) *Design Patterns: Elements of Reusable Object-Oriented Software*. Boston: Addison-Wesley.

Index

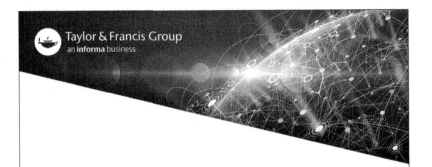